SO-ARE-722

Webster's

Travelers

Phrase Book

—◆—

English-German

—◆—

G. & C. MERRIAM CO.
SPRINGFIELD, MASSACHUSETTS 01101

Copyright © 1971

by

G. & C. MERRIAM CO.

All rights reserved. No part of this work covered
by the copyrights hereon may be reproduced or
copied in any form or by any means—graphic,
electronic, or mechanical, including photocopy-
ing, recording, taping, or information and re-
trieval systems—without written permission of
the publisher.

Standard Book Number:

0-87779-092-2

1B

MADE IN U.S.A.

Aboard

When can we go aboard?
Wann können wir an Bord gehen?
vahn könn-en veer ahnn BORT gay-en?

Accept

Do you accept U.S. currency (travelers checks, credit cards)?
Akzeptieren Sie Dollar (Reiseschecks, Kreditkarten)?
ahk-tsep-TEER-en zee DOH-lahr (RYE-zuh-shecks, kray-DEET kahrr-ten)?

Accident

There has been an accident.
Es ist ein Unfall passiert.
ess isst ine OONN-fahll pah-seert.

Get a doctor!
Holen Sie einen Arzt!
hoh-len zee eye-nen ARTST!

Call for the police!
Rufen Sie die Polizei!
roo-fen zee dee poh-lee-TSYE!

Send for an ambulance!
Bestellen Sie einen Krankenwagen!
buh-SHTELL-en zee eye-nen KRAHNNG-ken-vah-gen!

Take me (him, her) to the hospital.
Bringen Sie mich (ihn, sie) ins Krankenhaus.
bring-en zee mikh (een, zee) ins KRAHNNG-ken-house.

He (she) is injured.
Er (sie) ist verletzt.
air (zee) isst fehr-LETST.

Don't move him (her)!
Bewegen Sie ihn (sie) nicht!
buh-VAY-gen zee een (zee) nikht!

He (she) has fainted.
Er (sie) ist ohnmächtig.
air (zee) isst OHN-mehkh-tick.

Help me carry him (her).
Helfen Sie mir ihn (sie) tragen.
hell-fen zee meer een (zee) TRAH-GEN.

I feel dizzy.
Ich bin schwindlig.
ikh binn SHVINND-*lick.*

He (she) has a fracture (a bruise, a cut, a burn).
Er (sie) hat einen Knochenbruch (eine Quetschungen,
   eine Schnittwunden, eine Brandwunden).
air (zee) haht eye-nen KNAW-*khen-brookh (eye-nuh*
   KVET-*shoong-en, eye-nuh* SCHNITT-*voonn-duhn, eye-*
   nuh BRAHNT-*voonn-duhn).*

He (she) is bleeding.
Er (sie) blutet.
air (zee) BLOO-*tet.*

Are you all right?
Sind Sie verletzt?
*zinnt zee fehr-*LETST?

Where does it hurt?
Wo tut es weh?
VOH *toot ess* VAY?

It hurts here.
Hier tut es weh.
HEER *toot ess vay.*

I cannot move.
Ich kann mich nicht bewegen.
*ikh kahn mikh nikht buh-*VAY-*gen.*

Please notify my husband (wife).
Bitte, verständigen Sie meinen Mann (meine Frau).
*bit-tuh fehr-*SHTENN-*dig-en zee my-nen* MAHNN *(my-nuh*
   FROW).

Accommodate

Can you accommodate me (two, three, four)?
Haben Sie unterkunft für mich (für zwei, für drei, für
   vier)?
hah-ben zee OONN-*tehr-koonnft für* MIKH *(für* TSVYE, *für*
   DRY, *für* FEERR)?

Does the train to _____ have sleeping accommodations?
Hat der Zug nach _____ schlafwagen?
haht dair tsook nahkh _____ SHLAHF-*vah-gen?*

Accompany
May I accompany you?
Darf ich Sie begleiten?
*dahrf ikh zee buh-*GLITE-*en?*

Account (Bank)
I would like to (Where do I) open a checking account.
Ich möchte (Wo kann ich) ein Scheckkonto eröffnen.
ikh mökh-tuh (voh kahn ikh) ine SHECK-*kawnn-toh ehr-öff-nen.*

Account (Calculation)
May I see an account of the bill?
Kann ich die Abrechnung sehen?
kahn ikh dee AHPP-*rehkh-noong zay-en?*

Ache – see Hurt

Acquaintance – see also Meet
I am very happy to meet you (make your acquaintance).
Es freut mich sehr, Sie kennenzulernen (Ihre Bekanntschaft zu machen).
ess froyt mikh ZAIR *zie* KENN-*nen-tsoo-lehr-nen (ear-eh buh-*KAHNNT-*shahft tsoo mahkh-en).*

Address
Please forward all mail to this address.
Bitte senden Sie meine Post an diese Adresse.
bit-tuh zenn-den zie mine-uh PAWSST *ahnn dee-zuh ah-*DRESS-*uh.*

Here is my address.
Hier ist meine Adresse.
HEER *isst mine-uh ah-*DRESS-*uh.*

What is your address (and telephone number)?
Wie ist Ihre Adresse (und Telefonnummer)?
*vee isst ear-eh ah-*DRESS-*uh (oonnt tay-luh-*FOHN-*noomm-ehr)?*

Admission

What is the price of admission?
Wieviel kostet der Eintritt?
vee-feel kawss-tet dair INE-tritt?

Advertise

I would like to advertise for a _____.
Ich möchte nach _____ inserieren.
ikh MÖKH-tuh nahkh _____ inn-zehr-EER-en.

Advertisement

I am answering your advertisement.
Ich beantworte Ihr Inserat.
ikh buh-AHNNT-vor-tuh ear inn-zehr-RAHT.

I would like to run an advertisement.
Ich möchte ein Inserat aufgeben.
ikh MÖKH-tuh ine inn-zehr-RAHT OWF-gay-ben.

Afford

I cannot afford that.
Ich kann mir das nicht leisten.
ikh KAHN meer dahss nikht LICE-ten.

Afternoon

I would like to arrange it for the afternoon.
Ich möchte das für den Nachmittag arrangieren.
ikh MÖKH-tuh dahss für dane NAHKH-mit-tahk ahr-rahn-ZHEER-ren.

Again

I hope to see you again soon.
Ich hoffe, Sie bald wiederzusehen.
ikh HAWF-fuh zee bahllt VEE-dehr-tsoo-zay-en

Please say it again.
Bitte, sagen Sie das noch einmal.
bit-tuh ZAH-gen zee dahss NAWKH ine-mahl.

Age

What is your age?
Wie alt sind Sie?
vee AHLLT zinnt zee?

Aid – see Help

Air

My tire needs (my tires need) air.

Mein Reifen braucht (meine Reifen brauchen) Luft.

mine RYE-*fen browkht (my-nuh* RYE-*fen browkh-en)*
LOOFT.

Air Conditioning

Does it have air conditioning?

Hat es eine Klimaanlage?

haht ess eye-nuh KLEE-*mah*-AHNN-*lah-guh?*

I want a room with air conditioning, please.

Ich möchte ein Zimmer mit Klimaanlage, bitte.

ikh MÖK-*tuh ine* TSIMM-*mehr mitt* KLEE-*mah*-AHNN-
lah-guh, BIT-*tuh.*

Air Mail – see Mail

Airplane – see Flight

Airport

The airport, please.

Zum Flughafen, bitte.

tsoom FLOOK-*hah-fen,* BIT-*tuh.*

Airsick

I feel airsick.

Ich bin Luftkrank.

ikh binn LOOFFT-*krahnnk.*

A La Carte

Please show me the a la carte menu.

Bitte zeigen Sie mir die a la carte Speisekarte.

bit-tuh TSYE-*gen zee meer dee ah lah* KAHRRT SHPYE-
zuh-kahr-tuh.

All

This is all I have (need, want).

Das ist alles, was ich habe (brauche, wünsche).

dahss isst AHLL-*less vahss ikh* HAH-*buh (*BROW-*khuh,*
VÜN-*shuh).*

Allergy

I am allergic to this.

Ich bin allergisch dagegen.

ikh binn ahl-LEHR-*gisch dah*-GAY-*gen.*

All Right
It is all right.
Geht in Ordnung.
GAYT *inn* AWRD-*noong.*

Alone
Please leave me alone.
Bitte, lassen Sie mich in Ruhe.
BIT-*tuh* LAHSS-*senn zee mikh inn* ROO-*uh.*

Are you alone?
Sind Sie allein?
zinnt zee ahl-LINE*?*

I am (not) alone.
Ich bin (nicht) allein.
*ikh binn (*NIKHT*) ahl*-LINE*.*

Ambulance
Call me an ambulance.
Bestellen Sie einen Krankenwagen für mich.
buh-SHTELL-*en zee eye-nen* KRAHNNG-*ken-vah-gen für mikh.*

American
I am an American.
Ich bin amerikaner.
ikh binn ah-may-ree-KAH-*ner.*

Do you accept American money?
Akzeptieren Sie amerikanisches Geld (Dollar)?
ahk-tsep-TEER-*en zee ah-may-ree*-KAH-*nish-ess* GELT
(DOH-*lahr*)?

American Embassy
Please direct me (take me) to the American embassy.
Bitte sagen Sie mir den Weg (begleiten Sie mich) zur
amerikanischen Botschaft.
bit-tuh ZAH-*gen zee meer dane* VECK (*buh*-GLITE-*en zee
mikh*) *tsoor ah-may-ree*-KAH-*nish-en* BOAT-*shahft.*

American Express

Please direct me (take me) to the American Express office.

Bitte sagen Sie mir den Weg (begleiten Sie mich) zum American Express.

bit-tuh ZAH-*gen zee meer dane* VECK *(buh-*GLITE-*en zee mikh) tsoom ah-may-ree-kahn ek-spress.*

Do you accept the American Express credit card?

Akzeptieren Sie die American Express Kreditkarte?

*ahk-tsep-*TEER-*en zee dee ah-may-ree-kahn ek-spress kray-*DEET-*kahrr-tuh?*

Amount

What is the total amount?

Wie hoch ist der gesamte Betrag?

vee HOHKH *isst dair guh-*ZAHMM-*tuh buh-*TRAHK*?*

Another

Let's have another drink.

Trinken wir noch einen.

TRING-*ken veer* NAWKH *eye-nen.*

Please get me another drink.

Bitte bringen Sie mir noch ein Glas.

BIT-*tuh* BRING-*en zee meer* NAWKH *ine* GLAHSS.

Answer

They do not answer; please try again.

Es antwortet niemand; bitte versuchen Sie noch einmal.

ess AHNNT-*vor-tet* NEE-*mahnnt; bit-tuh fehr-*ZOOKH-*en zee* NAWKH *ine-nahl.*

Antiques

Please direct me (take me) to an antique shop.

Bitte sagen Sie mir den Weg (begleiten Sie mich) zu einem Antiquitäten-Laden.

bit-tuh ZAH-*gen zee meer dane* VECK *(buh-*GLITE-*en zee mikh) tsoo eye-nem ahn-tih-kvee-*TAY-*ten-lah-den.*

I am interested in antiques.

Ich interessiere mich für Antiquitäten.

*ikh in-tehr-ruh-*SEE-*ruh mikh für ahn-tih-kvee-*TAY-*ten.*

Do you sell antiques?
Verkaufen Sie Antiquitäten?
fehr-KOW-fen zee ahn-tih-kvee-TAY-ten?

Apologize
I apologize.
Ich bitte um Entschuldigung.
ikh BIT-tuh oomm ent-SCHOOL-dih-goong.

Appointment
I would like to make an appointment for _____.
Ich möchte eine Verabredung für _____ machen.
ikh MÖKH-tuh ine-uh fehr-AHPP-ray-doong für _____ mahkh-en.

Arrive
When does the plane (the bus, the boat, the train) arrive?
Wann kommt das Flugzeug (der Bus, das Schiff, der Zug) an?
VAHNN kawmmt dahss FLOOCK-tsoyk (dehr BOOSS, dass SHIFF, dehr TSOOK) AHNN?

When do we arrive at _____?
Wann kommen wir in _____ an?
vahnn KAWMM-en veer inn _____ AHNN?

Article-see Things

Asleep
My husband (wife) is asleep.
Mein Mann (meine Frau) schläft.
mine MAHNN (my-nuh FROW) SHLAYFT.

Assistance – see Help

Authority
I will report this to the authorities.
Ich werde das den Behörden melden.
ikh VAIR-duh dahss dane buh-HÖR-den MELL-den.

Automobile
I want to rent an automobile, please.
Ich möchte ein Auto mieten, bitte.
ikh MÖKH-tuh ine OW-toh MEE-ten, BIT-tuh.

Where is the next gas station (garage)?
Wo ist die nächste Tankstelle (Garage)?
voh isst dee NEX-*tuh* TAHNK-*shtell-uh (gah-*RAH-*zhuh)?*

My car has broken down.
Mein Auto hat eine Panne.
mine OW-*toh haht ine-uh* PAH-*nuh.*

I am out of gas.
Ich habe kein Benzin mehr.
ikh HAH-*buh kine ben-*TSEEN *mair.*

I have a flat tire.
Ich habe einen platten Reifen (einen "Plattfuss").
ikh HAH-*buh eye-nun* PLAHT-*ten* RYE-*fen (eye-nun*
    PLAHTT-*fooss).*

Can you help me?
Können Sie mir helfen?
könn-en zee meer HELL-*fen?*

Can you tow (push) me to a garage?
Können Sie mich zu einer Garage abschleppen
    (shieben)?
KONN-*en zee* MIKH *tsoo eye-nehr gah-*RAH-*zhuh* AHPP-
    *shlep-pen (*SHEE-*ben)?*

I have (I do not have) an international license.
Ich habe einen (ich habe keinen) internationalen
    Führerschein.
ikh HAH-*buh eye-nun (ikh* HAH-*buh* KINE-*un) in-tehr-*
    NAHTS-*yoh-nahl* FÜ-*rehr-shine.*

Here is my license.
Hier ist mein Führerschein.
HEER *isst mine* FU-*rehr-shine.*

Can you recommend a good mechanic?
Können Sie mir einen guten Mechaniker empfehlen?
KÖNN-*en zee meer eye-nun* GOO-*tun muh-*KAHN-*ee-kehr*
    *emp-*FAY-*len?*

Fill it up, please.
Auffüllen, bitte.
OWF-*fü-len,* BIT-*tuh.*

Give me _____ liters, please.
Geben Sie mir _____ Liter, bitte.
GAY-*ben zee meer* _____ LEE-*tehr*, BIT-*tuh.*

The _____ does not work.
Das _____ geht nicht.
dahss _____ GATE *nikht.*

Please check the _____.
Bitte prüfen Sie das _____.
bit-tuh PRÜ-*fen zee dahss* _____ .

Can you repair it while I wait?
Können Sie es reparieren, während ich warte?
KÖNN-*en zee ess reh-par-*REER-*en vay-rent ikh* VAHR-
tuh?

When?
Wann?
VAHNN*?*

What is wrong?
Was ist los?
vahss isst LOHSS*?*

Can you wash it (now)?
Können Sie es (jetzt) waschen?
KÖNN-*en zee ess (yettst)* VAHSH-*en?*

There is a rattle (squeak).
Etwas klappert (knarrt).
ett-vahss KLAHPP-*ehrt (*KNAHRRT*).*

Something is leaking here.
Hier läuft etwas aus.
heer LOYFT *ett-vahss* OWSS*.*

Will you accept this credit card (travelers checks, a
personal check)?
Akzeptieren Sie diese Kreditkarte (Reiseschecks, einen
persönlichen Scheck)?
*ahk-tsep-*TEER-*en zee dee-zuh kray-*DEET-*kahrr-tuh
(*RYE-*zuh-shecks, eye-nen pehr-*ZÖN-*likh-en* SHECK*)?*

I am staying at _____.
Meine Adresse ist _____.
*mine-uh ah-*DRESS-*uh isst* _____ .

I am a member of the automobile club.
Ich bin Mitglied des Automobilklubs.
ikh binn MITT-*gleet dess ow-toh-moh*-BEEL-*kloobs.*

Available

Are there any rooms (seats) available?
Haben Sie Zimmer (Sitzplätze) frei?
hah-ben zee TSIMM-*er (*ZITTS-*plet-zuh)* FRY?

Awaken – see Call

Away

Go away!
Gehen Sie weg!
GAY-*en zee* VECK!

Please take it away.
Bitte nehmen Sie das weg.
bit-tuh NAY-*men zee dahss* VECK.

Babysitter

Can you recommend a (an English-speaking) babysitter?
Können Sie mir eine (englisch-sprechende) Kinderhüterin empfehlen?
KÖNN-*en zee meer ine-uh (*ENG-*lish-*SHPREHKH-*en-duh) kinn-dehr-*HÜ-*tehr-inn emp-*FAY-*len?*

Bachelor

I am a bachelor.
Ich bin Junggeselle.
ikh binn YOONNG-*guh-zell-uh.*

Is he a bachelor?
Ist er Junggeselle?
isst air YOONNG-*guh-zell-uh?*

Back

How do I get back to _____?
Wie komme ich zurück nach _____?
VEE *kawmm-ah ikh tsoo-*RÜCK *nahkh* _____?

Please come back later.
Bitte kommen Sie später zurück.
bit-tuh kawmm-en zee SHPATE-*ehr tsoo-*RÜCK.

I (do not) want to sit in the back.
Ich möchte (nicht) rückwärts sitzen.
ikh MOKH-*tuh (*NIKHT) RUCK-*vehrts* ZITT-*sen.*

When are we due back?
Wann kommen wir zurück?
VAHNN KAWMM-*en veer tsoo-*RÜCK?

Please take me back to the _____.
Bitte bringen Sie mich zurück nach _____.
bit-tuh BRING-*en zee mikh tsoo-*RUCK *nahkh* _____.

Bad (= Unsatisfactory)
This is bad. (Please take it away.)
Das ist schlecht. (Bitte nehmen Sie es weg.)
dahss isst SHLEKHT. *(*BIT-*tuh* NAY-*men zee ess* VECK.)

Bags, Baggage
May I leave my bag (my baggage) here?
Darf ich meinen Koffer (mein Gepäck) hier lassen?
dahrff ikh my-nen KAWFF-*fehr (mine guh-*PECK) HEER
   lahss-senn?

Please help me with my bags.
Bitte helfen Sie mir mit dem Gepäck.
bit-tuh HELL-*fen zee meer mitt dame guh-*PECK.

Please take my bags to _____.
Bitte bringen Sie main Gepäck zu _____.
bit-tuh BRING-*en zee mine guh-*PECK *tsoo* _____.

Where is the baggage room?
Wo ist die Gepäck-Aufbewahrung?
VOH *isst dee guh-*PECK-OWF-*buh-*VAHR-*oong?*

How much baggage am I allowed?
Wieviel Gepäck ist erlaubt?
*vee-feel guh-*PECK *isst ehr-*LOWPT?

Where is my baggage?
Wo ist mein Gepäck?
VOH *isst mine guh-*PECK?

I cannot find my bags.
Ich kann mein Gepäck nicht finden.
ikh KAHNN *mine guh-*PECK *nikht* FINN-*den.*

I need a porter.
Ich brauche einen Gepäckträger.
ikh BROW-*khuh* *eye-nen* guh-PECK-*tray-gehr.*

Bank

Where is the nearest bank?
Wo ist die nächste Bank?
VOH *isst dee* NEX-*tuh* BAHNNK?

At what time does the bank open (close)?
Wann öffnet (schliesst) die Bank?
vahnn ÖFF-*net (*SHLEESST*) dee* BAHNNK?

Where can I cash this?
Wo kann ich das einlösen?
VOH *kahn ikh dahss* INE-*lö-zen?*

Will you cash a personal check?
Lösen Sie einen persönlichen Scheck ein?
LÖ-*zen zee eye-nen pehr-*ZÖN-*likh-en sheck* INE?

Can I cash a money order here?
Kann ich hier eine Postanweisung einlösen?
kahnn ikh HEER *ine-uh* PAWSST-*ahnn-vye-zoong* INE-*lö-zen?*

Where is the window for cashing traveler's checks?
Wo ist der Schalter für Reiseschecks?
VOH *isst dair* SHAHLLT-*ehr für* RYE-*zuh-shecks?*

Please give me (don't give me) large bills.
Bitte geben Sie mir (keine) grosse(n) Banknoten.
bit-tuh GAY-*ben zee meer (*KINE-*uh)* GROHSS-*suh(n)*
BAHNNK-*no-ten.*

Can you change this for me, please?
Können Sie das wechseln, bitte?
KÖNN-*en zee dahss* VECK-*seln,* BIT-*tuh?*

I would like to change some American dollars into
_____.
Ich möchte amerikanische Dollar in _____ umwechseln.
ikh MÖKH-*tuh ah-may-ree-*KAH-*nish-uh* DOH-*lahr inn*
_____ OMM-*veck-seln.*

What is the rate of exchange?
Wie ist der Umrechnungskurs?
VEE *isst dair* OOMM-*rehkh-noongs*-KOORRSS?

Bar

Where is the bar?
Wo ist die Bar?
VOH *isst dee* BAR?

Is there a bar open?
Ist eine Bar offen?
isst ine-uh BAR AWFF-*fen?*

When do the bars close (open)?
Wann schliessen (öffnen) die Bars?
vahnn SHLEE-*sen (*ÖFF-*nen) dee* BARZ?

Barber

Can you recommend a good barber?
Können Sie mir einen guten Herrenfriseur empfehlen?
KÖNN-*en zee meer eye-nen* GOOT-*en* HEHRR-*en-frih*-ZOOR
emp-FAY-*len?*

I want a haircut, please.
Ich möchte mir die Haare schneiden, bitte.
ikh MÖKH-*tuh meer dee* HAHR-*uh* SHNYE-*den,* BIT-*tuh.*

I want a shave, please.
Ich möchte mich rasieren lassen, bitte.
ikh MÖKH-*tuh mikh rah*-ZEE-*ren* LAHSS-*senn,* BIT-*tuh.*

Not too short, please.
Nicht zu kurz, bitte.
nikht tsoo KOORTS, BIT-*tuh.*

Don't cut any off the top.
Vorne nichts wegschneiden, bitte.
FORN-*uh nikhts* VECK-*shnye-den,* BIT-*tuh.*

I part my hair on the (other) side.
Ich trage den Scheitel auf der (anderen) Seite.
ikh TRAH-*guh dane* SHY-*tehl owf dair (*AHNN-*dehr-en)*
ZITE-*tuh.*

(Don't) use hair tonic, please.
(Kein) Haaröl, bitte.
(kine) HAHR-*öl,* BIT-*tuh.*

Bath

A room with a bath, please.
Ein Zimmer mit Bad, bitte.
ine TSIMMER-*mehr mitt* BAHT, BIT-*tuh.*

A private bath is not necessary.
Ich brauche kein Eigenbad.
ikh BROW-*khuh kine* EYE-*gen-baht.*

Bathing

Is bathing permitted here?
Darf man hier baden?
dahrf mahnn heer bah-den?

Bathing Suit

Where can I buy a bathing suit?
Wo kann ich einen Badeanzug kaufen?
VOH *kahnn ikh eye-nen* BAH-*duh-ahnn-tsook* KOW-FEN?

Bathroom (not Toilet)

Where is the bathroom?
Wo ist das Badezimmer?
VOH *isst dahss* BAH-*deh-tsimm-mehr?*

Bathtub

I prefer a bathtub (to a shower).
Ich ziehe eine Badewanne (einer Dusche) vor.
ikh TSEE-*uh ine-uh* BAH-*deh-vahn-nuh (eye-nehr* DOO-*shuh) for.*

Battery

Do you sell flashlight (radio, transistor, electric razor) batteries?
Verkaufen Sie Batterien für Taschenlampen (Radio, Transistor, elektrische Rasierapparate)?
*fehr-*KOW-*fen zee baht-teh-*REE-*ehn für* TAHSH-*en-lahm-puhn (*RAHD-*yoh, trahnn-*ZIHSS-*tohr, el-*LECK-*trish-uh rah-*ZEER-*ahp-pah-*RAHT*)?*

Beach

Is there a beach nearby?
Gibt es einen Badestrand hier in der Nähe?
GIPPT *ess eye-nen* BAH-*duh-shtrahnnt heer inn dair* NAY-*uh?*

Beauty Parlor

Can you recommend a good beauty parlor?
Können Sie mir einen guten Damenfriseur empfehlen?
KÖNN-en zee meer eye-nen GOO-ten DAH-*mehn-frih-*ZOOR *emp-*FAY-*len?*

Can I make an appointment for _____?
Ich möchte eine Verabredung für _____ machen.
ikh MÖKH-*tuh ine-uh fehr-*AHPP-*ray-doong fur* _____ MAHKH-*en.*

I (don't) have an appointment (with _____).
Ich habe eine (keine) Verabredung (mit _____).
ikh HAH-*buh ine-uh* (KINE-*uh) fehr-*AHPP-*ray-doong*
(mitt _____*).*

I want a wash, cut, and set, please.
Ich möchte Waschen, Schneiden und Legen, bitte.
ikh MÖKH-*tuh* VAHSH-*en* SHNYE-*den oonnt* LAY-*gen,* BIT-*tuh.*

Just trim it, please.
Nur stutzen, bitte.
noorr SHTOOTS-*en,* BIT-*tuh.*

Not too short.
Nicht zu kurz.
nikht tsoo KOORTS.

I want a permanent (a rinse), please.
Ich möchte Dauerwellen (einen Überguss), bitte.
ikh MÖKH-*tuh* DOW-*ehr-vell-en (eye-nen* Ü-*behr-goos),*
BIT-*tuh*

I want a facial (manicure, massage), please.
Ich möchte eine Gesichtsbehandlung (Maniküre, Massage), bitte.
ikh MOKH-*tuh ine-uh guh-*ZIKHTS-*buh-hahnnd-loong,* BIT-*tuh.*

I part my hair on the (other) side (in the middle).
Ich trage den Scheitel auf der (anderen) Seite (in der Mitte).
ikh TRAH-*guh dane* SHY-*tehl owf dair (*AHNN-*dehr-en)*
ZITE-*tuh (inn dair* MITT-*tuh).*

I wear bangs.
Ich trage Fransen.
ikh TRAH-*guh* FRAHNN-*zen.*

I want a French twist (chignon), please.
Ich möchte einen Twist (Knoten), bitte.
ikh MÖKH-*tuh eye-nen* TVEEST (KNOH-*ten*), BIT-*tuh.*

Can you (cut) wash and set my wig (fall)?
Können Sie meine Perücke (mein Haarteil) (schneiden)
    waschen and legen?
KÖNN-*en zee mine-uh* pay-RÜCK-*kuh (mine* HAHR-*tile)*
    SHNYE-*den* VAHSH-*en oonnt* LAY-*gen?*

Please (don't) tease it.
Bitte (nicht) toupieren.
bit-tuh (NIKHT) too-PEER-*ren.*

The water (the dryer) is too hot (cold).
Das Wasser (der Trockner) ist zu heiss (kalt).
dahss VAHSS-*ehr (dair* TRAWCK-*nehr) isst tsoo* HICE
    (KAHLLT).

Becoming
I'm sorry, it is not becoming to me.
Das steht mir leider nicht.
dahss SHTAYT *meer* LYE-*dehr* NIKHT.

Bed
A room with double bed (with twin beds), please.
Ein Zimmer mit Doppelbett (mit zwei Betten), bitte.
ine TSIMM-*mehr mitt* DAWPP-*pel-bet (mitt tsvy* BET-*ten*),
    BIT-*tuh.*

Please (do not) make up the bed (the beds) now.
Bitte machen Sie jetzt (nicht) das Bett (die Betten).
bit-tuh MAHKH-*en zee yettst* (NIKHT) *dahss* BET *(dee*
    BEE-*ten).*

Bedroom
We would like separate bedrooms.
Wir möchten getrennte Zimmer.
veer MÖKH-*ten guh*-TREN-*teh* TSIMM-*mehr.*

Bellboy
Please send the bellboy to me.
Bitte schicken Sie mir den Hotelpagen.
bit-tuh SHICK-*en zee meer dane ho-*TELL-*pah-gen.*

Berth
I want an upper (lower) berth.
Ich möchte eine obere (untere) Koje.
ikh MÖKH-*tuh ine-uh* OH-*beh-ruh (*OONN-*tehr-uh)* KOH-*yuh.*

Better
I like this one better (best).
Das gefällt mir besser (am besten).
*dahss guh-*FELT *meer* BESS-*sehr (ahmm* BESS-*ten).*

Have you anything better?
Haben Sie etwas Besseres?
HAH-*ben zee ett-vahss* BESS-*sehr-ess?*

Bicycle
Have you a bicycle repair outfit?
Haben Sie eine Fahrrad-Reparatur-Ausrüstung?
HAH-*ben zee ine-uh* FAR-*raht-reh-par-ah-*TOORR-*OWSS-rüss-toong?*

Where can I rent (buy) a bicycle?
Wo kann ich ein Fahrrad mieten (kaufen)?
VOH *kahn ikh ine* FAR-*raht* MEE-*ten?*

Where can my bicycle be repaired?
Wo kann ich mein Fahrrad reparieren lassen?
voh kahn ikh mine FAR-*raht reh-par-*REER-*en* LAHSS-*senn?*

Big
This is too big.
Das ist zu gross.
dahss isst tsoo GROHSS.

This is not big enough.
Das ist nicht gross genug.
dahss isst nikht GROHSS *guh-*NOOK.

I want something bigger.
Ich möchte etwas grösseres.
ikh MÖKH-*tuh ett-vahss* GRÖ-*sehr-ess.*

Bill (Currency)
Can you change this bill?
Können Sie diesen Schein wechseln?
KÖNN-*en zee dee-zen* SHINE VECK-*seln?*

Bill (Invoice)
The bill, please.
Die Rechnung, bitte.
dee REHKH-*noong,* BIT-*tuh.*

Blanket
May I have another blanket, please?
Könnte ich noch eine Wolldecke haben, bitte?
KÖNN-*tuh ikh* NAWKH *ine-uh* VAWLL-*deck-uh* HAH-ben,
   BIT-*tuh?*

Bleed – see Accident

Board
When can we board?
Wann können wir an Bord gehen?
VAHNN *könn-en veer ahnn* BORT GAY-*en?*

Are meals served on board?
Werden Mahlzeiten an Bord serviert?
vair-den MAHL-*tsite-ten ahnn* BORT *zehr-*VEERT*?*

Boardinghouse (Pension)
Can you recommend a boardinghouse?
Können Sie mir eine Pension empfehlen?
KÖNN-*en zee meer ine-uh pahn-see-*YOHNG *emp-*FAY-*len?*

Boat
Where can I rent a boat?
Wo kann ich ein Boot mieten?
VOH *kahnn ikh ine* BOAT MEE-*ten?*

I wish to rent a boat.
Ich möchte ein Boot mieten.
ikh MÖKH-*tuh ine* BOAT MEE-*ten.*

When does the boat leave for _____?
Wann fährt das Schiff nach _____ ab?
vahnn FEHRT *dahss* SHIFF *nahkh* _____ AHPP?

Book

I would like a book of tickets.
Ich möchte ein Fahrscheinheft.
ikh MÖKH-*tuh ine* FAHR-*shine-hefft.*

Do you have a book about _____?
Haben Sie ein Buch über _____?
HAH-*ben zee ine* BOOKH Ü-*behr* _____ *?*

I would like to book passage on _____ to _____.
Ich möchte eine Überfahrt mit _____ nach _____
  buchen.
ikh MÖKH-*tuh ine-uh* Ü-*behr-fahrrt mitt* _____ *nahkh*
  _____ BOO-*khen.*

Bookstore

Where is a bookstore?
Wo ist eine Buchhandlung?
VOH *isst ine-uh* BOOKH-*hahnnd-loong?*

Border

How many kilometers is it to the border?
Wie viele Kilometer ist es bis zur Grenze?
*vee fee-luh kee-loh-*MAY-*tehr isst ess biss tsoor* GRENT-
  suh?

When do we arrive at the border?
Wann kommen wir zur Grenze?
vahnn KAWMM-*en veer tsoor* GRENT-*suh?*

Borrow

May I borrow _____?
Kann ich _____ borgen?
kahnn ikh _____ BOR-*gen?*

Boss

Where is the boss?
Wo ist der Chef?
VOH *isst dair* SHEFF?

Both

I want both.
Ich möchte beide.
ikh MÖKH-*tuh* BY-*duh.*

I like both.
Mir gefallen beide.
*meer guh-*FAHLL*-en* BY*-duh.*

Bother

Stop bothering me.
Belästigen Sie mich nicht mehr.
*buh-*LESS*-tih-gen zee mikh nikht* MAIR.

They are bothering (he is bothering) me.
Sie belästigen (Er belästigt) mich.
*zee buh-*LESS*-tih-gen (air buh-*LESS*-tikht) mikh.*

Bottle – see Wine

Brand

Is this a good brand?
Ist das eine gute Marke?
isst DAHSS *ine-uh* GOO*-tuh* MAHRR*-kuh?*

What is the best brand?
Was ist die beste Marke?
vahss isst dee BESS*-tuh* MAHRR*-kuh?*

Break

The _____ is broken. (Please have it fixed.)
Das _____ ist zerbrochen. (Bitte lassen Sie es reparieren.)
dahss _____ *isst tsehr-*BRAWKH*-en. (bit-tuh* LAHSS*-senn zee ess reh-par-*REER*-en.)*

Breakfast

When is breakfast (lunch, supper) served?
Wann wird das Frühstück (Mittagessen, Abendessen) serviert?
vahnn veert dahss FRÜ*-shtück (*MITT*-tahg-ess-senn* AH*-bent-ess-sen) zehr-*VEERT?

I want breakfast (lunch, dinner) in my room.
Ich möchte das Frühstück (Mittagessen, Abendessen) auf meinem Zimmer.
ikh MÖKH*-tuh dahss* FRÜ*-shtuck (*MITT*-tahg-ess-senn* AH*-bent-ess-sen) owf my-nem* TSIMM*-mehr.*

Is breakfast included?
Ist das Frühstück inbegriffen?
isst dahss FRÜ*-shtück inn-buh-*GRIF*-fen?*

Bring

Please bring (me) a _____.
Bitte bringen Sie (mir) ein _____.
bit-tuh BRING-*en zee (meer) ine* _____.

I did not bring a _____.
Ich habe kein _____ mitgebracht.
ikh HAH-*buh kine* _____ MITT-*guh-brahkht.*

Building

What is that building?
Was ist dieses Gebäude?
vahss isst DEE-*zus guh-*BOY-*duh?*

Bus

When does the bus leave for _____?
Wann fährt der Bus nach _____ ab?
vahnn FAIRT *dair* BOOSS *nahkh* _____ AHPP?

How much is the bus fare?
Wieviel kostet der Bus-Fahrschein?
vee-feel KAWSS-*tet dair* BOOSS-*far-shine?*

Where is the bus stop (station)?
Wo ist die Bus-Haltestelle (Endstation)?
VOH *isst dee* BOOSS-*hahll-teh-*SHTELL-*uh (*END-*shtah-*TSYOHN)?

Which bus goes to _____?
Welcher Bus fährt nach _____?
vel-kher BOOSS *fairt nahkh* _____?

Business

I am here on business.
Ich bin geschäftlich hier.
*ikh binn guh-*SHEFFT-*likh heer.*

Where is the business district?
Wo ist das Geschäfts-Viertel?
*voh isst dahss guh-*SHEFFTS-FEERR-*tel?*

Busy

I am busy.
Ich bin beschäftigt.
*ikh binn buh-*SHEFF-*tickt.*

Are you busy?
Sind Sie beschäftigt?
zinnt zee buh-SHEFF-tickt?

The line is busy.
Die Leitung ist besetzt.
dee LYE-toong isst buh-ZETTST.

Buy

Where can I buy _____?
Wo kann ich _____ kaufen?
VOH *kahnn ikh* _____ KOW-*fen?*

I wish to buy _____.
Ich möchte _____ kaufen.
ikh MÖKH-*tuh* _____ KOW-*fen.*

Cab – see Taxi

Cabin

Where is cabin number _____?
Wo ist Kabine Nummer _____?
*voh isst kah-*BEE-*nuh* NOOMM-*ehr* _____?

Cablegram-see Telegram

Call

I want to put a call through to _____.
Ich möchte nach _____ telefonieren.
ikh MÖKH-*tuh nahkh* _____ *tay-luh-foh-*NEE-*ren.*

Please call me at _____.
Bitte wecken Sie mich um _____.
bit-tuh VECK-*en zee mikh oomm* _____.

How much is a call to _____?
Wieviel kostet ein Telefongespräch nach _____?
vee-feel KAWSS-*tet ine tay-luh-*FOHN-*guh-*SPREHKH
nahkh _____?

What is this (that) called?
Wie heisst das?
vee HYSST *dahss?*

Camera

Do you rent cameras?
Verleihen Sie Cameras?
*fehr-*LYE-*en zee kah-meh-*RAHZ?

I need film for this camera.
Ich brauche einen Film für diese Camera.
ikh BROW-*khuh* *eye-nen* FILM *für dee-zuh* kah-meh-RAH.

Something is the matter with this camera.
Etwas ist nicht in Ordnung mit dieser Camera.
ETT-*vahss isst* NIKHT *inn* AWRD-*noong mitt* DEE-*zehr kah-meh*-RAH.

Can you fix it?
Können Sie sie reparieren?
KONN-*en zee zee ray-pah*-REER-*en?*

Please direct me to a camera shop.
Bitte, wo ist hier ein Camera-Geschäft?
bit-tuh, VOH *isst* HEER *ine kah-meh*-RAH-*guh*-SHEFFT?

Camp

May we camp in your field?
Können wir auf Ihrer Wiese campieren?
KÖNN-*en veer owf ear-ehr* VEE-*zuh kam*-PEER-*ren?*

Is there a campsite nearby?
Ist ein Camping-Platz hier in der Nähe?
isst ine KAM-*ping-plahtts* HEER *inn dair* NAY-*uh?*

Can

Can you help me?
Können Sie mir helfen?
KÖNN-*en zee meer* HELL-*fen?*

Cancel

Please cancel my reservation.
Bitte annullieren Sie meine Buchung.
bit-tuh ah-noo-LEER-*rehn zee mine-uh* BOOKH-*oong.*

Is the flight cancelled?
Ist der Flug annulliert?
isst dair FLOOCK *ah-noo*-LEERT?

Candle

Do you have any candles?
Haben Sie Kerzen?
HAH-*ben zee* KEHR-*tsun?*

Car – see Automobile

Card (Calling)
May I have your calling card?
Kann ich Ihre Visitenkarte haben?
kahnn ikh EAR-eh vee-ZEE-ten-kahr-tuh HAH-ben?

Card (Post)
I wish to buy some postcards (postal cards).
Ich möchte Ansichtskarten (Postkarten) kaufen.
ikh MÖKH-tuh AHNN-zikhts-kahrr-ten (PAWSST-kahr-ten) KOW-fen.

Careful
Please be careful.
Bitte seien Sie vorsichtig.
bit-tuh ZY-en zee FOR-zikh-tick.

Please handle this with care.
Bitte behandeln Sie das mit Vorsicht.
bit-tuh buh-HAHNND-deln zee DAHSS mitt FOR-zikht.

Carry
Please carry this (my bags).
Bitte tragen Sie das (mein Gepäck).
bit-tuh TRAH-gen zee DAHSS (mine guh-PECK).

Cash
Can you cash this check?
Können Sie diesen Scheck einlösen?
KÖNN-en zee dee-zen SHECK INE-lö-zen?

Cashier
Where is the cashier?
Wo ist der Kassierer?
VOH ist dair kahss-SEER-ehr?

Castle
Are there tours of the castle?
Gibt es Führungen durch das Schloss?
gippt ess FU-roong-en doorrkh dahss SHLAWSS?

Catalog
May I have one of your catalogs?
Kann ich einen Ihrer Kataloge haben?
KAHNN ikh eye-nen EAR-ehr kah-tah-LOH-guh HAH-ben?

Catch
I have to catch a train.
Ich muss einen Zug erreichen.
ich MOOSS *eye-nen* TSOOK *ehr-*RYE-*khen.*

Cathedral
Please take me (direct me) to the cathedral.
Bitte bringen Sie mich (sagen Sie mir den Weg) zum Dom.
bit-tuh BRING-*en zee mikh (*ZAH-*gen zee meer dane* VECK*) tsoom* DOME.

Chamber of Commerce
Please direct me (take me) to the Chamber of Commerce.
Bitte sagen Sie mire den Weg (bringen Sie mich) zur Handelskammer.
bit-tuh ZAH-*gen zee meer dane* VECK (BRING-*en zee mikh) tsoor* HAHNN-*delss-kahmm-mehr.*

Change
Can you change this?
Können Sie das wechseln?
könn-en zee dahss VECK-*seln?*

May I have some change?
Kann ich etwas Kleingeld haben?
KAHNN *ikh ett-vahss* KLYNE-*gelt* HAH-*ben?*

Please change the sheets today.
Bitte wechseln Sie heute die Bettlaken.
bit-tuh VECK-*seln zee* HOY-*tuh dee* BET-*lahk-en.*

Where must I change for _____?
Wo muss ich nach _____ umsteigen?
VOH *mooss ikh nahkh* _____ OOMM-*shtye-gen?*

Chapel – see Church

Charge
What is this charge for?
Wofür ist dieser Betrag?
*voh-*FÜR *isst* DEE-*sehr buh-*TRAHK?

Is there a service charge?
Gibt es einen Bedienungszuschlag?
*gippt ess eye-nen buh-*DEEN-*oongs-*TSOO-*shlahk?*

What is the admission charge?
Wie hoch ist die Eintrittsgebühr?
vee HOHKH *isst dee* INE-*tritts-guh-*BÜR*?*

What is the charge per (minute, hour, day, week, kilogram, kilometer)?
Wieviel berechnen Sie pro (Minute, Stunde, Tag, Woche, Kilogramm, Kilometer)?
*vee-feel buh-*REHKH-*nen zee pro (mee-*NOO-*tuh,* SHTOONN-*duh,* TAHK, VAWKH-*uh,* KEE-*loh-grahm,* KEE-*loh-may-tehr)?*

Cheap
I prefer something cheaper.
Ich möchte etwas billigeres.
ikh MÖKH-*tuh ett-vahss* BILL-*ikh-ehr-ess.*

Check
The check, please.
Zahlen, bitte.
TSAH-*len,* BIT-*tuh.*

Will you cash a check?
Können Sie einen Scheck einlösen?
KONN-*en zee eye-nen* SHECK INE-*lö-sen?*

Here is the check for my baggage.
Hier ist mein Gepäckschein.
HEER *isst mine guh-*PECK-*shine.*

Is a traveler's check acceptable?
Akzeptieren Sie einen Reisescheck?
*ahk-tsepp-*TEER-*en zee eye-nen* RYE-*zuh-sheck?*

Checkout
What is checkout time?
Wann muss ich das Zimmer verlassen?
VAHNN *mooss ikh dahss* TSIMM-*ehr fehr-*LAHSS-*senn?*

Children
Are children allowed?
Nehmen Sie Kinder?
NAY-*men zee* KINN-*dehr?*

Chilly – see Cold

Christian

Are you a Christian?
Sind Sie ein Christ?
zinnt zee ine KRISST?

I am a Christian.
Ich bin ein Christ.
ikh binn ine KRISST.

Church

I would like to attend church services.
Ich möchte gern dem Gottesdienst beiwohnen.
ikh MOKH-*tuh* GEHRN *dame* GAWTT-*ess-deenst* BY-*voh-nen.*

When are church services held?
Wann wird der Gottesdienst gehalten?
vahnn VEERT *dair* GAWT-*tess-deenst guh*-HAHLL-*ten?*

Cigarette

A pack of cigarettes, please.
Eine Schachtel Zigaretten, bitte.
ine-uh SHAHKH-*tel tsee-gah*-RET-*ten,* BIT-*tuh.*

Citizen

Are you a citizen of _____?
Sind Sie _____ Staatsbürger?
zinut zee _____ SHTAHTS-*bür-gehr?*

I am a citizen of the United States.
Ich bin amerikanischer Staatsbürger.
ikh binn ah-may-ree-KAH-*nish-ehr* SHTAHTS-*bür-gehr.*

Clean

This is not clean.
Das ist nicht rein.
dahss isst nikht RINE.

I want this cleaned.
Ich möchte das reinigen lassen.
ikh MÖKH-*tuh dahss* RINE-*ih-gen* LAHSS-*senn.*

Clerk

I wish to speak to the room clerk.
Ich möchte mit dem Empfangschef sprechen.
ikh MÖKH-*tuh mitt dame emp*-FAHNNGS-*sheff* SHPREH-*khen.*

Climate – see Weather

Climb

Can one climb _____ at this time of year?
Kann man um diese Jahreszeit den _____ ersteigen?
kahn MAHNN *oomm* um DEE-*zuh* YAH-*ress-tsite dane*
_____ *air*-SHTYE-*gen?*

How long does it take to climb _____?
Wie lange braucht man, um den _____ zu ersteigen?
vee LAHNNG-*uh* BROWKHT *mahnn oomm dane* _____
tsoo ehr-SHTYE-*gen?*

I cannot climb stairs.
Ich kann keine Treppen steigen.
ikh KAHNN *kine-uh* TREPP-*en* SHTYE-*gen.*

Close

Are you closed?
Haben Sie geschlossen?
HAH-*ben zee gun*-SHLAWSS-*en?*

When do you open?
Wann öffnen Sie?
VAHNN ÖFF-*nen zee?*

When does it close (open)?
Wann schliesst (öffnet) es?
vahnn SHLEEST (ÖFF-*net) ess?*

Close the door (the window), please.
Schliessen Sie die Tür (das Fenster), bitte.
SHLEE-*sen zee dee* TÜRR *(dahss* FENN-*stehr),* BIT-*tuh.*

Clothing

What kind of clothing should be worn?
Was für Kleidung soll man tragen?
vahss für KLYE-*doong zawll mahnn* TRAH-*gen?*

Can you recommend a good clothing store?
Können Sie mir ein gutes Kleidergeschäft empfehlen?
KONN-*en zee* MEER *ine* GOO-*tess* KLYE-*dehr-guh*-SHEFFT
emp-FAY-*len?*

Coach

Are there any coach seats available?
Gibt es noch Sitzplätze im Autobus?
gippt ess nawkh ZITTS-*plett-zuh imm* OW-*toh-boos?*

Coast

How far is the coast from here?
Wie weit ist es von hier zur Küste?
vee VITE *isst ess fawnn* HEER *tsoor* KÜSS-*tuh?*

How long does it take to reach the coast?
Wie lange braucht man bis zur Küste?
vee LAHNNG-*uh* BROWKHT *mahnn biss tsoor* KÜSS-*tuh?*

Coat

Should I wear a coat (and tie)?
Soll ich eine Jacke (und Krawatte) tragen?
zawll ikh ine-uh YAHCK-*uh (oonnt krah-*VAHTT-*tuh)*
   TRAH-*gen?*

Cocktail

Do you serve cocktails?
Servieren Sie Cocktails?
*zehr-*VEER-*en zee* KOCK-*tehls?*

Would you like a cocktail?
Möchten Sie einen Cocktail?
MÖKH-*ten zee eye-nen* KOCK-*tehl?*

Cold

This is cold.
Das ist kalt.
dahss ist KAHLLT.

I am cold.
Mir ist kalt.
MEER *isst* KAHLLT.

Color

I do not like the color.
Die Farbe gefällt mir nicht.
dee FAR-*buh guh-*FELLT *meer nikht.*

Do you have other colors?
Haben Sie andere Farben?
hah-ben zee AHNN-*dehr-uh* FAR-*ben?*

Do you have a brighter (darker) color?
Haben Sie eine hellere (dunklere) Farbe?
hah-ben zee ine-uh HELL-*ehr-uh (*DOONNG-*klehr-uh)*
   FAR-*buh?*

Come

Please come back later.
Bitte kommen Sie später zurück.
bit-tuh KAWMM-*en zee* SHPAY-*tehr tsoo-*RÜCK.

Come here, please.
Kommen Sie her, bitte.
KAWMM-*en zee* HEHR, BIT-*tuh.*

Come in.
Kommen Sie herein.
KAWMM-*en zee hehr-*INE.

Companion

I am traveling with a companion.
Ich reise mit einem Gefährten.
ikh RYE-*zuh mitt eye-nem guh-*FAIR-*ten.*

Have you seen my companion?
Haben Sie meinen Gefährten gesehen?
HAH-*ben zee myc-nen guh-*FAIR-*ten guh-*ZAY-*en?*

Company

I am traveling on company business.
Ich reise für die Firma.
ikh RYE-*zuh für dee* FEERR-*muh.*

What company are you with?
Bei welcher Firma sind Sie?
by vel-kher FEERR-*muh zinnt zee?*

Compartment

I would like a compartment.
Ich möchte ein Abteil.
ikh MÖKH-*tuh ine* AHPP-*tile.*

Complaint

I have a complaint.
Ich habe eine Beschwerde.
ikh HAH-*buh ine-uh buh-*SHVAIR-*duh.*

Confirm

Can you confirm my reservation on flight number
_____?

Können Sie meine Buchung für Flug Nummer _____
bestätigen?

KÖNN-*en zee mine-uh* BOOKH-*oong für* FLOOCK *noom-ehr*
_____ *buh-*SHTAY-*tih-gen?*

Consulate

Please direct me to the U.S. Consulate (to the American Embassy).

Bitte sagen Sie mir den Weg zum amerikanischen Konsulat (zur amerikanischen Botschaft).

bit-tuh ZAH-*gen zee meer dane* VECK *tsoom ah-may-ree-*KAH-*nish-en kawwn-zool-*AHTT *(tsoor ah-may-ree-*KAH-*nish-en* BOAT-*shahft).*

Contents

What are the contents (ingredients) of this dish?

Welche Zutaten enthält diese Speise?

VEL-*khuh tsoo-*TAH-*ten ent-*HELLT *dee-zuh* SHPYE-*zuh?*

Convention

I am attending a convention.

Ich wohne einer Tagung bei.

ikh VOH-*nuh eye-nehr* TAH-*goong* BY.

Cook

Can you recommend a good cook?

Können Sie mir eine gute Köchin empfehlen?

könn-en zee MEER *ine-uh goo-tuh* KÖ-*khen emp-*FAY-*len?*

I want it thoroughly cooked.

Ich möchte es gut durchgebraten.

ikh MÖKH-*tuh ess goot* DOORRKH-*guh-*BRAH-*ten.*

Must this be cooked before being eaten?

Muss das gekocht werden, bevor es gegessen wird?

*mooss dahss guh-*KAWKHT *vair-den buh-for ess guh-*GESS-*en veert?*

Correct

That is (not) correct.
Das ist (nicht) korrekt.
*dahss isst (*NIKHT*) kaw-*REKT.

Correspond

I would like to correspond with you.
Ich möchte gern mit Ihnen korrespondieren.
ikh MÖKH-*tuh* GEHRN *mitt* EEN-*en kaw-res-pawnn-*DEE-*ren.*

May I have your address?
Kann ich Ihre Adresse haben?
*kahnn ikh ear-uh ah-*DRESS-*uh hah-ben?*

Cost

How much does it cost (per liter, per kilogram)?
Wieviel kostet es (pro Liter, pro Kilogramm)?
vee-feel KAWSS-*tet ess (pro* LEE-*tehr, pro* KEE-*loh-grahmm)?*

It costs too much.
Es kostet zu viel.
ess KAWSS-*tet tsoo* FEEL.

Costly

It is too costly.
Es ist zu kostspieling.
ess isst tsoo KAWSST-*shpee-lick.*

Costume

Where do the people wear native costume?
Wo tragen die Leute Landestracht?
voh TRAH-*gen dee* LOY-*tuh* LAHNND-*ess-trahkht?*

Cot–see Bed

Cotton

Do you have any made of cotton?
Haben Sie welche aus Baumwolle?
hah-ben zee VEL-*khuh owss* BOWM-*vawll-uh?*

Country

What country are you from?
Aus welchem Land sind Sie?
owss vell-khem LAHNNT *zinnt zee?*

Can this be taken out of the country?
Kann man das aus dem Land herausbringen?
kahnn MAHNN *dahss owss dame* LAHNNT *hehr-*OWSS-*bring-en?*

Credit Card
What credit cards do you honor?
Welche Kreditkarten akzeptieren Sie?
VELL-*kheh* kray-DEET-*kahrr-ten* ahk-tsepp-TEER-*en zee?*

Cup
Please bring me another cupful.
Bitte bringen Sie mir noch eine Tasse.
bit-tuh BRING-*en zee meer* NAWKH *ine-uh* TAHSS-*suh.*

Currency
Do you accept U.S. currency?
Akzeptieren Sie amerikanisches Geld?
ahk-tsepp-TEER-*en zee ah-may-ree-*KAH-*nish-es* GELT?
Where can I exchange currency?
Wo kann ich Devisen umwechseln?
VOH *kahnn ikh deh-*VEE-*zen* OOMM-*veck-seln?*

Current
Are there any dangerous currents?
Gibt es eine gefährliche Gegenströmung?
*gippt ess ine-uh guh-*FAIR-*likh-uh gay-gen-shtrö-moong?*

Customhouse
Where is the customhouse?
Wo ist das Zollamt?
VOH *isst dahss* TSAWLL-*ahmmt?*

Customs
Where is the customs office?
Wo ist die Zoll-Stelle?
voh isst dee TSAWLL-*shtell-uh?*

Do we have to go through customs?
Müssen wir durch den Zoll gehen?
MÜSS-*en veer doorrkh dane* TSAWLL *gay-en?*

Cut-see Accident

Cycle – see also Bicycle, Hostel

I am (we are) cycling to _____.
Ich (wir) fahre(n) mit dem Fahrrad nach _____.
ikh (veer) FAR-*eh(n) mitt dame* FAR-*raht nahkh* _____.

How long does it take to cycle to _____?
Wie lange braucht man mit dem Fahrrad nach _____?
vee LAHNNG-*uh* BROWKHT *mahnn mitt dame* FAR-*raht nahkh* _____?

Dance

May I have this dance?
Darf ich um diesen Tanz bitten?
DAHRFF *ikh oomm dee-zen* TAHNNTS BIT-*ten?*

Where can we go to dance?
Wo können wir tanzen gehen?
VOH *könn-en veer* TAHNNTS-*sen* GAY-*en?*

Dangerous

Is it dangerous?
Ist es gefährlich?
*isst ess guh-*FARE-*likh?*

Date

What is the date today?
Welches Datum ist heute?
vell-khus DAH-*toomm isst* HOY-*tuh?*

Do you have a date?
Haben Sie eine Verabredung?
HAH-*ben zee ine-uh fehr-*AHPP-*ray-doong?*

Day

What is the rate per day?
Wieviel kostet es pro Tag?
vee-feel KAWSS-*tet ess pro* TAHK?

Declare

I have nothing to declare.
Ich habe nichts zu verzollen.
ikh hah-beh NIKHTS *tsoo fehr-*TSAWLL-*en.*

Deep

Is it very deep?
Ist es sehr tief?
isst ess zair TEEF?

How deep is it?
Wie tief ist es?
vee TEEF *isst ess?*

Delay

Has there been a delay?
Gibt es eine Verspätung?
GIPPT *ess ine-uh fehr-*SHPAY*-toong?*

Will there be a delay?
Wird es eine Verspätung geben?
VEERT *ess ine-uh fehr-*SHPAY*-toong* GAY*-ben?*

Deliver

Please deliver this to this address.
Bitte liefern Sie das an diese Adresse.
bit-tuh LEE*-fehrn zee dahss ahnn* DEE*-zuh ah-*DRESS*-uh.*

Dentist

Can you recommend a good (English-speaking) dentist?
Können Sie mir einen guten (englisch-sprechenden)
    Zahnarzt empfehlen?
KÖNN*-en zee* MEER *eye-nen* GOO*-ten (eng-lish-*
    SHPREHKH*-en-den)* TSAHN*-artst emp-*FAY*-len?*

Can you give me an appointment as soon as possible?
Können Sie mich so bald wie möglich darannehmen?
KÖNN*-en zee mikh zoh* BAHLLT *vee* MÖG*-likh dahr-*
    AHNN*-nay-men?*

I (don't) have an appointment.
Ich bin (nicht) bestellt.
*ikh binn (*NIKHT*) buh-*SHTELLT.

I have a terrible toothache.
Ich habe fürchterliche Zahnschmerzen.
ikh hah-beh FÜRKH*-tehr-likh-uh* TSAHN*-shmehr-tsen.*

I have lost a filling.
Ich habe eine Plombe verloren.
ikh hah-beh ine-uh PLOH*-muh fehr-*LOH*-ren.*

The filling is loose.
Die Plombe ist locker.
dee PLOH-*muh isst* LAWCKH-*ehr.*

Can you put in a temporary filling?
Können Sie eine provisorische Füllung hineingeben?
KÖNN-*en zee* ine-*uh* pro-vee-ZOH-*rish-uh* FÜLL-*oong*
   *hinn-*INE-*gay-ben?*

Please don't pull it unless you must.
Bitte ziehen Sie ihn nicht, wenn es nicht sein muss.
bit-tuh TSEE-*en zee een* NIKHT *venn ess nikht* ZINE
   mooss.

Please (don't) use novocaine.
Bitte verwenden Sie (kein) Novocain.
*bit-tuh fehr-*VENN-*den zee (*KINE*)* NOH-*voh-kane.*

When can you give me another appointment?
Wann können Sie mich wieder vornehmen?
VAHNN *könn-en zee* MIKH VEE-*dehr* FOR-*nay-men?*

Deposit
Is a deposit required?
Ist eine Anzahlung nötig?
isst ine-uh AHNN-*tsah-loong* NÖ-*tick?*

How much deposit is required?
Wieviel Anzahlung ist nötig?
vee-feel AHNN-*tsah-loong isst* NÖ-*tick?*

Dessert
What do you have for dessert?
Was haben Sie als Nachspeise?
vahss HAH-*ben zee ahllss* NAHKH-*shpye-zuh?*

Is dessert included?
Ist Nachspeise inbegriffen?
isst NAHKH-*shpye-zuh inn-buh-*GRIFF-*en?*

Dining Car
Where is the dining car?
Wo ist der Speisewagen?
VOH *isst dair* SHPYE-*zuh-vah-gen?*

Does the train have a dining car?
Hat der Zug einen Speisewagen?
haht dair TSOOK *eye-nen* SHPYE-*zuh-vah-gen?*

Dining Room
Where is the dining room?
Wo ist der Speisesaal?
VOH *isst dair* SHPYE-*zuh-zahl?*

Dinner
When is dinner served?
Wann wird das Abendessen serviert?
vahnn veert dahss AH-*bent-ess-en zehr*-VEERT?

Will you have dinner with me?
Darf ich Sie zum Abendessen einladen?
DAHRFF *ikh zee tsoom* AH-*bent-ess-en* INE-*lah-den?*

Direct
What is the most direct route to _____?
Welches ist der kürzeste Weg nach _____?
VELL-*khehs isst dair* KÜRTS-*ess-tuh* VECK *nahkh* _____?

Please direct me to _____.
Bitte sagen Sie mir den Weg nach _____.
bit-tuh ZAH-*gen zee meer dane* VECK *nahkh* _____.

Direction
In which direction is _____?
In welcher Richtung ist _____?
inn vell-kher RIKH-*toong ist* _____?

Dirty
This is dirty. (Please bring me another.)
Das ist schmutzig. (Bitte bringen Sie mir ein anderes.)
dahss isst SHMOOTTS-*ick. (bit-tuh* BRING-*en zee meer ine*
  AHNN-*dehr-ess.)*

Discount
Is there a discount for students?
Gibt es einen Rabatt für Studenten?
*gippt ess eye-nen rah-*BAHTT *für shtoo-*DEN-*ten?*

Dish

What is in this dish?
Was ist in dieser Speise?
VAHSS isst inn dee-zehr SHPYE-zuh?

Which dish do you recommend?
Welche Speise empfehlen Sie mir?
vell-khuh SHPYE-zuh emp-FAY-len zee meer?

Is this dish served hot or cold?
Wird diese Speise warm order kalt serviert?
veert dee-zuh SHPYE-zuh VAHRRM oh-dehr KAHLLT zehr-VEERT?

Disinfected

Please have this disinfected.
Bitte lassen Sie das desinfizieren.
bit-tuh LAHSS-sen zee dahss dess-inn-fee-TSEER-ren.

Distance

What is the distance to _____?
Wie weit ist es nach _____?
vee VITE isst ess nahkh _____?

District

Please take me to the _____ district.
Bitte bringen Sie mich nach dem _____ Distrikt.
bit-tuh BRING-en zee mikh nahkh dame _____ DISS-trikt.

Disturb

Please do not disturb me until _____.
Bitte stören Sie mich nicht bis _____.
bit-tuh SHTÖ-ren zee mikh NIKHT biss _____.

He is disturbing me.
Er belästigt mich.
air buh-LESS-tickt mikh.

Divorced

I am divorced (about to be divorced).
Ich bin geschieden (in Scheidung).
ikh binn guh-SHEE-den (inn SHY-doong).

Dock

When will the ship dock?
Wann legt das Schiff an?
vahnn LAYGT dahss SHIFF AHNN?

Is our baggage on the dock?
Ist unser Gepäck im Dock?
isst OONN-*zehr guh*-PECK *imm* DAWCK?

Doctor – see also Medical

Can you recommend a good doctor?
Können Sie mir einen guten Arzt empfehlen?
könn-en zee MEER *eye-nen* GOO-*ten* ARTST *emp*-FAY-*len?*

I would like to see the doctor (dentist).
Ich möchte den Arzt (Zahnarzt) sprechen.
ikh MOKH-*tuh dane* ARTST *(*TSAHNN-*artst)* SHPREHKH-*en.*

Send for a doctor.
Holen Sie einen Arzt.
HOH-*len zee eye-nen* ARTST.

Dog

Are dogs allowed?
Sind Hunde erlaubt?
zinnt HOON-*duh ehr*-LOWPT?

Dollar

How much (how many) can I get for a dollar?
Wieviel (wie viele) kann ich für einen Dollar bekommen?
vee-FEEL *(vee* FEEL-*uh) kahnn ikh für eye-nen* DOH-*lahr buh*-KOMM-*en?*

How many _____ are exchanged for one dollar?
Wie viele _____ geben Sie für einen Dollar?
vee FEEL-*uh* _____ *gay-ben zee für* EYE-*nen* DOH-*lahr?*

Door

Please open (close) the door.
Bitte öffnen (schliessen) Sie die Tür.
bit-tuh ÖFF-*nen (*SHLEE-*sen) zee dee* TURR.

I cannot lock my door.
Ich kann meine Zimmertür nicht verschliessen.
ikh KAHNN *mine-uh* TSIMM-*mehr-türr nikht fehr*-SHLEE-*sen.*

I cannot unlock my door.
Ich kann meine Zimmertür nicht aufschliessen.
ikh MOKH-*tuh dane* ARTST *(*TSAHNN-*artst)* SHPREHKH-
en.

Double Bed

Do you have a room with a double bed?
Haben Sie ein Zimmer mit Doppelbett?
hah-ben zee ine TSIMM-*ehr mitt* DAWPP-*el-bet?*

Dozen

How much is a dozen?
Wieviel kostet ein Dutzend?
vee-feel KAWSS-*tet ine* DOOTT-*sent?*

I'll take a dozen.
Ich nehme ein Dutzend.
ikh NAY-*muh ine* DOOTT-*sent.*

Draft

There is a draft.
Hier ist ein Luftzug.
HEER *isst ine* LOOFFT-*tsook.*

Dressed

I am not dressed.
Ich bin nicht angekleidet.
ikh binn nikht AHNN-*guh-klye-dett.*

Dresses

I wish to look at dresses.
Ich möchte mir Kleider ansehen.
ikh MÖKH-*tuh meer* KLYE-*dehr* AHNN-*zay-en.*

Dressing Room

Where is the men's (women's) dressing room?
Wo ist die Herren- (Damen-) Garderobe?
voh isst dee HEHRRN- *(*DAH-*men-) gahr-duh-*ROH-*buh?*

Dressing (Salad)

Vinegar and oil only.
Nur Essig and Öl, bitte.
noor ESS-*ikh oonnt* ÖL, BIT-*tuh.*

Drink

Where can I get something to drink?
Wo bekomme ich etwas zu trinken?
*voh buh-*KOMM-*uh ikh ett-vahss tsoo* TRINK-*en?*

What do you have to drink?
Was haben Sie zu trinken?
vahss HAH-*ben zee tsoo* TRINK-*en?*

Would you like a drink?
Möchten Sie etwas trinken?
MÖKH-*ten zee* ETT-*vahss* TRINK-*en?*

Drive

Please drive me to _____.
Bitte fahren Sie mich nach _____.
bit-tuh FAH-*ren zee mikh nahkh* _____.

Please drive more carefully (more slowly).
Bitte fahren Sie vorsichtiger (langsamer).
bit-tuh FAH-*ren zee* FOR-*zikh-tick-ehr* (LAHNNG-*zahm-ehr*).

Can you drive?
Können Sie chauffieren?
KÖNN-*en zee show-*FEER-*en?*

Driver

I want to hire a driver.
Ich möchte einen Chauffeur engagieren.
ikh MÖKH-*tuh eye-nen shoh-*FUHR *ahnn-gah-*ZHEE-*ren.*

I have (do not have) an international driver's license.
Ich habe einen (keinen) internationalen Führerschein.
ikh HAH-*beh eye-nen (kine-en) inn-tehr-nahts-yoh-*NAHL
FÜ-*rehr-shine.*

Drugstore

Please direct me (take me) to a drugstore.
Bitte sagen Sie mir den Weg (bringen Sie mich) zu einer Apotheke.
bit-tuh ZAH-*gen zee meer dane* VECK (BRING-*en zee
mikh) tsoo eye-nehr ah-poh-*TAY-*kuh.*

Dry Clean-see Laundry

Duty

Must I pay duty on this?
Muss ich Zoll dafür zahlen?
mooss ikh TSAWLL *dah-für* TSAH-*len?*

What is the duty on this?
Wie hoch ist der Zoll dafür?
vee HOHKH *isst dair* TSAWLL *dah-für?*

Early

It is too early.
Es ist zu früh.
ess isst tsoo FRÜ.

Are we too early?
Sind wir zu früh gekommen?
zinnt-veer tsoo FRÜ *guh-*KOMM-*en?*

Eat

What do you have to eat?
Was haben Sie zu essen?
vahss HAH-*ben zee tsoo* ESS-*en?*

Where can I get something to eat?
Wo bekomme ich etwas zu essen?
*voh buh-*KOMM-*uh ikh* ETT-*vahss tsoo* ESS-*en?*

Do you want to eat now?
Wollen Sie jetzt essen?
VAWLL-*en zee yettst* ESS-*en?*

Either

Either one will do.
Beides ist mir recht.
BY-*duhs isst meer* REHKHT.

Electricity

Is there an electrical outlet here?
Gibt es eine Steckdose?
gippt ess ine-uh SHTECK-*doh-zuh?*

Elevator

Is there an elevator here?
Gibt es einen Lift?
gippt ess eye-nen LIFT?

Embassy – see Consulate

Emergency

This is an emergency.
Es ist dringend.
ess isst DRING-*ent.*

Engaged

I am engaged.
Ich bin beschäftigt.
*ikh binn buh-*SHEFF*-tickt.*

I am engaged to be married.
Ich bin verlobt.
*ikh binn fehr-*LOHPT.

English

Do you speak English?
Sprechen Sie englisch?
SHPREHKH-*en zee* ENG-*lish?*

I need an English-speaking guide.
Ich brauche einen englisch-sprechenden Führer.
ikh BROWKH-*uh eye-nen* ENG-*lish-*SHPREHKH-*en-den* FÜ-*rehr.*

I speak only English
Ich spreche nur englisch.
ikh SHPREHKH-*uh noorr* ENG-*lish.*

Is there a church service in English?
Gibt es einen Gottesdienst in englischer Sprache?
gippt ess eye-nen GAWT-*tess-deenst inn* ENG-*lish-ehr* SHPRAKH-*uh?*

Enough

That is enough.
Das ist genug.
*dahss isst guh-*NOOK.

It isn't hot enough.
Es ist nicht heiss genug.
ess isst nikht HICE *guh-*NOOK.

I have enough, thank you.
Ich habe genug, danke.
ikh HAH-*beh guh-*NOOK, DAHNNG-*kuh.*

I do not have enough money with me.
Ich habe nicht genug Geld bei mir.
ikh HAH-*beh nikht guh*-NOOK GELLT *by meer.*

Is that enough?
Ist das genug?
isst dahss guh-NOOK*?*

Entrance
Where is the entrance to _____?
Wo ist der Eingang zu _____?
VOH *isst dair* INE-*gahng tsoo* _____*?*

Envelope
May I have an envelope?
Kann ich einen Umschlag haben?
KAHNN *ikh eye-nen* OOMM-*shlahk* HAH-*ben?*

Equipment
Do you rent equipment for _____?
Verleihen Sie Ausrüstungen für _____?
fehr-LYE-*en zee* OWSS-*rüss-toong für* _____*?*

Error
There is an error here, I believe.
Hier ist ein Irrtum, glaube ich.
HEER *isst ine* EERR-*toomm,* GLOW-*buh ikh.*

Escort
May I escort you home?
Darf ich Sie nach Hause begleiten?
dahrf ikh zee nahkh HOW-*zuh buh*-GLITE-*en?*

Evening
See you this evening!
Bis heute Abend!
bis HOY-*tuh* AH-*bent!*

Excess
What is the rate for excess baggage?
Wie ist der Tarif für Übergewicht?
vee isst dair TAH-*reef für* Ü-*behr-guh-vikht?*

Is my baggage in excess of the weight allowance?
Hat mein Gepäck Übergewicht?
haht mine guh-PECK Ü-*behr-guh-vikht?*

Exchange

What is the exchange rate for the dollar?

Wie ist der Umrechnungskurs für den Dollar?

vee isst dair OOMM-*rehkh-noongs-koorrss für dane* DOH-*lahr?*

Can I exchange this?

Kann ich das umtauschen?

kahnn ikh dahss OOMM-*tow-shen?*

I would like to exchange these dollars for _____.

Ich möchte diese Dollar in _____ umwechseln.

ikh MÖKH-*tuh dee-zuh* DOH-*lahr inn* _____ OOMM-*veck-seln.*

Excursion

I would like to buy an excursion ticket.

Ich möchte eine Ausflugs-Fahrkarte lösen.

ikh MÖKH-*tuh ine-uh* OWSS-*floocks-far-kahrr-tuh* LÖ-*zen.*

When does the excursion boat run?

Wann geht das Ausflugs-Schiff?

VAHNN *gayt dahss* OWSS-*floocks-shiff.*

How long does the excursion trip last?

Wie lange dauert der Ausflug?

vee LAHNNG-*uh dow-ehrt dair* OWSS-*floock?*

Excuse

Excuse me!

Entschuldigen Sie!

*ent-*SHOOL-*dih-gen zee!*

Exit

Where is the exit?

Wo ist der Ausgang?

VOH *isst dair* OWSS-*gahng?*

Expensive

It is too expensive.

Es ist zu teuer.

ess isst tsoo TOY-*ehr.*

Do you have anything less expensive?

Haben Sie etwas Billigeres?

HAH-*ben zee ett-vahss* BILL-*ig-ehr-ess?*

Express

Where do I catch the express to _____?

Wo kann ich in den Express Zug nach _____ einstei-
gen?

VOH *kahnn ikh inn dane ex*-PRESS-*tsook nahkh* _____
INE-*shtye-gen?*

Is this the express?

Ist das der Express-Zug?

isst dahss dair ex-PRESS-*tsook?*

Fade

Will this color fade?

Verblasst diese Farbe?

fehr-BLAHSST *dee-zuh* FAR-*buh?*

Family

Do you have family rates?

Haben Sie einen Sondertarif für Familien?

hah-ben zee eye-nen ZAWNN-*dehr*-TAHR-*reef für fah*-
MEEL-*yen?*

Far

How far is it (to _____)?

Wie weit ist es (nach _____)?

vee VITE *isst ess (nahkh* _____)?

Fare

How much is the fare (to _____)?

Wieviel kostet die Fahrkarte (nach _____)?

vee-feel KAWSS-*tet dee* FAR-*kahrr-tuh (nahkh* _____)?

Fast

Don't go so fast, please.

Fahren Sie nicht so schnell, bitte.

FAH-*ren zee nikht zoh* SHNELL, BIT-*tuh.*

Fat

There is too much fat on this. (Take it back.)

Da ist zu viel Fett darauf. (Nehmen Sie es zurück.)

dah isst tsoo-FEEL FETT *dahr*-OWF. *(*NAY-*men zee ess
tsoo*-RÜCK.*)*

Fee

What is your fee?
Wie ist Ihr Honorar?
*VEE isst ear hoh-noh-*RAHRR*?*

What is the admission fee?
Wie hoch ist die Eintritts-Gebühr?
vee HOHKH *isst dee* INE-*tritts-guh-*BÜR*?*

Ferry

Is there a ferry to _____?
Gibt es eine Fähre nach _____ ?
gippt ess ine-uh FARE-*uh nahkh* _____?

When does the ferry leave?
Wann geht die Fähre ab?
VAHNN gayt dee FARE-*uh* AHPP*?*

What is the fare for the ferry?
Wieviel kostet die Fahrkarte für die Fähre?
vee-feel KAWSS-*tet dee* FAR-*kahrr-tuh für dee* FARE-*uh?*

Fill

Please fill the glass (the tub, the cup, the tank, the bottle).
Bitte füllen Sie das Glas (die Wanne, die Tasse, den Tank, die Flasche).
bit-tuh FÜLL-*en zee dahss* GLAHSS *(dee* VAHNN-*nuh, dee* TAHSS-*suh, dane* TAHNNK*, dee* FLAHSH-*uh).*

Filling

I have lost a filling from my tooth.
Ich habe eine Plombe aus meinem Zahn verloren.
ikh hah-beh ine-uh PLOH-*muh owss mine-em* TSAHN *fehr-*LOH-*ren.*

Film

Please develop this film.
Bitte entwickeln Sie diesen Film.
*bit-tuh ent-*VICK-*el'n zee dee-zun* FILM*.*

When will the film be ready?
Wann ist der Film fertig?
vahnn isst dair FILM *fare-tick?*

Do you have film for this camera?
Haben Sie einen Film für diese Camera?
hah-ben zee eye-nen FILM *für dee-zuh* KAH-*meh-rah?*

Find
Please find my _____.
Bitte versuchen Sie, mein _____ zu finden.
*bit-tuh fehr-*ZOO-*ken zee mine* _____ *tsoo* FINN-*den.*

I cannot find my _____.
Ich kann mein _____ nicht finden.
*ikh kahnn mine*_____ *nikht* FINN-*den.*

Finish
Please wait until I finish.
Bitte warten Sie, bis ich fertig bin.
bit-tuh VAHR-*ten zee biss ikh* FARE-*tick binn.*

Are you finished?
Sind Sie fertig?
zinnt zee FARE-*tick?*

Fire
Please light a fire in the fireplace.
Bitte zünden Sie ein Feuer im Kamin an.
bit-tuh TSÜN-*den zee ine* FOY-*ehr imm kah-*MEEN AHNN.

The fire has gone out.
Das Feuer ist ausgegangen.
dahss FOY-*ehr isst* OWSS-*guh-gahnng-en.*

Fishing
I would like to go fishing.
Ich möchte gern fischen gehen.
ikh MÖKH-*tuh* GEHRN FISH-*en* GAY-*en.*

Where can I rent (buy) fishing gear?
Wo bekomme ich Fischergerät geliehen (zu kaufen)?
*voh buh-*KOMM-*uh ikh* FISH-*ehr-guh-*RATE *guh-*LEE-*en
(tsoo* KOW-*fen)?*

Fit – see also Shopping
It does not fit me.
Es passt mir nicht.
ess PAHSST *meer nikht.*

Fix

Can you fix it?

Können Sie es reparieren?

KÖNN-*en zee ess reh-par-*REER-*en?*

Flag

What flag is that?

Was für eine Flagge ist das?

VAHSS *für ine-uh* FLAH-*guh isst dahss?*

Flat – see also Automobile

Can you fix the flat tire?

Können Sie den platten Reifen reparieren?

könn-en zee dane PLAHTT-*en* RYE-*fen reh-par-*REER-*en?*

Please fix the flat tire.

Bitte reparieren Sie den platten Reifen.

*bit-tuh reh-par-*REER-*en zee dane* PLAHTT-*en* RYE-*fen.*

Please help me fix the flat tire.

Bitte helfen Sie mir, den platten Reifen zu reparieren.

bit-tuh HELL-*fen zee meer dane* PLAHTT-*en* RYE-*fen tsoo reh-par-*REER-*en.*

Flight

When does the next flight leave for _____?

Wann ist der nächste Flug nach _____?

VAHNN *isst dair* NEXT-*uh* FLOOCK *nahkh* _____?

Could I make a reservation on flight number _____ to _____?

Kann ich einen Platz mit Flug Nummer _____ nach _____ buchen?

kahnn ikh eye-nen PLAHTTS *mitt* FLOOCK *noomm-ehr* _____ *nahkh* _____ BOOKH-*en?*

Are there any seats on flight number _____ to _____?

Gibt es noch Plätze für Flug Nummer _____ nach _____?

gippt ess NAWKH PLETTS-*uh für* FLOOCK *noomm-ehr* _____ *nahkh* _____?

Is there a connecting flight for _____?

Gibt es einen Flug-Anschluss nach _____?

gippt ess eye-nen FLOOCK-*ahnn-shlooss nahkh* _____?

Is a meal served on this flight?

Wird auf diesem Flug eine Mahlzeit serviert?

VEERT owff dee-zem FLOOCK *ine-uh* MAHL-*tsite zehr-*
VEERT?

Floor

On what floor is my room?

In welchem Stock ist mein Zimmer?

inn VELL-*khem* SHTAWCK *isst mine* TSIMM-*ehr?*

I want to move to a higher (lower) floor.

Ich möchte in einen höheren (tieferen) Stock übersiedeln.

ikh MÖKH-*tuh inn eye-nem* HÖ-*ehr-en* (TEE-*fehr-en)*
*shtawck ü-behr-*SEE-*deln.*

Floor Show

When does the floor show start?

Wann beginnt die Dielendarbietung?

*vahnn buh-*GINNT *dee* DEE-*lent-ahr-bee-toong?*

Food – see Meals

Forget

I forgot my money (my key, my passport).

Ich habe mein Geld (meinen Schlüssel, meinen Pass)
vergessen.

ikh hah-beh mine GELLT *(mine-em* SHLÜSS-*el mine-em*
PAHSS*) fehr-*GESS-*en.*

I am sorry, I have forgotten your name.

Entschuldigen Sie, ich habe Ihren Namen vergessen.

*ent-*SHOOL-*dih-gen zee, ikh hah-beh ear-en* NAH-*men*
*fehr-*GESS-*en.*

Fork

Please bring me another fork.

Bitte bringen Sie mir noch eine Gabel.

bit-tuh BRING-*en zee meer* NAWKH *ine-uh* GAH-*bel.*

Forward

Please forward all mail to this address.

Bitte senden Sie meine ganze Post an diese Adresse
nach.

bit-tuh ZENN-*den zee mine-uh* GAHNNTS-*uh* PAWSST
ahnn DEE-*zuh ah-*DRESS-*uh* NAHKH.

Found
Where is the lost and found?
Wo ist das Fundbüro?
VOH *isst dahss* FOONT-*bü*-ROH*?*

Fragile
Handle this carefully, please; it is fragile.
Gehen Sie vorsichtig damit um, bitte; es ist zerbrechlich.
gay-en zee FOR-*zikh-tick dah-mitt* OOMM, BIT-*tuh; ess isst
tsehr-* BREHKH-*likh.*

Free
Will you be free this afternoon (this evening, tomorrow)?
Haben Sie heute nachmittag (heute abend, morgen) frei?
hah-ben zee HOY-*tuh* NAHKH-*mitt-tahk (*HOY-*tuh* AH-bent, MOR-*gen)* FRY*?*

Is the admission free?
Ist der Eintritt frei?
isst dair INE-*tritt* FRY*?*

Is that table free?
Ist dieser Tisch frei?
isst DEE-*zehr* TISH FRY*?*

Fresh
Is this fresh?
Ist das frisch?
isst dahss FRISH*?*

Friend(s)
Have you seen my friends?
Haben Sie meine Freunde gesehen?
hah-ben zee mine-uh FROYN-*duh guh-*ZAY-*en?*

I am with a friend (a girlfriend).
Ich bin mit einem Freund (einer Freundin).
ikh binn mitt eye-nem FROYNT *(eye-nehr* FROYN-*dinn).*

Front
I want to sit up front.
Ich möchte vorne sitzen.
ikh MOKH-*tuh* FOR-*nuh* ZITT-*sen.*

Furnished

I want a (n) (un)furnished apartment.

Ich möchte eine (un)möblierte Etagenwohnung.

ikh MOKH-*tuh ine-uh (*OONN-*)mö-*BLEER-*tuh* ay-TAHZH-*en-voh-noong.*

Is the linen furnished?

Ist Tisch-und Bettwäsche inbegriffen?

isst TISH *oonnt* BET-VESH-*uh inn-buh-*GRIFF-*en?*

Gamble

Please direct me (take me) to a gambling house.

Bitte sagen Sie mir den Weg (bringen Sie mich) zu einem Spielclub.

bit-tuh ZAH-*gen zee meer dane* VECK *(*BRING-*en zee mikh) tsoo eye-nem* SHPEEL-*kloop.*

Game

Will you have a game of _____ with me?

Möchten Sie eine Partie _____ mit mir spielen?

MÖKH-*ten zee ine-uh pahr-*TEE _____ *mitt meer* SHPEE-*len?*

Garage

Where is the nearest garage?

Wo ist die nächste Garage?

voh isst dee NEXT-*uh gah-*RAH-*zhuh?*

Does the hotel have a garage?

Hat das Hotel eine Garage?

*haht dahss ho-*TELL *ine-uh gah-*RAH-*zhuh?*

Garbage

Where do I dispose of the garbage?

Wo kann ich die Abfälle hintun?

VOH *kahnn ikh dee* AHPP-*fell-uh* HINN-*toon?*

Will you please take care of the garbage?

Würden Sie bitte die Abfälle wegschaffen?

VÜRR-*den zee bit-tuh dee* AHPP-*fell-uh* VECK-*shahff-en?*

Gardens

I would like to see the gardens.

Ich möchte gern die Gärten sehen.

ikh MOKH-*tuh gairn dee* GEHR-*ten zay-en.*

Gas, Gasoline – see Automobile

Gate

What gate does it leave from?
Von welchem Ausgang geht es ab?
fawnn VELL-*khem* OWSS-*gahng gate ess* AHPP?

Where is gate number _____?
Wo ist Ausgang Nummer_____?
VOH *isst* OWSS-*gahng* NOOMM-*ehr* _____?

Get

How do I get to _____?
Wie komme ich zu _____?
VEE KAWMM-*uh ikh tsoo* _____?

Will you tell me where to get off?
Können Sie mir sagen, wo ich aussteigen muss?
könn-en zee meer ZAH-*gen voh ikh* OWSS-*shtye-gen*
MOOSS?

Where can I get _____?
Wo bekomme ich _____?
*voh buh-*KAWMM-*uh ikh* _____?

Glass

Please bring me a glass of water (milk, wine).
Bitte bringen Sie mir ein Glas Wasser (Milch, Wein).
bit-tuh BRING-*en zee meer ine glahss* VAHSS-*ehr*
(MILLKH, VINE).

Please bring me another glass.
Bitte bringen Sie mir noch ein Glas.
bit-tuh BRING-*en zee meer* NAWKH *ine* GLAHSS.

Glasses

I have lost my glasses.
Ich habe meine Brille verloren.
ikh HAH-*beh mine-uh* BRILL-*uh fehr-*LOH-*ren.*

Can you repair my glasses?
Können Sie meine Brille reparieren?
KÖNN-*en zee mine-uh* BRILL-*uh reh-pah-*REER-*en?*

Here is my prescription for eyeglasses.
Hier ist mein Brillen-Rezept.
HEER *isst mine* BRILL-*en-ray-*TSEPT.

I do not have my eyeglass prescription.
Ich habe mein Brillen-Rezept nicht dabei.
ikh hah-beh mine BRILL-*en-ray*-TSEPT *nikht dah*-BY.

Go (by Vehicle)

I want to go to _____.
Ich möchte nach _____ fahren.
ikh MÖKH-*tuh nahkh* _____ FAH-*ren*.

How do I go to _____?
Wie fahre ich nach _____?
vee FAH-*ruh ikh nahkh* _____?

I am going to _____.
Ich fahre nach _____.
ikh FAH-*ruh nahkh* _____.

Golf

Do you play golf?
Spielen Sie Golf?
SHPEEL-*en zee* GAWLF?

Where is the nearest (best) golf course?
Wo ist der nächste (beste) Golfplatz?
VOH *isst dair* NEXT-*uh* (BEST-*uh*) *gawlf*-PLAHTTS?

Good

It is (not) very good.
Es ist (nicht) sehr gut.
ess isst NIKHT *zair* GOOT.

Goodbye

Goodbye.
Auf Wiedersehen.
OWFF VEE-*dehr-zay-en*.

Good Evening

Good evening.
Guten Abend.
GOO-*ten* AH-*bent*.

Good Morning

Good morning.
Guten Morgen.
GOO-*ten* MOR-*gen*.

Good Night
Good night.
Gute Nach.
GOO-*tuh* NAHKHT.

Grateful
I am very grateful to you.
Ich bin Ihnen sehr dankbar.
ikh binn EEN-*en zair* DAHNNK-*bar.*

Grocery
Where is a grocery store?
Wo ist ein Lebensmittel-Laden?
voh isst ine LAY-*bens-mit-tell*-LAH-*den?*

Guest
This lady (gentleman) is my guest.
Die Dame (der Herr) ist mein Gast.
dee DAH-*muh (dair* HEHRR*) isst mine* GAHSST.

Will you be my guest?
Wollen Sie mein Gast sein?
VAWLL-*en zee mine* GAHSST *zine?*

Guide
Where can we get a guide?
Wo können wir einen Führer bekommen?
VOH *könn-en veer eye-nen* FÜ-*rehr buh*-KAWMM-*en?*

I want an English-speaking guide.
Ich möchte einen englisch-sprechenden Führer.
ikh MÖKH-*tuh eye-nen* ENG-*lish*-SHPREHKH-*end-en* FÜ-*rehr.*

Do you sell guide books?
Verkaufen Sie Reiseführer?
fehr-KOW-*fen zee* RYE-*zuh*-FÜ-*rehr?*

Hair – see also Barber, Beauty Parlor
Where can I get my hair cut?
Wo kann ich mir die Haare schneiden lassen?
VOH *kahnn ikh* MEER *dee* HAHR-*uh* SHNYE-*den* LAHSS-*senn?*

Hanger

Please bring me some hangers.
Bitte bringen Sie mir ein paar Kleiderbügel.
bit-tuh BRING-*en zee* MEER *ine pahr* KLYE-*dehr-bü-gel.*

Happy

I am happy to meet you.
Ich freue mich, Sie kennenzulernen.
ikh FROY-*uh mikh zee* KENN-*en-tsoo-*LEHR-*nen.*

Harbor

Is swimming permitted in the harbor?
Ist Schwimmen im Hafen erlaubt?
isst SHVIMM-*men imm* HAH-*fen ehr-*LOWPT?

Hat

Is this your hat?
Ist das Ihr Hut?
isst dahss ear HOOT?

Have you seen my hat?
Haben Sie meinen Hut gesehen?
HAH-*ben zee my-nen* HOOT *guh-*ZAY-*en?*

Have

Have you any _____?
Haben Sie _____?
HAH-*ben zee* _____?

Headwaiter

Please ask the headwaiter to come over here.
Könnten Sie den Oberkellner bitten, hierher zu kommen?
KÖNN-*ten zee dane* OH-*behr-kell-nehr bit-ten heer-*HEHR *tsoo* KAWMM-*en?*

Health

My health has been poor.
Es geht mir gesundheitlich nicht gut.
ess GATE *meer guh-*ZOONNT-*hite-likh nikht* GOOT.

How is your health?
Wie geht es Ihnen gesundheitlich?
vee GATE *ess* EEN-*en guh-*ZOONNT-*hite-likh?*

To your health!
Auf Ihr Wohl!
owff ear VOHL*!*

Hear

I did not hear you. Please repeat.
Ich habe Sie nicht gehört. Bitte wiederholen Sie.
ikh HAH-*beh zee* NIKHT *guh*-HÖRT. *bit-tuh vee-dehr*-HOLE-*en zee.*

Heater

Please show me how to operate the heater.
Bitte zeigen Sie mir, wie man die Heizung reguliert.
bit-tuh TSYE-*gen zee meer vee mahnn dee* HITE-*tsoong ray-goo*-LEERT.

Heavy

It is very (too) heavy.
Es ist sehr (zu) schwer.
ess isst zair (tsoo) SHVAIR.

Heel

Please replace the heels.
Bitte machen Sie neue Absätze darauf.
bit-tuh MAHKH-*en zee* NOY-*uh* AHPP-*zetts-uh dahr*-OWFF.

Help – see also Accident

Help!
Hilfe!
HILL-*fuh!*

Can you help me?
Können Sie mir helfen?
KÖNN-*en zee meer* HELL-*fen?*

Here

Come here, please.
Kommen Sie her, bitte.
KAWMM-*en zee* HEHR, BIT-*tuh.*

When will it be here?
Wann wird es hier sein?
vahnn veert ess HEER *zine?*

Here is my _____.
Hier ist mein _____.
HEER *isst mine* _____.

High

The price is too high.

Der Preis ist zu hoch.

dehr PRICE *isst tsoo* HOHKH.

Hire

How much would it cost to hire _____?

Wieviel würde es kosten, ein _____ zu mieten?

vee-feel VÜRR-*duh ess* KAWSS-ten *ine* _____ *tsoo* MEE-ten?

Hitchhiking

Is hitchhiking allowed?

Ist per Anhalter fahren erlaubt?

isst pehr AHNN-*hahl-tehr* FAH-*ren ehr*-LOWPT?

Holiday

When is the next holiday?

Wann ist der nächste Feiertag?

vahnn isst dair NEXT-*uh* FYE-*ehr-tahk?*

Is today a holiday?

Ist heute ein Feiertag?

isst HOY-*tuh ine* FYE-*ehr tahk?*

Home

May I take you home?

Darf ich Sie nach Hause bringen?

DAHRFF *ikh zee nahkh* HOW-*zuh bring-en?*

Honeymoon

We are on our honeymoon.

Wir sind auf der Hochzeitsreise.

veer zinnt owff dair HOHKH-*tsytes*-RYE-*zuh.*

Horse

Where can I get a horse?

Wo bekomme ich ein Pferd?

voh buh-KAWMM-*uh ikh ine* PFAIRT?

Would you like to go horseback riding with me?

Möchten Sie mit mir reiten gehen?

MÖKH-*ten zee mitt meer* RYE-*ten* GAY-*en?*

Is there any horseracing here?

Gibt es hier Pferderennen?

gippt ess heer PFAIR-*duh-ren-nen?*

Hospital — see also Accident, Medical

Where is the hospital?
Wo ist das Krankenhaus?
VOH isst dahss KRAHNNG-*ken-house?*

Please take me (direct me) to the hospital.
Bitte bringen Sie mich (sagen Sie mir den Weg) zum
    Krankenhaus.
bit-tuh BRING-*en zee* MIKH *(*ZAH-*gen zee meer dane*
    VECK) tsoom* KRAHNNG-*ken-house.*

Hostel

Is there a youth hostel nearby?
Ist hier in der Nähe eine Herberge?
isst heer inn dair NAY-*uh ine-uh hehr-*BEHR-*guh?*

May I have a list of the member hostels?
Kann ich eine Liste der gemeinnützigen Herbergen
    haben?
kahnn ikh ine-uh LISS-*tuh dair guh-*MINE-*nütts-ih-gen*
    *hehr-*BEHR-*gen hah-ben?*

I am staying at a hostel.
Ich wohne in einer Herberge.
ikh VOH-*nuh inn eye-nehr hehr-*BEHR-*guh.*

Hot

May I have some hot water?
Kann ich heisses Wasser haben?
KAHNN *ikh* HICE-*ess* VAHSS-*ehr hah-ben?*

This is not hot enough. (Please take it back.)
Das ist nicht heiss genug. (Bitte tragen Sie es zurück.)
dahss isst nikht HICE *guh-*NOOK. *(bit-tuh* TRAH-*gen zee*
    *ess tsoor-*RÜCK.*)*

There is no hot water.
Es gibt kein heisses Wasser.
ess GIPPT *kine* HICE-*ess* VAHSS-*ehr.*

Hotel

Can you recommend a good hotel?
Können Sie mir ein gutes Hotel empfehlen?
könn-en zee meer ine GOO-*tess ho-*TELL *emp-*FAY-*len?*

Where is the _____ hotel?
Wo ist das _____ Hotel?
*voh isst dahss _____ ho-*TELL?

Please send it to my hotel.
Bitte senden Sie es ins Hotel.
bit-tuh ZENN-*den zee ess innss ho-*TELL.

Hour

What is the charge per hour?
Wieviel kostet es pro Stunde?
vee-feel KAWSS-*tet ess pro* SHTOONN-*duh?*

At what hour should we meet?
Um wieviel Uhr sollen wir uns treffen?
oomm vee-feel OOR *zawll-en veer oonns* TREFF-*en?*

At what hour should I come?
Um wieviel Uhr soll ich kommen?
oomm vee-feel OOR *zawll ikh* KAWMM-*en?*

How

How do you do?
Wie geht's?
vee GATES?

How long?
Wie lang?
vee LAHNNG?

How far?
Wie weit?
vee VITE?

How many?
Wie viele?
vee FEEL-*uh?*

How much?
Wieviel?
*vee-*FEEL?

How long will it take?
Wie lange dauert es?
vee LAHNNG-*uh* DOW-*ehrt ess?*

How do you say _____ in _____?
Wie heisst _____ auf _____?
VEE *hysst* _____ *owff* _____*?*

Hungry
I am (not) hungry.
Ich bin (nicht) hungrig.
ikh binn (nikht) HOONNG-*rick.*

Hurry
Please hurry.
Bitte beeilen Sie sich.
bit-tuh buh-EYE-*len zee* ZIKH.

Hurt
Does it hurt?
Tut es Weh?
toot ess VAY*?*
Are you hurt?
Sind Sie verletzt?
zinnt zee fehr-LETTST*?*

Ice
Please bring me some ice.
Bitte bringen Sie mir etwas Eis.
bit-tuh BRING-*en zee meer ett-vahss* ICE.

Do you have an ice bag?
Haben Sie einen Eisbeutel?
HAH-*ben zee eye-nen* ICE-*boy-tel?*

Identification
Here is my identification.
Hier ist mein Ausweis.
heer isst mine OWSS-*vice.*

Ill – see also Medical, Accident
I am ill.
Ich bin krank.
ikh binn KRAHNNK.

Immediately
Call a doctor immediately.
Rufen Sie sofort einen Arzt!
ROO-*fen zee zoh*-FORT *eye-nen* ARTST*!*

Please do it immediately.
Bitte tun Sie es sofort.
bit-tuh TOON *zee ess zoh*-FORT.

I want to leave immediately.
Ich möchte sofort abreisen.
ikh MÖKH-*tuh zoh*-FORT AHPP-*rye-zen.*

I need it immediately.
Ich brauche es sofort.
ikh BROW-*khuh ess zoh*-FORT.

Important
It is very important.
Es ist sehr wichtig.
ess isst zair VIKH-*tick.*

Include
Are all meals included?
Sind alle Mahlzeiten inbegriffen?
zinnt AHL-*luh* MAHL-*tsite-en inn-buh*-GRIFF-*en.*

Is breakfast (lunch, supper) included?
Ist Frühstück (Mittagessen, Abendessen) inbegriffen?
isst FRÜ-*shtück* (MITT-*tahg-ess-senn,* AH-*bent-ess-senn) inn-buh*-GRIFF-*en?*

Is the tip included?
Ist Trinkgeld inbegriffen?
isst TRINK-*gellt inn-buh*-GRIFF-*en?*

Is coffee (dessert) included?
Ist Kaffee (Dessert) inbegriffen?
isst KAHFF-*ay (day*-SAIR*) inn-buh*-GRIFF-*en?*

Incorrect
This is incorrect.
Das ist nicht Korrekt.
dahss isst nikht kaw-REKT.

Indigestion
I have indigestion. (Please bring me a _____.)
Ich habe einen verdorbenen Magen. (Bitte bringen Sie mir ein _____.)
ikh hah-beh eye-nen fehr-DOHR-*ben-en* MAH-*gen. (bit-tuh*
BRING-*en zee meer ine _____.)*

Indoors

I will stay indoors (in the hotel) today (this morning, this evening, this afternoon).

Ich bleibe heute (heute vormittag, heute abend, heute nachmittag) zu Hause (im Hotel).

ikh blibe-uh HOY-*tuh (hoy-tuh* FOR-*mitt-tahg, hoy-tuh* AH-*bent, hoy-tuh* NAHKH-*mitt-tahg) tsoo* HOW-*zuh (imm ho-*TELL*).*

Inexpensive

Can you recommend an inexpensive restaurant?

Können Sie mir ein billigeres Restaurant empfehlen?

KÖNN-*en zee meer ine* BILL-*ikh-ehr-ess ress-toh-*RAHNG *emp-*FAY-*len?*

I want something inexpensive.

Ich möchte etwas billiges.

ikh MÖKH-*tuh ett-vahss* BILL-*ikh-ess.*

Informal

Can I dress informally?

Kann ich nicht-formelle Kleidung tragen?

kahn ikh NIKHT-*for-mel-uh* KLYE-*doong* TRAH-*gen?*

Information

I would like some information.

Ich möchte eine Auskunft.

ikh MÖKH-*tuh ine-uh* OWSS-*koonft.*

Where is the information desk (the information window)?

Wo ist die Auskunfts-Stelle (der Auskunfts-Schalter)?

voh isst dee OWSS-*koonfts-shtell-uh (dair* OWSS-*koonfts-shahllt-ehr)?*

Please direct me to the information bureau.

Wie komme ich zum Auskunfts-Büro, bitte?

VEE *kawmm-uh ikh tsoom* OWSS-*koonfts-bü-roh,* BIT-*tuh?*

Inland

What is the best route inland?

Welcher ist der beste Weg ins Landesinnere?

VELL-*khehr isst dehr* BESS-*tuh veck innss* LAHNNT-*ess-INN-ehr-uh?*

Inn

Can you recommend a good inn?

Können Sie mir einen guten Gasthof empfehlen?

könn-en zee MEER *eye-nen* GOO-*ten* GAHSST-*hohf* emp-FAY-*len?*

Insect

Have you any insect repellent?

Haben Sie ein Insekten vertreibendes Mittel?

hah-ben zee ine inn-SEKT-*en fehr-*TRY-*ben-des mitt-tel?*

Interpreter

I want to hire an interpreter.

Ich möchte einen Dolmetscher engagieren.

ikh MÖKH-*tuh eye-nen* DAWL-*metch-ehr ahnn-gah-*ZHEER-*en.*

Where can I find an interpreter?

Wo kann ich einen Dolmetscher finden?

VOH *kahnn ikh eye-nen* DAWL-*metch-ehr* FINN-*den?*

Introduce

May I introduce _____?

Darf ich _____ vorstellen?

dahrf ikh _____ FOR-*shtell-en?*

Invite

Thank you for the invitation.

Ich danke Ihnen für die Einladung.

ikh DAHNNK-*uh een-en für dee* INE-*lah-doong.*

I invite you to come with me (be my guest).

Ich lade Sie ein, mitzukommen (mein Gast zu sein).

ikh LAH-*duh zee* INE MITT-*tsoo-*KAWMM-*en (mine* GAHSST *tsoo* ZINE*).*

Jacket

Do I need to wear a jacket?

Muss ich eine Jacke tragen?

mooss ikh ine-uh YAHCK-*uh trah-gen.*

Jewelry

I would like to leave my jewelry in your safe.

Ich möchte meinen Schmuck in Ihrem Safe lassen.

ikh mökh-tuh mine-em SHMOOCK *inn ear-em* SAFE *lahss-senn.*

Jewish

I am Jewish.
Ich bin Jude (Jüdin).
ikh binn YOO-*duh (*YÜ-*dinn).*

Are you Jewish?
Sind Sie Jude (Jüdin)?
zinnt zee YOO-*duh (*YÜ-*dinn)?*

Job

What kind of job do you have?
Was für einen Job haben Sie?
VAHSS *für eye-nem* JAWPP *hah-ben zee?*

Key

I have lost my key.
Ich habe meinen Schlüssel verloren.
ikh hah-beh mine-en SHLÜSS-*el fehr-*LOH-*ren*

May I have another key?
Kann ich noch einen Schlüssel haben?
kahnn ikh nawkh eye-nen SHLÜSS-*el hah-ben?*

Kilogram

How much per kilogram for excess baggage?
Wieviel kostet Ubergewicht pro Kilo?
vee-feel KAWSS-*tet* Ü-*behr-guh-vikht pro* KEE-*loh?*

*Kilometer

How many kilometers to _____?
Wieviele Kilometer ist es nach _____?
*vee-*FEEL-*uh* KEE-*loh-may-tehr isst ess nahkh* _____?

How many kilometers from _____ to _____?
Wieviele Kilometer ist es von _____ nach _____?
*vee-*FEEL-*uh* KEE-*loh-may-tehr isst ess fawnn* _____
nahkh _____?

Knife

Please bring me a (another) knife.
Bitte bringen Sie mir (noch) ein Messer.
bit-tuh BRING-*en zee meer (*NAWKH*) ine mess-ehr.*

*One kilometer = 3/5 of a mile

Know

Do you know where _____ is?
Wissen Sie, wo _____ ist?
VISS-en zee VOH _____ *isst?*

I (don't) know how.
Ich kann das (nicht).
ikh KAHNN *dahss (*NIKHT*).*

Please let me know when we get to _____.
Bitte lassen Sie mich wissen, wenn wir in _____ ankommen.
bit-tuh LAHSS-*senn zee mikh* VISS-*en venn veer inn*
_____ AHNN-*kawmm-en.*

Kosher

Do you serve kosher meals?
Servieren Sie koscheres Essen?
*zehr-*VEER-*en zee* KOH-*shehr-ess* ESS-*sen?*

Do you sell kosher foods?
Verkaufen Sie koschere Esswaren?
*fehr-*KOW-*fen zee* KOH-*shehr-uh* ESS-*vahr-en?*

Laundry and Dry Cleaning

Do you have overnight laundry service?
Haben Sie 24 Stunden Wäsche-Dienst?
hah-ben zee FEER-*oont-TSVAHNN-tsick* SHTOON-*den*
VESH-*uh-deenst?*

I want this (these) washed (cleaned, pressed).
Ich möchte das (diese Sachen) waschen (reinigen,
bügeln) lassen.
ikh mökh-tuh dahss (dee-zuh ZAHKH-*en)* VAHSH-*en*
(*RINE-ih-gen* BÜ-*geln)* LAHSS-*sen.*

Can you remove this spot (stain)?
Können Sie diesen Fleck entfernen?
könn-en zee dee-zen FLECK *ent-*FEHR-*nen?*

Don't wash this in hot water.
Waschen Sie das nicht in heissem Wasser.
VAHSH-*en zee dahss* NIKHT *inn* HICE-*em* VAHSS-*ehr.*

No starch, please.
Keine Stärke, bitte
kine-uh SHTEHR-*kuh*, BIT-*tuh*.

I would like this button sewn on.
Ich möchte diesen Knopf angenäht haben.
ikh mökh-tuh dee-zen KNAWPF AHNN-*guh-nayt hah-ben*.

I would like this mended.
Ich möchte das geflickt haben.
ikh mökh-tuh dahss guh-FLICKT *hah-ben*.

When can I have it (them) back?
Wann kann ich es (sie) zurück bekommen?
VAHNN *kahnn ikh ess (zee) tsoo*-RÜCK *buh*-KAWMM-*en*?

Will it (will they) be ready today (tonight, tomorrow)?
Wird es (werden sie) heute (heute abend, morgen) fertig sein?
VEERT *ess (vair-den zee)* HOY-*tuh (hoy-tuh* AH-*bent* MOR-*gen)* FEHR-*tick zine*?

A button (the belt) is missing.
Ein Knopf (der Gürtel) fehlt.
ine KNAWPF *(dair* GÜRR-*tel)* FAILLT.

Less – see also Shopping
Do you have anything less expensive?
Haben Sie etwas Billigeres?
hah-ben zee ETT-*vahss* BILL-*ig-ehr-ess*?

Let
Let me know when we get to _____.
Lassen Sie mich wissen, wenn wir in _____ ankommen.
LAHSS-*sen zee mikh* VISS-*en venn veer inn* _____AHNN-*kawmm-en*.

Letter – see also Post Office
Are there any letters for me?
Sind Briefe für mich da?
zinnt BREEF-*uh für mikh* DAH?

Where can I mail some letters?
Wo kann ich Briefe einstecken?
VOH *kahnn ikh* BREE-*fuh* INE-*shteck-en*?

Please mail these letters for me.
Bitte senden Sie diese Briefe für mich ab.
bit-tuh ZENN-den zee dee-zuh BREE-fuh für mikh AHPP.

Library

Please take me (direct me) to the library.
Bitte bringen Sie mich (sagen Sie mir den Weg) zur Bibliothek.
bit-tuh BRING-en zee mikh (ZAH-gen zee meer dane VECK) tsoor bee-blee-oh-TAKE.

License – Driver

Lifeboats

Where are the lifeboats?
Wo sind die Rettungsboots?
VOH zinnt dee RETT-oongs-boat-uh?

Life Preservers

Where are the life preservers?
Wo sind die Schwimmgürtel?
voh zinnt dee SHVIMM-gürr-tel?

How do you use the life preservers?
Wie benutzt man die Schwimmgürtel?
vee buh-NOOTST mahnn dee SHVIMM-gürr-tel?

Light

May I have a light?
Darf ich Sie um Feuer bitten?
DAHRF ikh zee oomm FOY-ehr bit-ten?

Like – see also Shopping

I (don't) like _____.
Ich habe _____ (nicht) gern.
ikh hah-beh _____ (NIKHT) GAIRN.

Limit

What is the speed limit?
Was ist die Geschwindigkeitsbegrenzung?
vahss isst dee guh-SHVINN-dick-kites-buh-GRENTS-oong?

Limousine

Is there limousine service to the airport?
Gibt es einen Limousinen-Service zum Flughafen?
gippt ess eye-nen lih-moo-ZEE-nun-zehr-VEESS tsoom FLOOCK-hah-fen?

When does the limousine leave for the airport?
Wann fährt die Limousine zum Flughafen?
vahnn fehrt dee lih-moo-ZEE-nuh tsoom FLOOCK-*hah-fen?*

I want to hire a limousine.
Ich möchte eine Limousine mieten.
ikh MÖKH-*tuh ine-uh lih-moo-*ZEE-*nuh mee-ten.*

Liquor

Where can I buy some liquor?
Wo kann ich Spirituosen kaufen?
VOH *kann ikh shpih-*RIH-*too-*OH-*zen kow-fen?*

How much liquor can I take out?
Wieviel Spirituosen kann ich mitnehmen?
*vee-feel shpih-*RIH-*too-*OH-*zen kahn ikh* MITT-*nay-men?*

Little

I want just a little, please.
Ich möchte bloss ein wenig, bitte.
ikh mökh-tuh BLOHSS *ine* VAY-*nick,* BIT-*tuh.*

A little more, please.
Ein wenig mehr, bitte.
ine VAY-*nick mair,* BIT-*tuh*

A little less, please.
Etwas Weniger, bitte.
ett-vahss vay-nig-ehr, BIT-*tuh.*

Live

Where do you live?
Wo wohnen Sie?
voh VOH-*nen zee?*

Lobby

I'll meet you in the lobby.
Ich treffe Sie in der Vorhalle.
ikh TREFF-*uh zee inn dair* FOR-*hahll-uh.*

Local

Where do I get the local train?
Wo bekomme ich den Lokalzug?
*voh buh-*KAWMM-*uh ikh dane loh-*KAHL-*tsook?*

Lock

Please lock my door.
Bitte verschliessen Sie meine Tür
*bit-tuh fehr-*SHLEES-*sen zee mine-uh* TÜRR.

The lock does not work.
Das Schloss funktioniert nicht.
dahss SHLAWSS *foonk-tsee-oh-*NEERT *nikht.*

How does the lock work?
Wie funktioniert das Schloss?
VEE *foonk-tsee-oh-*NEERT *dahss* SHLAWSS.

I have lost the key for the lock.
Ich habe den Schlüssel für das Schloss verloren.
ikh hah-beh dane SHLÜSS-*el für dahss* SHLAWSS *fehr-*
    LOH-*ren.*

Locker

Where can I rent a locker?
Wo kann ich ein Schliessfach mieten?
VOH *kahnn ikh ine* SHLEES-*fahck* MEE-*ten?*

Long

How long will it take (last)?
Wie lange wird es dauern (halten)?
vee LAHNNG-*uh veert ess* DOW-*ehrn (*HAHLL-*ten)?*

How long is the stop at _____?
Wie lange ist der Aufenthalt in _____?
vee LAHNNG-*uh isst dair* OWFF-*ent hahllt inn* _____?

How long must I wait?
Wie lange muss ich warten?
vee LAHNNG-*uh mooss ikh* VAHRR-*ten?*

How long does it stay open?
Wie lange bleibt es geöffnet?
vee LAHNNG-*uh blypt ess guh-*ÖFF-*net?*

Lost

I am lost.
Ich habe den Weg verloren.
ikh hah-beh dane VECK *fehr-*LOH-*ren.*

Where is _____?
Wo ist _____?
VOH *isst _____?*

I have lost my key (my passport, my wallet).
Ich habe meinen Schlüssel (meinen Pass, meine Brief-
    tasche) verloren.
ikh hah-beh mine-em SHLÜSS-*el (mine-en* PAHSS, *mine-
    uh* BREEF-*tahsh-uh) fehr-*LOH-*ren.*

Love

I love you.
Ich liebe dich.
ikh LEE-*buh* DIKH.

I love my wife (my husband).
Ich liebe meine Frau (meinen Mann).
ikh LEE-*buh mine-uh* FROW *(mine-en* MAHNN*).*

I love _____.
Ich liebe _____.
ikh LEE-buh.

Lower

I want a lower berth.
Ich möchte eine untere Koje.
ikh MÖKH-*tuh ine-uh* OONN-*tehr-uh* KOH-*yuh.*

I want a room on a lower floor.
Ich möchte ein Zimmer in einem tieferen Stock.
ikh mökh-tuh ine TSIMM-*ehr inn eye-nem* TEE-*fehr-en*
    SHTAWCK.

Lunch

Can we have lunch now?
Können wir jetzt das Mittagessen haben?
könn-en veer YETST *dahss* MITT-*tahg-ess-senn* HAH-*ben?*

When is lunch served?
Wann wird das Mittagessen serviert?
vahnn VEERT *dahss* MITT-*tahg-ess-senn zehr-*VEERT?*

How late (how early) do you serve lunch?
Bis wann (von wann ab) wird Mittagessen serviert?
biss VAHNN *(fawnn* VAHNN AHPP*) veert* MITT-*tahg-
    ess-sen zehr-*VEERT?*

Will you have lunch with me?
Möchten Sie mit mir Mittagessen?
mökh-ten zee mitt meer MITT-*tahg-ess-sen?*

Does that include lunch?
Ist Mittagessen inbegriffen?
isst MITT-*tahg-ess-sen inn-buh-*GRIFF-*en?*

Magazine
Where are magazines sold?
Wo werden Zeitschriften verkauft?
VOH *vair-den* TSITE-*shrift-en fehr-*KOWFFT?

Maid
Please send the maid to my room.
Bitte schicken Sie das Studenmädchen auf mein Zimmer.
bit-tuh SHICK-*en zee dahss* SHTOO-*ben-maid-knen owff mine* TSIMM-*mehr.*

Mail – see also Post Office
Is there any mail for me?
Ist Post für mich da?
isst PAWSST *für mikh* DAH?

When is the mail delivered?
Wann wird die Post ausgetragen?
vahnn VEERT *dee* PAWSST *owss-guh-*TRAH-*gen?*

Please mail this for me.
Bitte senden Sie das für mich ab.
bit-tuh ZENN-*den zee* DAHSS *für mikh* AHPP.

Mail Box
Where is a mail box, please?
Wo ist ein Briefkasten, bitte?
VOH *isst ine* BREEF-*kahss-ten,* BIT-*tuh?*

Make
Please make the bed.
Bitte machen Sie das Bett.
bit-tuh MAHKH-*en zee dahss* BET.

Man-see also Men's Room
Who is that man?
Wer ist dieser Mann?
VAIR *isst* DEE-*zehr* MAHNN?

Manager

I want to see the manager.
Ich möchte den Manager sprechen.
ikh MÖKH-*tuh dane* MEN-*ih-zher* SHPREHKH-*en.*

Are you the manager?
Sind Sie der Manager?
zinnt zee dair MEN-*ih-zher?*

Manicure – see Beauty Parlor

Map

Do you have a map of _____?
Haben Sie eine Landkarte von _____?
hah-ben zee ine-uh LAHNNT-*kahrr-tuh fawnn* _____?

I need a map of _____, please.
Ich brauche eine Landkarte von _____, bitte.
ikh BROW-*khuh ine-uh* LAHNNT-*kahrr-tuh fawnn* _____,
BIT-*tuh.*

Married

I am (not) married.
Ich bin (nicht) verheiratet.
*ikh binn (*NIKHT*) fehr-*HYE-*rah-tett.*

Are you married?
Sind Sie verheiratet?
*zinnt zee fehr-*HYE-*rah-tett?*

Mass

What time is mass?
Um wieviel Uhr ist die Messe?
oomm vee-feel OOR *isst dee* MESS-*uh?*

Massage

I would like to have a massage.
Ich möchte eine Massage haben.
ikh MÖKH-*tuh ine-uh muh-*SAH-*zhuh hah-ben.*

Match

Excuse me, do you have a match?
Entschuldigen Sie, haben Sie ein Streichholz?
*ent-*SHOOL-*dih-gen zee, hah-ben zee ine* SHTRIKE-*hawllts?*

Matinee

Is there a matinee today?

Gibt es heute eine Nachmittagsvorstellung?

gippt ess HOY-*tuh* *ine-uh* NAHKH-*mitt-tahgs*-FOR-*shtell-oong?*

Matter

What is the matter?

Was ist los?

vahss isst LOHSS*?*

Mattress

I would like another mattress.

Ich möchte eine andere Matratze.

ikh MÖKH-*tuh* *ine-uh* AHNN-*dehr-uh mah*-TRAHT-*suh.*

The mattress is too hard (soft, lumpy).

Diese Matratze ist zu hart (weich, klumpig).

dee-zuh mah-TRAHT-*suh isst tsoo* HAHRT *(*VYEKH, KLOOMM-*pick).*

Meals

When are meals served?

Wann werden die Mahlzeiten serviert?

VAHNN *vair-den dee* MAHL-*tsite-en zehr*-VEERT*?*

Does that include meals?

Sind Mahlzeiten inbegriffen?

zinnt MAHL-*tsite-en inn-buh*-GRIFF-*en?*

What meals are included?

Welche Mahlzeiten sind inbegriffen?

vell-khuh MAHL-*tsite-en zinnt inn-buh*-GRIFF-*en?*

Mean

What do you mean?

Was meinen Sie?

vahss MINE-*en zee?*

This is (not) what I mean.

Das meine ich (nicht).

dahss MINE-*uh ikh (*NIKHT*).*

What does _____ mean?

Was bedeutet _____?

*vahss buh-*DOY-*tet _____?*

Medical — see also Accident

Is there a (an English-speaking) doctor near here (in the hotel)?

Gibt es einen (englisch-sprechenden) Arzt hier in der Nähe (im Hotel)?

GIPPT *ess eye-nem* (ENG-*lish*-SHPREHKH-*en-den*) ARTST *heer inn dair* NAY-*uh (imm ho-*TELL*)?*

Can you recommend a good (English-speaking) doctor?

Können Sie mir einen guten (english-sprechenden) Arzt empfehlen?

KONN-*en zee* MEER *eye-nen* GOO-*ten* (ENG-*lish*-SHPREHKH-*en-den*) ARTST *emp-*FAY-*len?*

Can you give me an appointment as soon as possible?

Können Sie mich so bald wie möglich darannehmen?

könn-en zee MIKH *zoh* BAHLLT *vee* MÖG-*likh dahr-*AHNN-*nay-men?*

Can I come right now?

Kann ich sofort kommen?

*kahnn ikh zoh-*FORT KAWMM-*en?*

I (don't) have an appointment.

Ich bin (nicht) bestellt.

*ikh binn (*NIKHT*) buh-*SHTELLT.

I am having trouble breathing.

Ich habe Atembeschwerden.

ikh hah-beh AH-*tem-buh-*SHVAIR-*den.*

I am having trouble sleeping.

Ich leide an Schlaflosigkeit.

ikh lye-duh ahnn shlaff-lohss-ikh-kite.

I have a stomach ache (food poisoning, nausea, cramps).

Ich habe Magenschmerzen (eine Nahrungsmitt-elver-giftung, Brechreiz, Krämpfe).

ikh hah-beh MAH-*gen-shmehr-tsen (ine-uh* NAH-*roongs-mitt-tel-fehr-*GIFF-*toong,* BREHKH-*rites,* KREHMMPF-*uh).*

I have diarrhea (dysentery).

Ich habe Durchfall (Dysenterie).

ikh hah-beh DOORRKH-*fahll (düs-en-tuh-*REE*).*

I am constipated.
Ich leide an Verstopfung.
ikh LYE-*duh ahnn fehr*-SHTOPF-*oong.*

I have a pain in my chest (my back, my arm, my leg, my hand, my foot).
Ich habe Schmerzen in der Brust (im Rücken, im Arm, im Bein, in der Hand, im Fuss).
ikh hah-beh SHMEHRTS-*en inn dair* BROOST *(imm* RÜCK-*en, imm* ARM, *imm* BINE, *inn dair* HAHNNT, *imm* FOOSS).*

I have an earache.
Ich habe Ohrenschmerzen.
ikh hah-beh OAR-*en-shmehr-tsen.*

I have a bad cough (a sore throat).
Ich habe einen starken Husten (Halsschmerzen).
ikh hah-beh eye-nen SHTARK-*en* HOOS-*ten* (HAHLLS-*shmehr-tsen).*

I have a splitting headache.
Ich habe entsetzliche Kopfschmerzen.
ikh hah-beh ent-ZETTS-*likh-uh* KAWPPF-*shmehr-tsen.*

I have a bad sunburn (sunstroke).
Ich habe einen starken Sonnenbrand (Sonnenstich).
ikh hah-beh eye-nen SHTARK-*en* ZAWNN-*en-brahnnt* (ZAWNN-*en-shtikh).*

I have a fever (chills).
Ich habe Fieber (Schüttelfrost).
ikh hah-beh FEE-*behr* (SHÜTT-*tel-frawsst).*

I have sprained my wrist (my ankle).
Ich habe mir die Hand (den Fuss) verstaucht.
ikh hah-beh meer dee HAHNNT *(dane* FOOSS) *fehr*-SHTOWKHT.

Are you going to take X-rays?
Werden Sie eine Röntgenaufnahme machen?
vair-den zee ine-uh RÖNT-*gen*-OWF-*nah-muh mahkh-en?*

Do I have to go to the hospital?
Muss ich ins Krankenhaus?
MOOSS *ikh innss* KRAHNNG-*ken-house?*

I have something in my eye.
Ich habe etwas im Auge.
ikh hah-beh ETT-*vahss imm* OW-*guh.*

I am allergic to _____.
Ich bin allergisch gegen _____.
*ikh binn ahl-*LEHR-*gish gay-gen* _____.

Please don't use anesthesia.
Bitte werwenden Sie keine Anästhesie.
*bit-tuh fehr-*VENN-*den zee kine-uh ah-ness-tay-*ZEE.

Can I have a tranquilizer (aspirin, a sleeping pill)?
Kann ich ein Beruhigungsmittel (Aspirin, eine Schlaf-
    tablette) haben?
*kahnn ikh ine buh-*ROO-*ih-goongs-mitt-tel (ah-spih-*
    REEN, *ine-uh* SHLAHFF-*tah-*BLETT-*uh) hah-ben?*

Do I have to stay in bed?
Muss ich im Bett bleiben?
MOOSS *ikh imm* BET BLIBE-*en?*

For how long?
Wie lange?
vee LAHNNG-*uh?*

When do you think I will be better?
Wann, glauben Sie, wird mir wieder besser sein?
VAHNN, GLOW-*ben, zee veert meer* VEE-*dehr* BESS-*sehr*
    ZINE?

Where can I have this prescription filled?
Wo kann ich dieses Rezept machen lassen?
voh KAHNN *ikh* DEE-*zehs ray-*TSEPT MAHKH-*en* LAHSS-
    senn?

When should I see you again?
Wann soll ich wiederkommen?
VAHNN *zawll ikh* VEE-*dehr-kawmm-en?*

Medium

I like my meat medium (medium rare).
Ich möchte das Fleisch gern leicht durchgebraten
    (nicht durchgebraten).
ikh mökh-tuh dahss FLYSH *gairn lyekht* DOORRKH-*guh-*
    BRAH-*ten (nikht* DOORRKH-*guh-*BRAH-*ten).*

Meet

Let's meet at _____.
Treffen wir uns bei _____.
TREFF-en veer oonns by _____.

I am meeting my husband (wife, friend).
Ich warte auf meinen Mann (meine Frau, meinen Freund).
ikh VAHRR-tuh owff mine-en MAHNN (mine-uh FROW, mine-en FROYNT).

I am very please to meet you.
Es freut mich sehr, Sie kennenzulernen.
ess FROYT mikh ZAIR zee KENN-nen-tsoo-LEHR-nen.

I would like to meet him (her).
Ich möchte ihn (sie) gern kennenlernen.
ikh mökh-tuh EEN (ZEE) gairn KENN-nen-LEHR-nen.

Men's Room

Where is the men's room?
Wo ist die Herrentoilette?
voh isst dee HEHRR-ren-too-ah-LETT-tuh?

Mend – see Laundry

Menu

The menu, please.
Die Speisekarte, bitte.
dee SHPYE-zuh-kahr-tuh, BIT-tuh.

Is _____ on the menu?
Ist _____ auf der Speisekarte?
isst _____ owff dair SHPYE-zuh-kahr-tuh?

Message

I would like to leave a message for _____.
Ich möchte eine Botschaft für _____ hinterlassen.
ikh MÖKH-tuh ine-uh BOAT-shahft für _____ HINN-tehr-lahss-senn.

Are there any telephone messages for me?
Gibt es irgendwelche (telefonische) Mitteilungen für mich?
gippt ess ear-gent-VELL-khuh (tay-luh-FOH-nish-uh) MITT-tile-oong-en für MIKH?

Milk

May I have a glass of milk, please?

Kann ich ein Glas Milch haben, bitte?

KAHNN *ikh ine glahss* MILLKH *hah-ben,* BIT-*tuh?*

Is the milk pasteurized?

Ist die Milch pasteurisiert?

isst dee MILLKH *pahss-toor-ih-*ZEERT*?*

Mind

Do you mind if I smoke?

Haben Sie etwas dagegen, wenn ich rauche?

hah-ben zee ETT-*vahss dah-*GAY-*gen venn ikh* ROWKH-*uh?*

Mine

That is mine.

Das gehört mir.

*dahss guh-*HÖRT MEER.

Minister

Where can I find a (an English-speaking) minister?

Wo kann ich einen (englisch-sprechenden) Pfarrer finden?

VOH *kahnn ikh eye-nen (*ENG-*lish-*SHPREHKH-*en-den)* PFAHRR-*ehr* FINN-*den?*

Minutes

I'll see you again in _____ minutes.

Ich sehe Sie in _____ Minuten wieder.

ikh ZAY-*uh zee inn* _____ *mee-*NOO-*ten* VEE-*dehr.*

Missed

I missed my plane (train).

Ich habe das Flugzeug (den Zug) verpasst.

ikh hah-beh dahss FLOOK-*tsoyk (dane* TSOOK*) fehr-*PAHSST.

When is the next one?

Wann geht das (der) nächste?

VAHNN *gayt dahss (dair)* NEXT-*uh?*

Mistake

Is there a mistake?
Ist da ein Fehler?
isst dah ine FAY-*lehr?*

There must be some mistake.
Da muss ein Fehler sein.
dah MOOSS *ine* FAY-*lehr zine.*

Moderate

Can you recommend a moderate-priced hotel (restaurant)?
Können Sie mir ein Hotel (Restaurant) mit mässigen Preisen empfehlen?
*könn-en zee meer ine ho-*TELL *(ress-toh-*RAHNG*) mitt* MESS-*ick-en* PRY-*zen emp-*FAY-*len?*

Moment

Wait a moment.
Warten Sie einen Moment.
VAHR-*ten zee eye-nen moh-*MENT.

Stop here a moment, please.
Halten Sie hier einen Moment, bitte.
HAHLL-*ten zee* HEER *eye-nen moh-*MENT, BIT-*tuh.*

I'll see you in a moment.
Gedulden Sie sich noch einen Moment, bitte.
*guh-*DOOLLT-*en zee zikh nawkh eye-nen mon-*MENT, BIT-*tuh.*

Money – see also Bank

I need some _____ money.
Ich brauche etwas _____ Geld.
ikh BROW-*khuh ett-vahss* _____ GELLT.

Will you accept American money?
Akzeptieren Sie amerikanischer Geld?
*akh-tsep-*TEER-*en zee ah-may-ree-*KAH-*nish-es* GELLT?

I have no money with me.
Ich habe kein Geld bei mir.
ikh hah-beh kine GELLT *by meer.*

Money order

I wish to send a money order.
Ich möchte eine Postanweisung schicken.
ikh mökh-tuh ine-uh PAWSST-*ahnn-vye-zoong* SHICK-*en.*

More

I would like some more, please.
Ich möchte gern etwas mehr, bitte.
ikh MÖKH-*tuh* GAIRN *ett-vahss* MAIR, BIT-*tuh.*

Please speak more slowly.
Bitte Sprechen Sie langsamer.
bit-tuh SHPREHKH-*en zee* LAHNNG-*zahm-ehr.*

Morning

We will leave tomorrow morning.
Wir reisen morgen früh ab.
veer RYE-*zen mor-gen* FRÜ AHPP.

I'll see you in the morning.
Wir können uns am vormittag sehen.
veer KÖNN-*en oonns ahmm* FOR-*mitt-tahg* ZAY-*en.*

Most

What is the most I can take?
Wieviel darf ich mitnehmen?
vee-feel dahrf ikh MITT-*nay-men?*

Motor – see also Automobile

There is something wrong with the motor.
Der Motor ist nicht in Ordnung.
*dair moh-*TOR *isst* NIKHT *inn* AWRD-*noong.*

Move

I want to move to another room (hotel).
Ich möchte in ein anderes Zimmer (Hotel) übersiedeln.
ikh mökh-tuh inn ine AHNN-*dehr-ess* TSIMM-*mehr (ho-
TELL) ü-behr-*SEE-*deln.*

Movie

What movie is being shown?
Welcher Film wird gespielt?
vell-khehr FILM *veert guh-*SHPEELT?

Would you like to go to a movie with me?
Möchten Sie mit mir ins Kino gehen?
MÖKH-*ten zee mitt meer innss* KEE-*no gay-en?*

Much

How much is it?
Wieviel kostet es?
vee-feel KAWSS-*tet ess?*

That is too much.
Das ist zu viel.
dahss isst tsoo FEEL.

I like you (it) very much.
Ich habe Sie (es) sehr gern.
ikh hah-beh ZEE *(ESS) zair* GAIRN.

Museum

Where is the ____ museum, please?
Wo ist das ____ Museum, bitte?
VOH *isst dahss* ____ *moo-*ZAY-*oomm,* BIT-*tuh?*

Music

Where can we hear some good music?
Wo können wir gute Musik hören?
voh KÖNN-*en veer* GOO-*tuh moo-*ZEEK *hö-ren?*

Must

I must leave now.
Ich muss jetzt gehen.
ikh MOOSS *yetst* GAY-*en.*

Name

What is your name?
Wie heissen Sie?
VEE HICE-*en zee?*

My name is ____.
Ich heisse ____.
ikh HICE-*uh* ____.

Napkin

May I have a (another) napkin, please?
Könnte ich (noch) eine Serviette haben, bitte?
KÖNN-*tuh ikh (*NAWKH*) ine-uh zehrv-*YET-*tuh hah-ben,*
BIT-*tuh?*

National

What is the national dish?
Was ist die Nationalspeise?
VAHSS *isst dee nahts-yoh-*NAHL-*shpye-zuh?*

Near

Are we near it?
Sind wir in der Nähe?
ZINNT *veer inn dair* NAY-*uh?*

How near are we?
Wie nah sind wir?
vee NAH ZINNT *veer?*

How near is _____?
Wie nah ist _____?
vee NAH *isst* _____?

Necessary

It is (not) necessary.
Es ist (nicht) notwendig.
*ess isst (*NIKHT*)* NOTE-*venn-dick.*

Need

I need _____.
Ich brauche _____.
ikh BROW-*khuh* _____.

Do I need tokens (reservations)?
Brauche ich Belege (Reservierungen)?
BROW-*khuh ikh buh-*LAY-*guh (ray-zehr-*VEER-*oong-en)?*

How much (many) do you need?
Wieviel (Wie viele) brauchen Sie?
vee-feel (vee FEEL-*uh)* BROWKH-*en zee?*

Needle

I would like to buy some needles and thread.
Ich möchte Nähnadeln und Nähfaden kaufen.
ikh mökh-tuh NAY-*nah-deln oonnt* NAY-*fah-den* KOW-*fen.*

New

This is something new to me.
Das ist mir neu.
dahss isst meer NOY.

Newspaper

Where can I buy a (an American, English) newspaper?

Wo kann ich eine (amerikanische, englische) Zeitung kaufen?

VOH kahnn ikh ine-uh (ah-may-ree-KAHNN-ish-uh, ENG-lish-uh) TSYE-toong KOW-fen?

May I look at your newspaper for a moment?

Kann ich mir Ihre Zeitung einen Moment ansehen?

kahnn ikh MEER ear-eh TSYE-toong eye-nen moh-MENT AHNN-zay-en?

Next

What is the next town (stop)?

Wie heisst die nächste Stadt (Station)?

VEE hysst dee NEXT-uh SHTAHTT (shtahtts-YOHN)?

When is the next boat (the next train, the next plane)?

Wann geht das nächste Schiff (der nächste Zug, das nächste Flugzeug)?

VAHNN gate dahss NEXT-uh SHIFF (dair NEXT-uh TSOOK dahss NEXT-uh FLOOCK-tsoyk?

Next stop, please.

Die nächste Haltestelle, bitte.

dee NEXT-uh HAHLL-tuh-shtell-uh, BIT-tuh.

Nice

It is nice to meet you.

Es freut mich, Sie kennenzulernen.

ess FROYT mikh zee KENN-en-tsoo-LAIR-nen.

That is very nice of you.

Das ist sehr nett von Ihnen.

dahss isst zair NETT fawnn EEN-en.

She (he) is very nice.

Sie (er) ist sehr nett.

zee (air) isst zair NETT.

Nightclub

Can you recommend a good nightclub?

Können Sie mir ein gutes Nachtlokal empfehlen?

könn-en zee meer ine GOO-tess NAHKHT-loh-kahl emp-FAY-len?

Let's go to a nightclub.
Gehen wir in ein Nachtlokal.
GAY-*en veer inn ine* NAHKHT-*loh-kahl.*

Noisy

My room is too noisy.
Mein Zimmer ist zu lärmend.
mine TSIMM-*mehr isst tsoo* LAIR-*mehnt.*

I want to change it.
Ich möchte ein anderes.
ikh MÖKH-*tuh ine* AHNN-*dehr-ess.*

Noon

We are leaving at noon.
Wir reisen am Mittag ab.
veer RYE-*zen ahmm mitt-tahg* AHPP.

Nothing

I have nothing to declare.
Ich habe nichts zu verzollen.
ikh hah-beh NIKHTS *tsoo fehr-*TSAWLL-*en.*

Nothing, thank you.
Nichts, danke.
NIKHTS, DAHNNG-*kuh.*

Number

What is your telephone (room) number?
Wie ist Ihre Telefon-(Zimmer-) Nummer?
VEE *isst* EAR-*eh tay-luh-*FON-*(*TSIMM-*mehr-)*NOOMM-*ehr?*

What is my room number?
Welche Zimmer-Nummer habe ich?
VELL-*khuh* TSIMM-*ehr-noomm-ehr hah-beh ikh?*

What number bus do I take to _____?
Welche Nummer hat der Bus nach _____?
VELL-*khuh* NOOMM-*ehr haht dair* BOOS *nahkh* _____?

I am in number _____.
Ich bin in Nummer _____.
ikh binn inn NOOMM-*ehr* _____.

Nurse
Is there a doctor or nurse aboard?
Ist ein Arzt oder eine Krankenschwester an Bord?
isst ine ARTST *oh-dehr ine-uh* KRAHNNG-*ken-shvess-tehr ahnn* BORT?

Obtain
Where can I obtain _____?
Wo kann ich _____ bekommen?
VOH *kahnn ikh* _____ *buh*-KAWMM-*en*?

Occupation
What is your occupation?
Was sind Sie von Beruf?
vahss ZINNT *zee fawnn buh*-ROOF?

Occupy
Is this _____ occupied?
Ist dieses _____ besetzt?
isst dee-zus _____ *buh*-ZETTST?

Off
How do you turn it off?
Wie dreht man das ab?
vee DRAYT *mahnn dahss* AHPP?

Please tell me when (where) to get off.
Bitte sagen Sie mir, wenn (wo) ich aussteigen muss.
bit-tuh ZAG-*en zee meer* VENN (VOH) *ikh* OWSS-*shty-gen* MOOSS.

Off at the next stop, please.
Nächste Haltestelle aussteigen, bitte.
NEXT-*uh* HAHLL-*tuh-shtell-uh* OWSS-*shtye-gen*, BIT-*tuh*.

Often
How often do you come here?
Wie oft kommen Sie hierher?
vee AWFFT KAWMM-*en zee* HEER-*hehr*?

How often do the buses (trains, planes, boats) run?
Wie häufig gehen die Busse (Züge, Flugzeuge, Schiffe)?
vee HOY-*fick gay-en dee* BOOSS-*uh* (TSÜ-*guh*, FLOOCK-*tsoy-guh* SHIFF-*uh*)?

Do you come here often?
Kommen Sie oft hierher?
KAWMM-*en zee* AWFFT HEER-*hehr?*

I (don't) come here often.
Ich komme (nicht) oft hierher.
ikh KAWMM-*uh (*NIKHT*)* AWFFT HEER-*hehr.*

Old

How old are you?
Wie alt sind Sie?
vee AHLLT *zinnt zee?*

I am _____ years old.
Ich bin _____ Jahre alt.
ikh binn _____ YAHR-*uh* AHLLT.

How old is this building?
Wie alt ist dieses Gebäude?
vee AHLLT *isst dee-zehs guh-*BOY-*duh?*

It is (not) old.
Es ist (nicht) alt.
ess isst (nikht) AHLLT.

On

How do you turn it on?
Wie dreht man das auf?
vee DRAYT *mahnn dahss* OWFF?

What flight are you on?
Mit welchem Flug reisen Sie?
mitt VELL-*khem* FLOOCK RYE-*zen zee?*

One-Way

A one-way ticket to _____, please.
Eine einfache Fahrkarte nach _____, bitte.
ine-uh INE-*fahkh-uh* FAR-*kahrr-tuh nahkh* _____, BIT-*tuh.*

Is this street one-way?
Ist das eine Einbahn-Strasse?
isst DAHSS *ine-uh* INE-*bahn-*SHTRAH-*suh?*

Only

I speak only English.
Ich spreche nur English.
ikh SHPREHKH-*uh noorr* ENG-*lish.*

Open

May I open the door (the window)?
Darf ich die Tür (das Fenster) öffnen?
dahrf ikh dee TÜRR *(dahss* FENN-*stehr)* ÖFF-*nen?*

Is it still open?
Ist es noch offen?
isst ess NAWKH AWFF-*fen?*

When do you open?
Wann öffnen Sie?
vahnn ÖFF-*nen zee?*

I cannot get it open.
Ich kann es nicht öffnen.
ikh kahnn ess nikht ÖFF-*nen*

How long does it stay open?
Wie lange bleibt es geöffnet?
vee LAHNNG-*uh blypt ess guh-*ÖFF-*net?*

Opener

Excuse me, but have you a can (bottle) opener?
Entschuldigen Sie, haben Sie einen Büchsen- (Flaschen-) Öffner?
*ent-*SHOOL-*dih-gen zee,* HAH-*ben zee eye-nen* BÜKH-*senn-* (FLAHSH-*en-) öff-nehr?*

Opera

Where is the opera house?
Wo ist das Opernhaus?
voh isst dahss OH-*pehrn-howss?*

What opera is being given tonight?
Welche Oper wird heute abend gegeben?
vell-khuh OH-*pehr veert hoy-tuh ah-bent guh-*GAY-*ben?*

Would you like to go to the opera with me?
Möchten Sie mit mir in die Oper gehen?
MÖKH-*ten zee mitt meer inn dee* OH-*pehr gay-en?*

Operator – see Telephone

Opposite

What is that building opposite _____?

Was ist das Gebäude gegenüber _____?

VAHSS *isst dahss guh*-BOY-*duh gay-gen*-Ü-*behr* _____?

Orchestra

Is the orchestra playing tonight?

Spielt das Orchester heute abend?

SHPEELT *dahss awr*-KEHSST-*ehr hoy-tuh* AH-*bent?*

Order

May I order, please?

Kann ich bestellen, bitte?

kahnn ikh buh-SHTELL-*en,* BIT-*tuh?*

Where can I cash a money order?

Wo kann ich eine Postanweisung einlösen?

VOH *kahnn ikh ine-uh* PAWSST-*ahnn-vye-zoong* INE-*lö-zen?*

I did not order this.

Ich habe das nicht bestellt.

ikh hah-beh DAHSS NIKHT *buh*-SHTELLT.

This is (not) what I ordered.

Das ist (nicht) was ich bestellt habe.

*dahss isst (*NIKHT*) vahss ikh buh*-SHTELLT *hab-beh.*

Outlet

Where is the electrical outlet?

Wo ist die Steckdose?

VOH *isst dee* SHTECK-*doh-zuh?*

Overcooked

This is overcooked.

Das ist zu gar.

dahss isst tsoo GAHR.

Please take it back.

Bitte nehmen Sie es zurück.

bit-tuh NAY-*men zee ess tsoo*-RÜCK.

Overnight

We will be staying overnight.
Wir werden hier übernachten.
veer VAIR-*den* HEER *ü-behr*-NAHKHT-*en.*

May I leave my car here overnight?
Kann ich mein Auto übernacht hier lassen?
kahnn ikh mine OW-*toh ü-behr*-NAHKHT HEER *lahss-senn?*

Overtime

What is the charge for overtime?
Wie hoch werden Überstunden berechnet?
vee HOHKH *vair-den ü-behr*-SHTOON-*den buh*-REHKH-*net?*

Is there a charge for overtime?
Werden Überstunden berechnet?
vair-den ü-behr-shtoon-den buh-REHKH-*net?*

Owe

How much do I owe?
Wieviel bin ich schuldig?
VEE-*feel binn ikh* SHOOL-*dick?*

Owner

May I see the owner, please?
Kann ich den Eigentümer sprechen, bitte?
kahnn ikh dane EYE-*gen-tü-mehr* SHPREHKH-*en,* BIT-*tuh?*

Are you the owner?
Sind Sie der Eigentümer?
zinnt zee dair EYE-*gen-tü-mehr?*

Pack

Pack this carefully (well).
Verpacken Sie das sorgfältig (gut).
fehr-PAHCK-*en zee dahss* ZAWRK-*fell-tick (*GOOT*).*

Package

Has a package arrived for me?
Ist ein Paket für mich gekommen?
isst ine pah-KATE *für mikh guh*-KAWMM-*en?*

Page

Please page _____.

Bitte lassen Sie _____ ausrufen.

bit-tuh LAHSS-*senn zee* _____ OWSS-*roo-fen.*

Pain

Do you feel any pain?

Haben Sie schmerzen?

hah-ben zee SHMEHR-*tsen?*

Paper

Where can I buy a paper?

Wo kann ich eine Zeitung kaufen?

VOH *kahnn ikh ine-uh* TSITE-*toong* KOW-*fen?*

May I have some writing paper?

Kann ich Briefpapier haben?

kahnn ikh BREEF-*pah-*PEER *hah-ben?*

Parcel

What will it cost to send this parcel?

Wieviel kostet es, dieses Paket abzusenden?

vee-feel KAWSS-*tet ess, dee-zehs pah-*KATE AHPP-*tsoo-*ZEN-*den?*

Parcel Post – see Post Office

Pardon

Pardon me!

Verzeihen Sie!

*fehr-*TSYE-*en zee!*

Park

May I park here for a while?

Kann ich eine Weile hier parken?

KAHNN *ikh ine-uh* VYE-*luh heer* PAHRR-*ken?*

Where can I park?

Wo kann ich parken?

VOH *kahnn ikh* PAHRR-*ken?*

Pass

Do I need a pass?

Brauche ich einen Passierschein?

BROW-*khuh ikh eye-nen pahs-*SEER-*shine?*

May I have a pass?
Kann ich einen Passierschein haben?
KAHNN *ikh eye-nen pahs*-SEER-*shine hah-ben?*

Passport
Here is my passport.
Hier ist mein Pass.
HEER *isst mine* PAHSS.

I don't have my passport with me.
Ich habe meinen Pass nicht bei mir.
ikh HAH-*beh mine-en* PAHSS *nikht* BY *meer.*

I have lost my passport.
Ich habe meinen Pass verloren.
ikh HAH-*beh mine-en* PAHSS *fehr*-LOH-*ren.*

Pastry
What kind of pastry do you have?
Was haben Sie an Kuchengebäck?
VAHSS *hah-ben zee ahnn* KOO-*khen-guh*-BECK?

Pawn; Pawnshop
I would like to pawn this.
Ich möchte das verpfänden.
ikh MÖKH-*tuh dahss fehr*-PFENN-*den.*

Could you direct me to a pawnshop?
Können Sie mir sagen, wo hier ein Pfandleiher ist?
könn-en zee meer ZAH-*gen voh* HEER *ine* PFAHNNT-*lye-ehr isst?*

Pay
Whom (where) do I pay?
Wem (Wo) habe ich zu zahlen?
VAIM *(*VOH*) hah-beh ikh tsoo* TSAHL-*len?*

How much must I pay?
Wieviel muss ich zahlen?
vee-feel mooss ikh TSAHL-*len?*

Do I pay now or later?
Soll ich gleich oder später zahlen?
zawll ikh GLYEKH *oh-dehr* SHPAY-*tehr* TSAHL-*len?*

Did you already pay?
Haben Sie schon bezahlt?
*hah-ben zee shone buh-*TSAHLLT*?*

I have already paid.
Ich habe schon bezahlt.
ikh hah-beh SHONE *buh-*TSAHLLT.

I have not paid yet.
Ich habe noch nicht bezahlt.
ikh hah-beh nawkh NIKHT *buh-*TSAHLLT.

Have you paid?
Haben Sie bezahlt?
*hah-ben zee buh-*TSAHLLT*?*

Pen (Pencil)
Have you a pen (a pencil) I could borrow for a moment?
Haben Sie eine Feder (einen Bleistift), die (den) ich mir
   für einen Moment ausborgen könnte?
hah-ben zee ine-uh FAY-*dehr (eye-nen* BLY-*shtift) dee
   (dane) ikh meer für eye-nen moh-*MENT OWSS-*bor-gen*
   KÖNN-*tuh?*

Pepper
May I have the pepper, please?
kann ich den Pfeffer haben, bitte?
kahnn ikh dane PFEFF-*ehr hah-ben,* BIT-*tuh?*

Performance
When does the (evening) performance begin?
Wann beginnt die (Abend-) Vorstellung?
*vahnn buh-*GINNT *dee (*AH-*bent-)* FOR-*shtell-oong?*

Permit
Do I need a permit?
Brauche ich eine Erlaubnis?
BROW-*khuh ikh ine-uh ehr-*LOWP-*niss?*

Personal
This is for my personal use.
Das ist für meinen persönlichen Gebrauch.
*dahss isst für mine-en pehr-*ZÖN-*likh-en guh-*BROWKH.

Will you accept (cash) a personal check?

Würden Sie einen persönlichen Scheck akzeptieren (einlösen)?

VÜRR-*den zee eye-nen pehr-*ZÖN-*likh-en* SHECK *ahk-tsepp-*TEER-*en (*INE-*lö-zen)?*

Phone – see also Telephone

I would like to make a phone call to _____.

Ich möchte einen Telefonanruf nach _____ machen.

ikh MÖKH-*tuh eye-nen tay-luh-*FON-*ahnn-roof nahkh* _____ MAHKH-*en.*

Photograph

Excuse me, but I would like you to take a photograph of me (us).

Entschuldigen Sie, könnten Sie ein Foto von mir (uns) machen?

*ent-*SHOOL-*dih-gen zee, könn-ten zee ine* FOH-*toh fawnn meer (oonnss)* MAHKH-*en?*

Am I allowed to take photographs here?

Darf man hier fotografieren?

*dahrf mahnn heer foh-toh-grah-*FEER-*en?*

Piano

I play the piano.

Ich spiele Klavier.

ikh SHPEEL-*uh klah-*VEER.

Do you play the piano?

Spielen Sie Klavier?

SHPEE-*len zee klah-*VEER?

Picnic

Let's have a picnic.

Machen wir ein Picknick.

mahkh-en veer ine PICK-*nick.*

Pillow

Please bring me a (another) pillow.

Bitte bringen Sie mir (noch) ein Kissen.

bit-tuh BRING-*en zee meer (*NAWKH*) ine* KISS-*en.*

Plane – see Flight

Plate

May I have a (clean, another) plate, please?
Kann ich (noch) einen (sauberen) Teller haben, bitte?
kahnn ikh (NAWKH) eye-nen (ZOW-behr-en) TELL-ehr hah-ben, BIT-tuh?

Platform

At which platform is the train for _____?
Auf welchem Bahnsteig ist der Zug nach _____?
owff VELL-khum BAHNN-shtyek isst dair TSOOCK nahkh _____?

Play

I want to see a play tonight.
Ich möchte heute abend ein Theaterstück sehen.
ikh mökh-tuh hoy-tuh AH-bent ine tay-AH-tehr-shtück ZAY-en.

Which play would you suggest?
Welches Stück schlagen Sie vor?
vell-khehs SHTÜCK shlah-gen zee FOR?

Will you attend the play with me?
Möchten Sie das Stück mit mir sehen?
mökh-ten zee dahss SHTÜCK mitt meer ZAY-en?

When does the play begin?
Wann beginnt die Vorstellung?
VAHNN buh-GINNT dee FOR-shtell-oong?

Do you play golf (tennis, chess, bridge)?
Spielen Sie Golf (Tennis, Schach, Bridge)?
SHPEE-len zee GAWLF (TENN-niss, SHAHKH, BRIDGE)?

Would you like to play golf (tennis, bridge, chess)?
Möchten Sie Golf (Tennis, Bridge, Schach) spielen?
mökh-ten zee GAWLF (TENN-niss, BRIDGE, SHAHKH) SHPEE-len?

I don't play (very well).
Ich spiele nicht (zehr gut).
ikh SHPEE-luh NIKHT (zair GOOT).

Please

Please don't do that.
Bitte tun Sie das nicht.
bit-tuh TOON zee dahss NIKHT.

Please pass the _____.
Bitte reichen Sie mir das (die, der) _____.
bit-tuh RYE-*khen zee meer* DAHSS *(*DEE, DAIR*)* _____.

Plenty

I have plenty, thanks.
Ich habe einen Menge, danke.
ikh hah-beh ine-uh MENNG-*uh,* DAHNNG-*kuh.*

Point

Please point the way to _____.
Bitte zeigen Sie mir den Weg nach _____.
bit-tuh TSYE-*gen zee meer dane* VECK *nahkh* _____.

Point to the phrase in this book.
Zeigen Sie mir die Phrase in diesem Buch.
TSYE-*gen zee meer dee* FRAH-*zuh inn dee-zehm* BOOKH.

Police

Call the police!
Rufen Sie die Polizei!
ROO-*fen zee dee poh-lee-*TSYE*!*

Where is the police station?
Wo ist die Polizeiwache?
VOH *isst dee poh-lee-*TSYE-*vahkh-uh?*

Policeman

Call a policeman!
Rufen Sie einen Schutzmann!
ROO-*fen zee eye-nen* SHOOTS-*mahnn!*

Polish

Would you polish my shoes, please?
Würden Sie meine Schuhe putzen, bitte?
VÜRR-*den zee mine-uh* SHOO-*uh* POOTS-*sen,* BIT-*tuh?*

Pool

Where is the pool?
Wo ist das Schwimmbad?
VOH *isst dahss* SHVIMM-*baht?*

Is there a charge for the pool?
Muss man für das Schwimmbad bezahlen?
MOOSS *mahnn für dahss* SHVIMM-*baht buh-*TSAH-*len?*

Port

What is the next port?
Welches ist der nächste Hafen?
VELL-khehs isst dair NEXT-*uh* HAH-*fen?*

When do we reach port?
Wann kommen wir im Hafen an?
vahnn KAWMM-*en veer imm* HAH-*fen* AHNN?

Porter

I need a porter.
Ich brauche einen Gepäckträger.
ikh BROW-*khuh eye-nen guh-*PECK-*tray-gehr.*

Possible

As soon as possible.
So bald wie möglich.
zoh BAHLLT *vee* MÖG-*likh.*

Postage – see also Post Office

What is the postage on this?
Wieviel Porto ist darauf?
vee-fell POR-*toh isst dahr-*OWFF?

Postcards

Do you sell postcards?
Verkaufen Sie Ansichtskarten?
*fehr-*KOW-*fen zee* AHNN-*zikhts-karr-ten?*

Do you have postcards of _____?
Haben Sie Ansichtskarten von _____?
HAH-*ben zee* AHNN-*zikhts-karr-ten fawnn* _____?

Please mail these postcards for me.
Bitte senden Sie diese Ansichtskarten für mich ab.
bit-tuh ZENN-*den zee dee-zuh* AHNN-*zikhts-karr-ten für mikh* AHPP.

Post Office

Where is the post office?
Wo ist das Postamt?
VOH *isst dahss* PAWSST-*ahmmt?*

Where can I buy air mail stamps for the United States?

Wo kann ich Luftpost-Briefmarken für die Vereinigten Staaten kaufen?

VOH kahnn isk LOOFFT-*pawsst* BREEF-*mahrr-ken für dee fehr-* INE-*ick-ten* SHTAH-*ten* KOW-*fen?*

How many stamps do I need for _____?

Wie viele Briefmarken brauche ich für _____?

vee FEEL-*uh* BREEF-*mahrr-ken* BROW-*khuh ikh für _____?*

How much is the postage?

Wieviel kostet das Porto?

vee-feel KAWSS-*tet dahss* POR-*toh?*

How long will it take to get to _____?

Wie lange wird es dauern, bis es in _____ ankommt?

vee LAHNNG-*uh veert ess* DOW-*ehrn, biss ess inn _____* AHNN-*kawmmt?*

Will it arrive within _____ days (weeks)?

Wird es innerhalb von _____ Tagen (Wochen) ankommen?

*veert ess inn-ehr-*HAHLP *fawnn _____* TAHG-*en (*VAWKH-*en)* AHNN-*kawmm-en?*

Please send this (these) by air mail (parcel post, registered, insured, special delivery).

Bitte senden Sie das (diese Sachen) per Luftpost (Paketpost, eingeschrieben, versichert, express).

bit-tuh ZENN-*den zee* DAHSS *(dee-zuh zahkh-en) pehr* LOOFFT-*pawsst (pah-*KATE-*pawsst,* INE-*guh-shree-ben, fehr-*ZIKH-*ehrt, ex-*PRESS*).*

Would you wrap this package for me?

Würden Sie dieses Paket für mich verpacken?

*VÜRR-den zee dee-zus pah-*KATE *für mikh fehr-*PAHCK-*en?*

Will the receiver have to pay duty?

Wird der Empfänger Zoll zahlen müssen?

*VEERT dair emp-*FENG-*ehr* TSAWLL TSAH-*len* MÜSS-*en?*

When does the postman arrive?

Wann kommt der Briefträger?

VAHNN kawmmt dair BREEF-*tray-gehr?*

Please give this to the postman.
Bitte geben Sie das dem Briefträger.
bit-tuh GAY-*ben zee dahss dame* BREEF-*tray-gehr.*

Pounds

How many pounds of baggage per person?
Wieviel Pfund Gepäck pro Person?

vee-feel PFOONT *guh-*PECK *pro pehr-*ZOHN?
How many pounds of overweight baggage do I have?
Wieviel Pfund Übergewicht hat mein Gepäck?
vee-feel PFOONT Ü-*behr-guh-*VIKHT *haht mine guh-*PECK?

Prefer

I prefer something cheaper (better).
Ich ziehe etwas Billigeres (Besseres) vor.
ikh TSEE-*uh ett-vahss* BILL-*ig-ehr-ess* (BESS-*ehr-ess*)
FOR.

Pregnant

I am pregnant.
Ich bin schwanger.
ikh binn SHVAHNNG-*ehr.*

Prescription – see also Medical

Can you fill this prescription?
Können Sie dieses Rezept machen?
KÖNN-*en zee dee-zus ray-*TSEPT *mahkh-en?*

When will my prescription be ready?
Wann wird mein Rezept fertig sein?
vahnn VEERT *mine ray-*TSEPT FEHR-*tick zine?*

Press – see Laundry

Priest

Where can I find a (an English-speaking) priest?
Wo kann ich einen (englisch-sprechenden) Pfarrer
finden?
VOH *kahnn ikh eye-nen* (ENG-*lish-*SHPREHKH-*en-den*)
PFAHRR-*ehr finn-den?*

Private

I want a private room (bathroom, compartment).
Ich möchte ein Privat-Zimmer (-Bad, -Abteil).
*ikh mökh-tuh ine pree-*VAHT-*tsimm-mehr (-baht,-*AHPP-
tile).

Profession

What is your profession?
Was sind Sie von Beruf?
vahss ZINNT *zee fawn buh-*ROOF*?*

Program

Where can I get a program?
Wo kann ich ein Programm bekommen?
VOH *kahnn ikh ine pro-*GRAHMM *buh-*KAWMM-*en?*

Is there a charge for the program?
Muss man für das Programm zahlen?
MOOSS *mahnn für dahss pro-*GRAHMM *tsah-len?*

When does the program begin?
Wann beginnt das Programm?
VAHNN *buh-*GINNT *dahss pro-*GRAHMM*?*

Pronounce

How do you pronounce this?
Wie spricht man das aus?
VEE SHPRIKHT *mahnn dahss* OWSS*?*

Protestant

I am a Protestant.
Ich bin Protestant.
*ikh binn pro-tess-*TAHNT.

Can you direct me to the nearest Protestant church?
Können Sie mir den Weg zur nächsten protestantischen Kirche sagen?
KÖNN-*en zee meer dane* VECK *tsoor* NEXT-*en pro-tess-*TAHNT-*ih-shehn* KEERRKH-*uh zah-gen?*

Public

Is this open to the public?
Hat das Publikum Zutritt?
haht dahss POO-*blee-koomm* TSOO-*tritt?*

Push

Can you give me a push?
Können Sie mir einen Stoss geben?
KÖNN-*en zee meer eye-nen* SHTAWSS *gay-ben?*

Put

Please put this in the safe (in my room).

Bitte legen Sie das ins Safe (in meinem Zimmer).

bit-tuh LAY-*gen zee dahss innss* SAFE *(inn mine-em* TSIMM-*mehr).*

Quality

I want the best quality.

Ich möchte die beste Qualität.

ikh mökh-tuh dee BESS-*tuh kvahl-ee-*TATE.

Quantity

What quantity may I take (have)?

Welche Quantität kann ich mitnehmen (haben)?

VELL-*khuh kvahn-tee-*TATE *kahnn ikh* MITT-*nay-men* (HAH-*ben)?*

Question

I have a question.

Ich habe eine Frage.

ikh hah-beh ine-uh FRAH-*guh.*

Quickly

Call a doctor quickly!

Rufen Sie schnell einen Arzt!

ROO-*fen zee* SHNELL *eye-nen* ARTST*!*

Call the police quickly!

Rufen Sie schnell die Polizei!

ROO-*fen zee* SHNELL *dee poh-lee-*TSYE*!*

Come here quickly!

Kommen Sie schnell her!

KAWMM-*en zee* SHNELL HEHR*!*

Quiet

Can you recommend a nice, quiet restaurant (hotel)?

Können Sie mir ein nettes, ruhiges Restaurant (Hotel) empfehlen?

KÖNN-*en zee* MEER *ine* NETT-*tes* ROO-*ih-gess ress-toh-*RAHNG *(ho-*TELL) *emp-*FAY-*len?*

Quiet, please.

Bitte um Ruhe!

BIT-*tuh ǫomm* ROO-*uh!*

Rabbi

Where can I find a (an English-speaking) Rabbi?

Wo kann ich einen (englisch-sprechenden) Rabbiner finden?

VOH *kahnn ikh eye-nen* (ENG-*lish*-SHPREHKH-*en-den*) *rah-*BEE-*nehr finn-den?*

Radio

May I have a radio for my room, please?

Kann ich ein Radio für mein Zimmer haben, bitte?

KAHNN *ikh ine* RAHD-*yoh für mine* TSIMM-*mehr hah-ben,* BIT-*tuh?*

The radio in my room does not work.

Das Radio in meinem Zimmer geht nicht.

dahss RAHD-*yoh inn mine-em* TSIMM-*mehr* GATE *nikht.*

Railroad – see also Train

Can you direct (take) me to the railroad station?

Wie komme ich (bitte bringen Sie mich) zum Bahnhof?

vee KAWMM-*uh ikh (bit-tuh* BRING-*en zee mikh) tsoom* BAHN-*hohf?*

Rain

There will be rain this morning (afternoon, evening).

Heute vormittag (nachmittag, abend) wird es Regen geben.

hoy-tuh FOR-*mitt-tahg* (NAHKH-*mitt-tahg,* AH-*bent) veert ess* RAY-*gen gay-ben.*

Is it raining?

Regnet es?

RAYG-*net ess?*

Rare

I want my meat rare (medium rare), please.

Ich möchte das Fleisch nicht durchgebraten (leicht durchgebraten).

ikh MÖKH-*tuh dahss* FLYSH NIKHT DOORRKH-*guh-*BRAH-*ten (lyekht* DOORRKH-*guh-*BRAH-*ten).*

I ordered this rare; please take it back.
Ich habe es nicht durchgebraten bestellt; bitte tragen
  Sie es zurück.
ikh hah-beh ess NIKHT DOORRKH-*guh*-BRAH-*ten buh*-
  SHTELLT; *bit-tuh* TRAH-*gen zee ess tsoo*-RÜCK.

This is too rare; please take it back.
Das ist zu roh; bitte tragen Sie es zurück.
dahss isst tsoo ROH; *bit-tuh* TRAH-*gen zee ess tsoo*-RÜCK.

Rate – see also Bank
What is the rate per kilometer (per minute, per hour,
  per day, per week, per month, per word)?
Wie hoch ist der Tarif pro Kilometer (pro Minute, pro
  Stunde, pro Tag, pro Woche, pro Monat, pro Wort)?
vee HOHKH *isst dair* TAH-*reef pro* KEE-*loh-may-tehr*
  (pro mee-NOO-*tuh, pro* SHTOON-*duh, pro* TAHG, *pro*
  VAWKH-*uh, pro* MOH-*naht, pro* VAWRT*)?*

What is your rate to _____?
Wieviel kostet es nach _____?
vee-feel KAWSS-*tet ess nahkh* _____?

What is the rate of exchange?
Wie ist der Umrechnungskurs?
vee isst dair OOMM-*rehkh-noongz*-KOORRSS?

Rather
I would rather see _____ than _____.
Ich möchte lieber _____ sehen als _____.
ikh MÖKH-*tuh* LEE-*behr* _____ *zay-en ahllss* _____.

I would rather not.
Ich möchte lieber nicht.
ikh MÖKH-*tuh* LEE-*behr* NIKHT.

Raw
I like my meat nearly raw.
Ich habe das Fleisch gern fast roh.
ikh HAH-*beh dahss* FLYSH *gairn fahsst* ROH.

This is raw; please take it back.
Das ist roh; bitte tragen Sie es zurück.
dahss isst ROH; *bit-tuh* TRAH-*gen zee ess tsoo*-RÜCK.

Razor

Where is the electrical outlet for the razor?

Wo ist die Steckdose für den Rasierer?

voh isst dee SHTECK-*doh-zuh für dane rah-*ZEER-*ehr?*

Where can I buy razor blades?

Wo kann ich Rasierklingen kaufen?

VOH *kahnn ikh rah-*ZEER-*kling-en* KOW-*fen?*

Ready

When will it (will you, will they) be ready?

Wann wird es (werden Sie, werden sie) fertig sein?

VAHNN *veert ess (*VAIR-*den zee,* VAIR-*den zee)* FEHR-*tick zine?*

Are you (they) ready?

Sind Sie (sie) fertig?

zinnt zee (zee) FEHR-*tick?*

I am (not) ready.

Ich bin (nicht) fertig.

*ikh binn (*NIKHT*)* FEHR-*tick.*

Reasonable

Can you recommend a hotel with reasonable rates?

Können Sie mir ein Hotel mit mässigen Preisen empfehlen?

*könn-en zee meer ine ho-*TELL *mitt* MACE-*ih-gen* PRIZE-*en emp-*FAY-*len?*

Receipt

Give me a receipt, please.

Geben Sie mir einen Quittung, bitte.

GAY-*ben zee meer ine-uh* KVITT-*toong,* BIT-*tuh.*

Recipe

Would you (would the chef) give me the recipe for this dish?

Könnten Sie (könnte der Koch) mir das Rezept für diese Speise geben?

KÖNN-*ten zee (könn-tuh dair* KOHKH*)* MEER *dahss ray-*TSEPT *für dee-zuh* SHPYE-*zuh gay-ben?*

Recommend

Can you recommend a good restaurant (hotel)?

Können Sie mir ein gutes Restaurant (Hotel) empfehlen?

KÖNN-*en zee* MEER *ine* GOO-*tess ress-toh-*RAHNG *(ho-*TELL*) emp-*FAY-*len?*

What do you recommend?

Was empfehlen Sie mir?

VAHSS *emp-*FAY-*len zee* MEER?

Record

Can you tell me where phonograph records are sold?

Können Sie mir sagen, wo man Schallplatten verkauft?

KÖNN-*en zee meer* ZAH-*gen voh mahnn* SHAHLL-*plahtt-en fehr-*KOWFT?

Reduce

I am trying to reduce.

Ich versuche abzunehmen.

*ikh fehr-*ZOOKH-*uh* AHPP-*tsoo-nay-men.*

Refrigerator

I would like a room with a refrigerator.

Ich möchte ein Zimmer mit einem Kühlschrank.

ikh MÖKH-*tuh ine* TSIMM-*mehr mitt eye-nem* KÜL-*shrahnnk.*

Refund

Will you give me a refund?

Werden Sie mir das Gelt zurückerstatten?

vair-den zee MEER *dahss* GELLT *tsoo-*RÜCK-*ehr-*SHTAHTT-*en?*

Refuse (Garbage)

Where does one dispose of refuse?

Wohin tut man die Abfälle?

*voh-*HINN *toot mahnn dee* AHPP-*fell-uh?*

Remember

I do not remember your name (your address).

Ich kann mich nicht an Ihren Namen (Ihre Adresse) erinnern.

ikh kahnn mikh NIKHT *ahnn ear-ehn* NAH-*men (ear-eh ah-*DRESS-*uh) ehr-*IN-*ehrn.*

Rent

Where can I rent a _____?
Wo kann ich ein _____ mieten?
VOH *kahnn ike ine* _____ MEE-*ten?*

How much would it cost to rent a _____?
Wieviel kostet es ein _____ zu mieten?
vee-feel KAWSS-*tet ess ine* _____ *tsoo* MEE-*ten?*

Repair

Can you repair this?
Können Sie das reparieren?
KÖNN-*en zee* DAHSS *reh-pahr-*REER-*en?*

Do you know who can?
Können Sie mir sagen, wer es kann?
könn-en zee meer ZAH-*gen vair ess* KAHNN?

Repeat

Repeat it, please.
Wiederholen Sie es, bitte.
*vee-dehr-*HOH-*len zee ess,* BIT-*tuh.*

Request

I have a request.
Ich habe eine Bitte.
ikh hah-beh ine-uh BIT-*tuh.*

Reservation

I want to confirm (cancel) my reservation to _____.
Ich möchte meine Reservierung nach _____ bestätigen
(annullieren).
*ikh mökh-tuh mine-uh ray-zehr-*VEE-*roong nahkh* _____
*buh-*SHTETT-*ih-gen (ah-noo-*LEER-*en).*

I (don't) have a reservation.
Ich habe (keine) eine Reservierung.
*ikh hah-beh (*KINE-*uh) ine-uh ray-zehr-*VEE-*roong.*

Should we make a reservation for _____ in advance?
Sollen wir im Voraus _____ reservieren?
zawll-en veer imm FOR-*owss* _____ *ray-zehr-*VEE-*ren?*

Could I make a reservation on the flight to _____?
Könnte ich einen Platz für den Flug nach _____ reservieren?
KÖNN-*tuh ikh eye-nen* PLAHTTS *für dane* FLOOCK *nahkh* _____ *ray-zehr*-VEE-*ren?*

Reserve

Can I reserve a (front, window) seat?
Kann ich einen Sitzplatz (vorne, beim Fenster) reservieren?
kahn ikh eye-nen ZITTS-*plahtts* (FOR-*nuh, bime* FENN-*stehr) ray-zehr*-VEE-*ren?*

Is this reserved?
Ist das reserviert?
isst dahss ray-zehr-VEERT?

Resident

Are you a resident of _____?
Sind Sie in _____ Ansässig?
zinnt zee inn _____ AHNN-*sess-ick?*

Resort

Can you recommend a good resort?
Können Sie mir einen guten Kurort empfehlen?
KÖNN-*en zee* MEER *eye-nen* GOO-*ten* KOOR-*ort emp*-FAY-*len?*

Restaurant

Can you recommend a good (inexpensive) restaurant?
Können Sie mir ein gutes (billiges) Restaurant empfehlen?
KÖNN-*en zee meer ine* GOO-*tess* (BILL-*ig-ess) ress-toh*-RAHNG *emp*-FAY-*len?*

Return

I want to return on _____.
Ich möchte am _____ zurückfahren.
ikh MOKH-*tuh ahmm* _____ *tsoo*-RÜCK-*fah-ren.*

When will he (she) return?
Wann kommt er (sie) zurück?
VAHNN *kawmmt air (zee) tsoo*-RÜCK?

Reverse

I would like to reverse the charges.
Ich möchte ein R-Gespräch führen.
ikh MÖKH-*tuh ine* AIR-*guh*-SHPREHKH FÜ-*ren*.

How do you get it into reverse?
Wie reversiert man?
*vee ray-vehr-*ZEERT *mahnn?*

Reward

I am offering a reward of _____.
Ich setze eine Belohnung von _____ aus.
ikh ZET-*suh ine-uh buh-*LOH-*noong fawnn* _____ OWSS.

Ride

May I have a ride?
Kann ich mitfahren?
Kahnn ikh MITT-*fah-ren?*

Let's go for a ride.
Machen wir eine Spazierfahrt.
MAHKH-*en veer ine-uh shpahtts-*EER-*fahrrt.*

River

What river is this?
Welcher Fluss ist das?
vell-khehr FLOOSS *isst dahss?*

Road

Is this the road to _____?
Ist das die Strasse nach _____?
isst DAHSS *dee* SHTRAH-*suh nahkh* _____?

Which is the road to _____?
Welche Strasse führt nach _____?
vell-khuh SHTRAH-*suh* FÜRRT *nahkh* _____?

Which road should I take?
Welche Strasse muss ich nehmen?
vell-khuh SHTRAH-*suh mooss ikh* NAY-*men?*

Where does that road go?
Wohin führt diese Strasse?
*voh-*HINN FÜRRT *dee-zuh* SHTRAH-*suh?*

Is the road paved (bumpy)?
Ist die Strasse gepflastert (holprig)?
isst dee SHTRAH-*suh guh-*PFLAHSS-*tehrt (*HOLE-*prikh)?*

Robbed

I have been robbed!
Man hat mich beraubt!
*mahnn hahtt mikh buh-*ROWPT*!*

Call the police (the manager)!
Rufen Sie die Polizei (den Manager)!
ROO-*fen zee dee poh-lee-*TSYE *(dane* MEN-*ih-zhehr)!*

Room

I want a room with a double bed (single bed, twin beds)
    and bath.
Ich möchte ein Zimmer mit Doppelbett (Einzelbett,
    zwei Einzelbetten) und Bad.
ikh mökh-tuh ine TSIMM-*mehr mitt* DAWPP-*pel-bet (*INE-
    tsell-bet, TSVYE INE-*tsell-bet-ten) oont* BAHT*.*

Do you have a room?
Haben Sie ein Zimmer?
hah-ben zee ine TSIMM-*mehr?*

Is there room for us?
Ist hier Platz für uns?
isst heer PLAHTTS *für* OONNSS*?*

I am in room _____.
Ich bin in Zimmer _____.
ikh binn inn TSIMM-*mehr* _____.

Room service, please.
Zimmerbedienung, bitte.
TSIMM-*mehr-buh-*DEE-*noong,* BIT-*tuh.*

Round Trip

A round-trip ticket to _____, please.
Eine Hin-und Rückfahrkarte nach _____, bitte.
ine-uh HINN- *oonnt* RÜCK-FAR-*kahrr-tuh nahkh* _____,
    BIT-*tuh.*

How much is a round-trip ticket?
Wieviel kostet eine Hin-und Rückfahrkarte?
vee-feel KAWSS-*tet ine-uh* HINN-*oonnt* RÜCK-FAR-*kahrr-*
    tuh?

Route

Which is the best route to _____?

Welches ist der beste Weg nach _____?

VELL-*kehss isst dair* BESS-*tuh* VECK *nahkh* _____?

Rubbish

Please take care of this rubbish.

Bitte lassen Sie diese Abfälle wegschaffen.

bit-tuh LAHSS-*senn zee dee-zuh* AHPP-*fell-uh* VECK-*shahff-en.*

Ruins

Is there a tour of the ruins?

Gibt es eine Führung durch die Ruinen?

gippt ess ine-uh FÜ-*roong doorrkh dee* ROO-*ee-nen?*

Which way are the ruins?

Wie kommt man zu den Ruinen?

vee KAWMMT *mahnn tsoo dane roo-*EE-*nen?*

Safe

Is it safe?

Ist es ungefährlich?

*isst ess oonn-guh-*FARE-*likh?*

Please keep these in the safe for me.

Bitte halten Sie diese Sachen für mich im Safe.

bit-tuh HAHLL-*ten zee dee-zuh* ZAHKH-*en für mikh imm* SAFE.

Sale

Is this for sale?

Kann man das kaufen?

kahnn mahnn dahss KOW-*fen?*

Salt

May I have the salt, please?

Kann ich das Salz haben, bitte?

kahnn ikh dahss ZAHLLTS *hab-ben,* BIT-*tuh?*

Please cook it without salt.

Bitte kochen Sie es ohne Salz.

bit-tuh KAWKH-*en zee ess oh-nuh* ZAHLLTS.

Sandwiches
Do you have sandwiches?
Haben Sie belegte Brötchen?
*hah-ben zee buh-*LAYK-*tuh* BRÖT-*khen?*

Say
How do you say _____ in _____?
Wie heisst _____ auf _____ ?
VEE HYSST _____ *owff* _____?

What did you (did he, did she) say?
Was haben Sie (hat er, hat sie) gesagt?
vahss HAH-*ben zee (*HAHTT *air, hahtt zee) guh-*ZAHKHT?

Schedule
May I have a copy of the schedule?
Kann ich einen Fahrplan haben?
kahnn ikh eye-nen FAR-*plahn hah-ben?*

School
Are you in school?
Sind Sie in der Schule?
zinnt zee inn dair SHOO-*luh?*

Where do you go to school?
Wo gehen Sie zur Schule?
VOH *gay-en zee tsoor* SHOO-*luh?*

Seasick
I am seasick.
Ich bin Seekrank.
ikh binn ZAY-*krahnnk.*

Seat
Is this seat taken?
Ist dieser Platz besetzt?
isst DEE-*zehr* PLAHTTS *buh-*ZETTST?

I want a window seat, please.
Ich möchte einen Fensterplatz, bitte.
ikh MOKH-*tuh eye-nen* FENN-*stehr-plahtts,* BIT-*tuh.*

Are there any seats available?
Gibt es noch Sitzplätze?
gippt ess NAWKH ZITTS-*pletts-uh?*

See

May I see you tonight?
Kann ich Sie heute abend sehen?
kahnn ikh ZEE *hoy-tuh* AH-*bent* ZAY-*en?*

Have you seen my _____?
Haben Sie mein _____ gesehen?
hah-ben zee mine _____ *guh-*ZAY-*en?*

I want to see _____.
Ich möchte _____ sehen.
ikh mökh-tuh _____ ZAY-*en.*

Sell

Would you sell this?
Würden Sie das verkaufen?
VÜRR-*den zee dahss fehr-*KOW-*fen?*

Separate

We want separate rooms.
Wir möchten getrennte Zimmer.
veer MÖKH-*ten guh-*TRENNT-*uh* TSIMM-*mehr.*

Servant

I would like to hire a servant.
Ich möchte einen Diener (ein Dienstmädchen) engagieren.
ikh mökh-tuh eye-nen DEE-*nehr (ine* DEENST-*maid-khen) ahnn-gah-*ZHEER-*en.*

I would like to advertise for a servant.
Ich möchte ein Inserat für einen Diener (ein Dienstmädchen) aufgeben.
*ikh mökh-tuh ine inn-sehr-*RAHT *für eye-nen dee-nehr (ine* DEENST-*maid-khen)* OWFF-*gay-ben.*

Service

Is the service charge included?
Ist Bedienungszuschlag inbegriffen?
*isst buh-*DEE-*noongs-*TSOO-*shlahk* INN-*buh-griff-en?*

Room service, please.
Zimmerbedienung, bitte.
TSIMM-*mehr-buh-*DEE-*noong,* BIT-*tuh.*

Is there bus (limousine) service to the airport (hotel)?
Gibt es einen Bus-(Limousinen-) Service zum Flughafen (Hotel)?
gippt ess eye-nen BOOSS-*(lee-moo-*ZEEN-*en)* ZEHR-*veess
tsoom* FLOOCK-*hah-fen (ho-*TELL*)?*

When is the church service?
Wann ist der Gottesdienst?
vahnn isst dair GAWTT-*ess-deenst?*

Sew – see Laundry

Share

I do not want to share a bath.
Ich will das Badezimmer nicht mit jemandem teilen.
ikh VILL *dahss* BAH-*duh-tsimm-mehr nikht mitt* YAY-*mahnt* TILE-*en.*

Sharp

This knife is not sharp enough.
Dieses Messer ist nicht scharf genug.
dee-zus MESS-*ehr isst nikht* SHAHRRF *guh-*NOOK.

Shave – see Barber

Shaver

Where can I plug in an electric shaver?
Wo kann ich meinen elektrischen Rasierer einschalten?
VOH *kahnn ikh mine-em eh-*LECK-*trish-en-rah-*ZEER-*ehr*
INE-*shahllt-en?*

Sheet

Please change the sheets.
Bitte wechseln Sie die Bettwäsche.
bit-tuh VECK-*seln zee dee* BET-*vehsh-uh.*

Shine

Please shine my shoes.
Bitte putzen Sie meine Schuhe.
bit-tuh POOTS-*en zee mine-uh* SHOO-*uh.*

Ship

When does the ship arrive?
Wann kommt das Schiff an?
vahnn KAWMMT *dahss* SHIFF AHNN*?*

When does the ship leave?
Wann fährt das Schiff ab?
vahnn FEHRT *dahss* SHIFF AHPP?

Shoe
Where can I get my shoes repaired?
Wo kann ich meine Schuhe reparieren lassen?
VOH *kahnn ikh mine-uh* SHOO-*uh reh-par*-REER-*en*
LAHSS-*senn*?

Shopping
Where is the shopping center?
Wo ist das Einkaufszentrum?
VOH *isst dahss* INE-*kowffs*-TSEN-*troom*?

Is there a salesman (a salesgirl) who speaks English?
Gibt es einen Verkäufer (eine Verkäuferin), der (die)
Englisch spricht?
gippt ess eye-nen fehr-KOY-*fehr (ine-uh fehr*-KOY-*fehr-inn) dair (dee)* ENG-*lish* SHPRIHKHT?

Do you speak English?
Sprechen Sie Englisch?
SHPREHKH-*en zee* ENG-*lish*?

May I help you?
Kann ich Ihnen helfen?
kahnn ikh een-en HELL-*fen*?

I am just looking, thank you.
Ich sehe mich bloss um, danke.
ikh ZAY-*uh mikh blohss* OOMM, DAHNNG-*kuh*.

I want to buy _____.
Ich möchte _____ kaufen.
ikh mökh-tuh _____ KOW-*fen*.

Do you sell _____?
Verkaufen Sie _____?
fehr-KOW-*fen zee* _____?

Can I see _____?
Kann ich _____ sehen?
kahnn ikh _____ ZAY-*en*?

I want to spend about _____.
Ich möchte etwa _____ ausgeben.
ikh MÖKH-*tuh ett-vah* _____ OWSS-*gay-ben.*

What else do you have?
Was haben Sie sonst noch?
VAHSS *hah-ben zee* ZAWNSST *nohkh?*

How much is it?
Wieviel kostet es?
vee-feel KAWSS-*tet ess?*

It is too expensive.
Es ist zu teuer.
ess isst tsoo TOY-*ehr.*

Can I see something else?
Kann ich etwas anderes sehen?
KAHNN *ikh ett-vahss* AHNN-*dehr-ess* ZAY-*en?*

Do you have anything better (less expensive)?
Haben Sie etwas Besseres (Billigeres)?
hah-ben zee ett-vahss BESS-*ehr-ess (*BILL-*ikh-ehr-ess)?*

I prefer this one.
Ich ziehe das vor.
ikh TSEE-*uh dahss* FOR.

I'll take this one.
Ich nehme das hier.
ikh NAY-*muh dahss* HEER.

May I try it on?
Kann ich es anprobieren?
kahnn ikh ess AHNN-*pro-*BEE-*ren?*

It does not fit.
Es passt nicht.
ess PAHSST *nikht.*

Do you make alterations here?
Machen Sie hier Änderungen?
MAHKH-*en zee heer* ENN-*duh-roong-en?*

Can you take it in (let it out, shorten it, lengthen it)?
Können Sie es enger (weiter, kürzer, länger) machen?
könn-en zee ess ENG-*ehr (*VITE-*ehr,* KÜRTS-*ehr,* LENG-*ehr) makh-en?*

Will you take my measurements?
Können Sie mein Mass nehmen?
könn-en zee mine MAHSS *nay-men?*

My size in the United States is _____.
Meine Grösse in den Vereinigten Staaten ist _____.
mine-uh GRÖ-*suh inn dane fehr*-INE-*ick-ten* SHTAH-*ten
isst* _____.

Does it come in other colors?
Gibt es das in anderen Farben?
gippt ess dahss inn AHNN-*dehr-en far-ben?*

Do you accept this credit card (American money, travelers' checks, a personal check)?
Akzeptieren Sie diese Kreditkarte (amerikanisches Geld, Reiseschecks, einen persönlichen Scheck)?
*ahk-tsep-*TEER-*en zee dee-suh* KRAY-*deet-kahrr-tuh
(ah-may-ree-*KAN-*nish-ess* GELLT, RYE-*zuh-shecks,
eye-nen pehr-*ZÖN-*likh-en* SHECK*)?*

Do you accept returns?
Nehmen Sie Ware zurück?
NAY-*men zee* VAHR-*uh tsoo-*RÜCK?

I bought it here.
Ich habe es hier gekauft.
ikh hah-beh ess HEER *guh-*KOWFFT.

I would like to exchange it for the next size.
Ich möchte es gegen die nächste Grösse umtauschen.
ikh mökh-tuh ess GAY-*gen dee* NEXT-*uh* GRÖ-*suh* OOMM-*tow-shen.*

Will you wrap this please?
Würden Sie das einpacken, bitte?
VURR-*den zee dahss* INE-*pahck-en,* BIT-*tuh?*

Do you deliver?
Haben Sie einen Lieferdienst?
hah-ben zee eye-nen LEE-*fehr-deenst?*

Please deliver it to my hotel.
Bitte schicken Sie es mir ins Hotel.
bit-tuh SHICK-*en zee ess meer innss ho-*TELL.

Please send it to _____.
Bitte senden Sie es an _____.
bit-tuh ZENN-*den zee ess ahnn* _____.

How much will it cost to insure it?
Wieviel kostet es, das Paket zu versichern?
vee-feel KAWSS-*tet ess dahss pah-*KATE *tsoo fehr-*ZIKH-*ehrn?*

I want to send it as a gift.
Ich möchte es als Geschenk senden.
ikh MÖKH-*tuh ess ahlss guh-*SHENK *zenn-den.*

Will the receiver have to pay duty?
Wird der Empfänger Zoll zahlen müssen?
*veert dair emp-*FENG-*ehr* TSAWLL TSAH-*len müss-en?*

Give me a receipt, please.
Geben Sie mir eine Quittung, bitte.
gay-ben zee meer ine-uh KVITT-*toong,* BIT-*tuh.*

Show
Please show me the way to _____.
Bitte zeigen Sie mir den Weg zu _____.
bit-tuh TSYE-*gen zee meer dane* VECK *tsoo* _____.

When is the next show?
Wann ist die nächste Vorstellung?
vahnn isst dee NEXT-*uh* FOR-*shtell-oong?*

Shower
I want a room with a shower, please.
Ich möchte ein Zimmer mit einer Dusche, bitte.
ikh mökh-tuh ine TSIMM-*mehr mitt eye-nehr* DOOSH-*uh,* BIT-*tuh.*

Shut
Please shut the door (the window).
Bitte schliessen Sie die Tür (das Fenster).
bit-tuh SHLEE-*sen zee dee* TÜRR *(dahss* FENN-*stehr).*

Sick
I am sick.
Ich bin krank.
ikh binn KRAHNNK.

Side Dish

May I have a side dish of _____, please?

Kann ich als Beilage _____ haben, bitte?

kahnn ikh ahlss BY-*lah-guh* _____ HAH-*ben,* BIT-*tuh?*

Sight

I would like to make a tour of the sights.

Ich möchte eine Rundfahrt zur Besichtigung der
Sehenswürdigkeiten machen.

ikh MÖKH-*tuh ine-uh* ROONNT-*fahrrt tsoor buh-*ZIKHT-
tih-goong dair ZAY-*ens-vürr-dikh-kite-en mahkh-en.*

Sightseeing

I want to go sightseeing.

Ich möchte die Sehenswürdigkeiten besichtigen.

ikh mökh-tuh dee ZAY-*ens vürr-dikh-kite-en buh-*ZIKHT-
tih-gen.

What tours can you arrange?

Was für Rundfahrten können Sie arrangieren?

vahss für ROONNT-*far-ten könn-en zee ah-rahn-*ZHEE-
ren?

Sign

What does that sign mean?

Was bedeutet dieses Strassenzeichen?

*vahss buh-*DOY-*tet dee-zus* SHTRAH-*sen-*TSYE-*khen?*

Signal

What is the signal for _____?

Wie ist das Signal für _____?

VEE *isst dahss zeeg-*NAHL *für* _____ *?*

Single

I want a room with single bed and bath.

Ich möchte ein Zimmer mit Einzelbett und Bad.

ikh mökh-tuh ine TSIMM-*mehr mitt* INE-*tsell-*BET *oonnt*
BAHT.

I am single.

Ich bin ledig.

ikh binn LAY-*dick.*

Are you single?

Sind Sie ledig?

zinnt zee LAY-*dick?*

Sit

I would like to sit down for awhile.
Ich möchte mich gern für eine Weile niedersetzen.
ikh MÖKH-*tuh mikh* GAIRN *für ine-uh* VYE-*luh* NEE-*dehr-zetts-en.*

Size

What size is it?
Welche Grösse ist es?
vell-khuh GRO-*suh isst ess?*

It is (not) the right size.
Es ist (nicht) die richtige Grösse.
ess isst (nikht) dee RIKH-*tick-uh* GRÖ-*suh.*

Skate

Do you like to skate?
Gehen Sie gern Schlittschuh laufen?
gay-en zee GAIRN SHLITT-*shoo* LOW-*fen?*

I cannot skate.
Ich kann nicht Schlittschuh laufen.
ikh kahn nikht SHLITT-*shoo* LOW-*fen.*

Where can I find a skating rink?
Wo gibt es einen Schlittschuhbahn?
VOH *gippt ess eye-nen* SHLITT-*shoo*-BAHN?

Ski

Do you like to ski?
Gehen Sie gern skilaufen?
gay-en zee GAIRN SHEE-*low-fen?*

Where is the best place to ski?
Wo ist der beste Ort zum skilaufen?
voh isst dehr BESS-*tuh ort tsoom* SHEE-*low-fen?*

Skin Dive

Do you like to skin dive?
Gehen Sie gern Schwimmtauchen?
gay-en zee GAIRN SHVIMM-*tow-khen?*

Where is the best place for skin diving?
Wo ist die beste Stelle zum Schwimmtauchen?
voh isst dee BESS-*tuh* SHTELL-*uh tsoom* SHVIMM-*tow-khen?*

Sleep

I am going to sleep.

Ich gehe schlafen.

ikh GAY-*uh* SHLAH-*fen.*

Sleeping

My wife (my husband) is sleeping.

Meine Frau (mein Mann) schläft.

mine-uh FROW *(mine* MAHNN*)* SHLAYFT.

Does the train have sleeping accommodations?

Hat der Zug Schlafwagen (Liegewagen)?

hahtt dair TSOOK SHLAHF-*vah-gen (*LEE-*guh*-VAH-*gen)?*

Slope

Where are the best slopes (for skiing)?

Wo sind die besten Abhänge (zum skilaufen)?

voh zinnt dee BESS-*ten* AHPP-*heng-uh (tsoom* SHEE-*low-fen)?*

Slow

Slow down!

Langsam, bitte!

LAHNNG-*zahm,* BIT-*tuh!*

Slower

Drive slower, please.

Fahren Sie langsamer, bitte.

FAH-*ren zee* LAHNNG-*zah-mehr,* BIT-*tuh.*

Slowly

Please speak (drive) more slowly.

Bitte sprechen (fahren) Sie langsamer.

bit-tuh SPREHKH-*en (*FAH-*ren) zee* LAHNNG-*zah-mehr.*

Small

This is too small.

das ist zu klein.

dahss isst tsoo KLINE.

This is not small enough.

Das ist nicht klein genug.

dahss isst nikht KLINE *guh*-NOOK.

Smoke

Do you smoke?

Rauchen Sie?

ROWKH-en zee?

Do you mind if I smoke?

Haben Sie etwas dagegen, wenn ich rauche?

hah-ben zee ett-vahss dah-GAY-gen venn ikh ROWKH-uh?

Smoking

Where is the smoking car?

Wo ist das Raucher-Abteil?

voh isst dahss ROW-khehr-ahpp-tile?

Snack

Where can I get a snack?

Wo kann ich einen kleinen Imbiss bekommen?

VOH kahnn ikh eye-nen KLINE-en IMM-biss buh-KAWMM-en?

Soap

Please bring me some soap.

Bitte bringen Sie mir Seife.

bit-tuh BRING-en zee meer ZIFE-uh.

Sole

A new pair of soles, please.

Neue Sohlen, bitte.

NOY-uh ZOH-len, BIT-tuh.

Soil

My _____ is soiled.

Mein _____ ist schmutzig.

mine _____ isst SHMOOTTS-ick.

Something

Can we get something to eat (drink)?

Können wir etwas zu essen (trinken) bekommen?

KÖNN-en veer ett-vahss tsoo ESS-sen (TRING-ken) buh-KAWMM-en?

Soon

I'll see you soon.

Bis später!

biss SHPAY-tehr!

How soon does the bus (the plane, the boat, the train) leave?

Wann fährt der Bus (das Flugzeug, das Schiff, der Zug) ab?

vahnn FEHRRT *dair* BOOSS *(dahss* FLOOCK-*tsoyg, dahss* SHIFF, *dair* TSOOK) AHPP?

How soon does the bus (the plane, the boat, the train) arrive?

Wann kommt der Bus (das Flugzeug, das Schiff, der Zug) an?

vahnn KAWMMT *dair* BOOSS *(dahss* FLOOCK-*tsoyg, dahss* SHIFF, *dair* TSOOK) AHNN?

Sorry
I am sorry.
Es tut mir Leid.
ess toot meer LITE.

Sound
What is that sound?
Was ist das für ein Geräusch?
vahss ISST *dahss für ine guh*-ROYSH?

Souvenir
Where can I find a souvenir shop?
Wo gibt es hier einen Geschenk-Laden?
VOH *gippt ess heer eye-nen guh*-SHENK-*lah-den*?

Speak
Do you speak English?
Sprechen Sie Englisch?
SHPREHKH-*en zee* ENG-*lish*?

I speak only English.
Ich spreche nur English.
ikh SHPREHKH-*uh noorr* ENG-*lish*.

Please speak more slowly.
Bitte sprechen Sie langsamer.
bit-tuh SHPREHKH-*en zee* LAHNNG-*zah-mehr*.

May I please speak with _____?
Kann ich bitte mit _____ sprechen?
kahnn ikh bit-tuh mitt _____ SHPREHKH-*en*?

I don't speak ——— (very well).
Ich spreche nicht (sehr gut) ———.
ikh SHPREHKH-*uh* NIKHT *(zair goot)* ———.

I want a guide (driver) who speaks English.
Ich möchte einen Führer (Chauffeur), der Englisch
    spricht.
ikh mökh-tuh eye-nen FÜ-*rehr (show-*FUR*) dair* ENG-*lish*
    SHPRIKHT.

Special Delivery – see Post Office

Spectacles – see Glasses

Speed
What is the speed limit?
Was ist die Höchstgeschwindigkeit?
*vahss isst dee hökhst-guh-*SHVINN-*dick-kite?*

Spoon
Please bring me another spoon.
Bitte bringen Sie mir noch einen Löffel.
bit-tuh BRING-*en zee meer* NAWKH *eye-nen* LÖ-*fell.*

Stables
Where are the stables?
Wo sind die Ställe?
VOH *zinnt dee* SHTELL-*uh?*

Stamps – see Post Office

Standby
Please put me on standby.
Bitte setzen Sie mich auf die Warteliste.
bit-tuh ZET-*sen zee mikh owff dee* VAHR-*tuh-liss-tuh.*

Stateroom
Where is the stateroom ———?
Wo ist Luxuskabine ———?
voh isst LOOX-*ooss-kah-*BEE-*nuh* ———?

I am in stateroom ———.
Ich bin in Luxuskabine ———.
ikh binn inn LOOX-*ooss-kah-*BEE-*nuh* ———.

Which stateroom are you in?
In welcher Luxuskabine sind Sie?
inn vell-khehr LOOX-*ooss-kah-*BEE-*nuh zinnt zee?*

Station

Can you direct me to the railroad station?
Wie komme ich zum Bahnhof, bitte?
vee KAWMM-*uh ikh tsoom* BAHN-*hof,* BIT-*tuh?*

Can you take me to the railroad station?
Können Sie mich zum Bahnhof bringen, bitte?
KÖNN-*en zee mikh tsoom* BAHN-*hohf* BRING-*en,* BIT-*tuh?*

Stay

I am going to stay for _____ days (weeks).
Ich bleibe _____ Tage (Wochen).
ikh BLIBE-*uh* _____ TAHG-*uh (*VAWKH-*en).*

How long are you planning to stay?
Wie lange wollen Sie bleiben?
vee LAHNNG-*uh vawll-en zee* BLIBE-*en?*

Where are you staying?
Wo wohnen Sie?
voh VOH-*nen zee?*

I am staying at _____.
Ich wohne im _____.
ikh VOH-*nuh imm* _____.

Stolen

My _____ has been stolen!
Mein _____ ist gestohlen worden!
mine _____ *isst guh-*SHTAWLL-*en vawrr-den!*

Call the police (the manager)!
Rufen Sie die Polizei (den Manager)!
*roo-fen zee dee poh-lee-*TSYE *(dane* MAHNN-*uh-zhehr)!*

Stop

Stop here, please.
Halten Sie hier, bitte.
HAHLL-*ten zee* HEER, BIT-*tuh.*

Next stop, please.
Nächste Haltestelle, bitte.
NEXT-*uh* HAHLLT-*uh-*SHTELL-*uh,* BIT-*tuh.*

Do we stop at _____?
Halten wir in _____?
HAHLLT-*en veer inn* _____?

When is the next stop?
Wann ist die nächste Endstation (Bus-Haltestelle)?
VAHNN *isst dee* NEXT-*uh* END-*shtahtts*-YOHN *(*BOOSS-
  HAHLLT-*uh*-SHTELL-*uh)?*

Stop!
Halt!
HAHLLT*!*

Stranger
I am a stranger here.
Ich bin Fremd hier.
ikh binn FREMMT *heer.*

Street
What street is this?
Welche Strasse ist das?
vell-khuh SHTRAH-*suh isst* DAHSS*?*

What street comes after _____?
Welche Strasse kommt nach _____?
vell-khuh SHTRAH-*suh kawmmt nahkh* _____?

It is on _____ street.
Es ist in der _____ Strasse.
ess isst inn dair _____ SHTRAH-*suh.*

Student
I am a student.
Ich bin Student.
*ikh binn shtoo-*DENT.

Are you a student?
Sind Sie Student?
*zinnt zee shtoo-*DENT*?*

Do you give student rates?
Haben Sie einen Sondertarif für Studenten?
hah-ben zee eye-nen ZAWNN-*dehr-*TAH-*reef für shtoo-*
  DENT-*en?*

Subtitles
Does the movie have English subtitles?
Hat der Film englische Untertitel?
hahtt dair FILM ENG-*lish-uh* OONN-*tehr-*TEE-*t'l?*

Subway

What subway do I take to _____?

Welche U-Bahn fährt nach _____?

vell-khuh OO-*bahn* FEHRRT *nahkh* _____?

Where can I find the subway for _____?

Wie komme ich zur U-Bahn nach _____?

VEE *kawmm-uh ikh tsoor* OO-*bahn nahkh* _____?

Sugar

May I have some sugar, please?

Kann ich Zucker haben, bitte?

kahnn ikh TSOOCK-*ehr hah-ben, bit-tuh?*

Suit

Where can I have a suit made (cleaned, pressed)?

Wo kann ich einen Anzug machen (reinigen, bügeln) lassen?

VOH *kahnn ikh eye-nen* AHNN-*tsook* MAHKH-*en* (RINE-*ih-gen,* BÜ-*geln*) LAHSS-*senn?*

Please clean (press) this suit.

Bitte reinigen (bügeln) Sie diesen Anzug.

bit-tuh RINE-*ih-gen* (BÜ-*geln*) *zee dee-zen* AHNN-*tsook.*

Suitcase

This is my suitcase.

Das ist mein Koffer.

dahss isst mine KAWFF-*fehr.*

Would you carry my suitcase, please?

Könnten Sie meinen Koffer tragen, bitte?

KÖNN-*ten zee mine-em* KAWFF-*fehr* TRAH-*gen,* BIT-*tuh?*

Sunburn

What do you have for sunburn?

Was haben Sie, um Sonnenbrand zu heilen?

vahss hah-ben zee oomm ZAWNN-*en-brahnnt tsoo* HYE-*len?*

Sweet

This is too sweet.

Das ist zu süss.

dahss isst tsoo ZÜSS

This is not sweet enough.
Das ist nicht süss genug.
dahss isst nikht ZÜSS *guh*-NOOK.

Swim
Where can I go swimming?
Wo kann man hier schwimmen?
voh kahnn mahnn heer SHVIMM-*men?*

I don't know how to swim.
Ich kann nicht schwimmen.
ikh kahnn nikht SHVIMM-*men.*

Synagogue
Can you direct me to the nearest synagogue, please?
Wie komme ich zur nächsten Synagoge, bitte?
VEE *kawmm-uh ikh tsoor* NEXT-*en zünn-uh*-GOH-*guh,*
BIT-*tuh?*

Can you take me to the nearest synagogue, please?
Können Sie mich zur nächsten Synagoge bringen,
bitte?
KÖNN-*en zee mikh tsoor* NEXT-*en zünn-uh*-GOH-*guh*
BRING-*en,* BIT-*tuh?*

Table
A table by the window (at the side, in the corner),
please.
Ein Tisch beim Fenster (an der Seite, in der Ecke),
bitte.
ine TISH *bime* FENN-*stehr (ahnn dair* ZITE-*tuh, inn dair*
ECK-*uh),* BIT-*tuh.*

A table for two (three, four, for just myself), please.
Ein Tisch für zwei (drei, vier, für mich allein), bitte.
ine TISH *für* TSVYE *(*DRY*,* FEER*, für mikh ahl*-LINE*),* BIT-
tuh.

Take
How long will it take?
Wie lange wird es dauern?
vee LAHNNG-*uh veert ess* DOW-*ehrn?*

Take me to the _____.
Bringen Sie mich zum _____.
BRING-*en zee mikh tsoom* _____.

Please take my order (my bags).
Bitte nehmen Sie meine Bestellung (mein Gepäck).
bit-tuh NAY-*men zee mine-uh buh*-SHTELL-*oong (mine*
  guh-PECK*).*

Take it away, please.
Nehmen Sie es weg, bitte.
NAY-*men zee ess* VECK, BIT-*tuh.*

Is this taken?
Ist dieser _____ besetzt?
isst dee-zehr _____ *buh*-ZETTST?

Taste

This has a strange taste.
Das hat einen merkwürdigen Geschmack.
dahss HAHTT *eye-nen* MAIRK-*vür-dih-gen guh*-SHMAHCK.

It does not taste right.
Es schmeckt nicht richtig.
ess SHMECKT *nikht* RIKH-*tick.*

May I taste it?
Kann ich es kosten?
kahnn ikh ess KAWSS-*ten?*

Tax

Is the tax included?
Ist Steuer inbegriffen?
isst SHTOY-*ehr inn-buh*-GRIFF-*en?*

How much is the tax?
Wie hoch ist die Steuer?
vee HOHKH *isst dee* SHTOY-*ehr?*

Taxi

Please get me a taxi.
Bitte besorgen Sie mir ein Taxi.
bit-tuh buh-ZAWR-*gen zee meer ine* TAHCK-*see.*

Where can I get a taxi?
Wo kann ich ein Taxi bekommen?
VOH *kahnn ikh ine* TAHCK-*see buh*-KAWMM-*en?*

Tea

May I please have some (more) tea?
Kann ich bitte (noch) etwas Tee haben?
kahnn ikh bit-tuh (NAWKH) *ett-vahss* TAY *hah-ben?*

With lemon (with milk, iced), please.
Mit Zitrone (mit Milch, mit Eis), bitte.
*mitt tsee-*TROH-*nuh (mitt* MILLKH, *mitt* ICE), BIT-*tuh.*

Teach

Will you teach me _____?
Könnten Sie mich _____ lehren?
könn-ten zee mikh _____ LAY-*ren?*

Telegram

Where can I go to send a telegram?
Wo kann ich ein Telegram absenden?
*voh kahnn ikh ine tay-luh-*GRAHMM AHPP-*zenn-den?*

I want to send a telegram to _____ at _____.
Ich möchte ein Telegram an _____ in _____ senden.
*ikh mökh-tuh ine tay-luh-*GRAHMM *ahnn* _____ *inn*
_____ ZENN-*den.*

What is the cost per word to _____?
Wieviel kostet es pro Wort nach _____?
vee-feel KAWSS-*tet ess pro* VAWRT *nahkh_____?*

What is the night rate to _____?
Wieviel kostet ein Nacht-Telegramm nach _____?
vee-feel KAWSS-*tet ine* NAHKHT-*tay-luh-*GRAHMM *nahkh*
_____?

It is urgent.
Es ist dringend.
ess isst DRING-*ent.*

When will it be delivered to _____?
Wann wird es in _____ ausgetragen?
VAHNN *veert ess inn* _____ OWSS-*guh-*TRAH-*gen?*

I want to pay for the answer.
Ich möchte die Antwort bezahlen.
ikh mökh-tuh dee AHNNT-*vort buh-*TSAH-*len.*

Please read it back to me.
Bitte lesen Sie es mir vor.
bit-tuh LAY-*zen zee ess meer* FOR.

Telephone

Where can I make a telephone call?
Wo kann ich telefonieren?
VOH *kahnn ikh tay-luh-foh*-NEER-*en?*

Do I need tokens?
Brauche ich Münzen?
BROW-*khuh ikh* MÜNT-*sen?*

Where can I get some tokens?
Wo kann ich Münzen bekommen?
VOH *kahnn ikh* MÜNT-*sen buh*-KAWMM-*en?*

Will you telephone for me?
Könnten Sie für mich telefonieren?
KÖNN-*ten zee für* MIKH *tay-luh-foh*-NEER-*en?*

A local call, number _____.
Ein Ortgespräch, Nummer _____.
ine ORT-*guh*-SHPREHKH *noomm-ehr* _____.

Long distance operator, please.
Fernamt, bitte.
FEHRN-*ahmmt,* BIT-*tuh.*

Overseas operator, please.
Amt für Überseegespräche, bitte.
AHMMT *für ü-behr*-ZAY-*guh*-SHPREH-*khuh,* BIT-*tuh.*

How much is a call to _____?
Wieviel kostet ein Gespräch nach _____?
vee-feel KAWSS-*tet ine guh*-SHPREHKH *nahkh* _____?

I want number _____ in _____.
Ich möchte Nummer _____ in _____.
ikh MÖKH-*tuh noomm-ehr* _____ *inn* _____.

Information, please.
Auskunft, bitte.
OWSS-*koonft,* BIT-*tuh.*

Operator, that's the wrong number.
Fraülein, ich bein falsch verbunden.
FROY-*line, ikh binn* FAHLLSH *fehr*-BOON-*den.*

There is no answer.
Es meldet sich niemand.
ess MELL-*det zikh* NEE-*mahnnt.*

The line is busy.
Die Linie ist besetzt.
dee LEEN-*yuh isst buh-*ZETTST.

Hold the line, please.
Bleiben Sie am Apparat, bitte.
BLIBE-*en zee ahmm ahp-pah-*RAHT, BIT-*tuh.*

May I speak with _____?
Kann ich mit _____ sprechen?
kahnn ikh mitt _____ SHPREHKH-*en?*

When (where) can I reach him?
Wann (Wo) kann ich ihn erreichen?
VAHNN *(*VOH*) kahnn ikh een ehr-*RYE-*khen?*

This is _____ speaking.
Hier spricht _____.
heer SHPRIHKHT _____.

Please take a message for _____.
Bitte übernehmen Sie eine Botschaft für _____.
*bit-tuh ü-behr-*NAY-*men zee ine-uh* BOAT-*shahft für*
_____.

Have him call _____ at number _____.
Sagen Sie ihm, er möchte _____, Nummer _____ anru-
fen.
ZAH-*gen zee* EEM *air* MÖKH-*tuh* _____, NOOM-*mehr*
_____ AHNN-*roo-fen.*

I'll call back later.
Ich werde später wieder anrufen.
ikh VAIR-*duh* SHPAY-*tehr* VEE-*dehr* AHNN-*roo-fen.*

Television

Is there a television in the room (in the lobby)?
Ist ein Fernseher im Zimmer (in der Halle)?
isst ine FEHRN-*zay-ehr imm* TSIMM-*mehr (inn dair*
HAHLL-*uh)?*

Can I have a television in my room?
Kann ich einen Fernseher in meinem Zimmer haben?
kahn ikh eye-nen FEHRN-*zay-ehr inn mine-em* TSIMM-*mehr hah-ben?*

The television in my room does not work.
Der Fernseher in meinem Zimmer geht nicht.
dair FEHRN-*zay-ehr inn mine-em* TSIMM-*mehr* GATE *nikht.*

Tell
Please tell me when (where) to get off.
Bitte sagen Sie mir, wenn (wo) ich aussteigen muss.
bit-tuh ZAH-*gen zee meer* VENN *(*VOH*) ikh* OWSS-*shtye-gen* MOOSS.

Temple – see Synagogue

Tennis
Let's play tennis.
Spielen wir Tennis.
SHPEE-*len veer* TENN-*niss.*

Where can we play tennis?
Wo können wir Tennis spielen?
VOH *könn-en veer* TEEN-*niss* SHPEE-*len?*

Thank You
Thank you very much.
Danke sehr.
DAHNNG-*kuh* ZAIR.

No, thank you.
Nein, danke.
NINE, DAHNNG-*kuh.*

That
What is that?
Was ist das?
VAHSS *isst* DAHSS*?*

What is that in _____?
Was ist das auf _____?
VAHSS *isst* DAHSS *owff* _____*?*

That will be all.
Das ist alles.
DAHSS *isst* AHLL-*less.*

Theater

I want to go to the theater tonight; what do you recommend?
Ich möchte heute abend ins Theater gehen; was empfehlen Sie?
ikh MÖKH-*tuh hoy-tuh* AH-*bent innss tay-*AH-*tehr* GAY-*en;* VAHSS *emp-*FAY-*len zee?*

Can you direct me to the theater, please?
Wie komme ich zum Theater, bitte?
VEE *kawmm-uh ikh tsoom tay-*AH-*tehr,* BIT-*tuh?*

Take me to the theater, please.
Bringen Sie mich zum Theater, bitte.
BRING-*en zee mikh tsoom tay-*AH-*tehr,* BIT-*tuh.*

Would you like to go to the theater with me?
Möchten Sie mit mir ins Theater gehen?
MÖKH-*ten zee mitt meer innss tay-*AH-*tehr gay-en?*

Thermometer

Where is the thermometer?
Wo ist das Thermometer?
*voh isst dahss tehr-moh-*MAY-*tehr?*

Things

Where are your things?
Wo sind Ihre Sachen?
VOH *zinnt ear-eh* ZAHKH-*en?*

Those are my things.
Das sind meine Sachen.
DAHSS *zinnt mine-uh* ZAHKH-*en.*

Thirsty

I am (not) thirsty.
Ich bin (nicht) durstig.
*ikh binn (*NIKHT*) *DOORSS-*tick.*

This

What is this in _____?
Was ist das auf _____?
VAHSS *isst* DAHSS *owff* _____?

What street (town) is this?
Welche Strasse (Stadt) ist das?
vell-khuh SHTRAH-*suh (*SHTAHT*) isst dahss?*

Is this the way?
Ist das der Weg?
isst DAHSS *dair* VECK?

Through

I want to check this through to ＿＿＿.
Ich möchte das direkt bis ＿＿＿ aufgeben.
ikh MÖKH-*tuh dahss dee-*REKT *biss* ＿＿＿ OWFF-*gay-ben.*

What city are we passing through?
Durch welche Stadt fahren wir?
doorrkh VELL-*khuh* SHTAHT FAH-*ren veer?*

I want to pass through ＿＿＿.
Ich möchte durch ＿＿＿ fahren.
ikh MÖKH-*tuh doorrkh* ＿＿＿ FAH-*ren.*

Ticket

A one-way ticket (round-trip ticket) to ＿＿＿, please.
Eine einfache Fahrkarte (Hin-und Rückfahrkarte) nach ＿＿＿, bitte.
ine-uh INE-*fahkh-uh far-karr-tuh (*HINN-*oonnt* RÜCK-FAR-*karr-tuh) nahkh* ＿＿＿, BIT-*tuh.*

How much is a ticket to ＿＿＿?
Wieviel kostet eine Fahrkarte nach ＿＿＿?
vee-feel KAWSS-*tet ine-uh* FAR-*karr-tuh nahkh* ＿＿＿?

Do you have tickets for tonight?
Haben Sie Billetts für heute abend?
*hah-ben zee bill-*YETTS *für hoy-tuh* AH-*bent?*

Where is the ticket window?
Wo ist der Fahrkarten-Schalter?
VOH *isst dair* FAR-*karr-ten-shahllt-ehr?*

Tide

When is high tide (low tide)?
Wann ist Flut (Ebbe)?
VAHNN *isst* FLOOT (EBB-*uh)?*

Time

What time is it?

Wieviel Uhr ist es?

vee-feel OOR *isst ess?*

What time is breakfast (lunch, dinner) served?

Um wieviel Uhr wird Frühstück (Mittagessen, Abendessen) serviert?

oomm vee-feel OOR *veert* FRÜ-*shtück (*MITT-*tahk-ess-senn,* AH-*bent-ess-senn) zehr-*VEERT*?*

Timetable

Please give me a timetable.

Bitte geben Sie mir einen Fahrplan.

bit-tuh GAY-*ben zee meer eye-nen* FAR-*plahn.*

Tip

Is the tip included?

Ist Trinkgeld inbegriffen?

isst TRINK-*gelt inn-buh-*GRIFF-*en?*

How much tip should I leave?

Wieviel Trinkgeld soll ich hinterlassen?

vee-feel TRINK-*gelt zawll ikh* HINN-*tehr lahss-senn?*

Tired

I am (not) tired.

Ich bin (nicht) müde.

*ikh binn (*NIKHT*) MÜ-duh.*

Tissues

Please bring me some tissues.

Bitte bringen Sie mir Papiertaschentücher.

bit-tuh BRING-*en zee meer pah-*PEER-TAHSH-*en-*TOOKH-*ehr.*

Tobacco

Where can I buy some tobacco?

Wo kann ich Tabak kaufen?

VOH *kahnn ikh tah-*BAHCK KOW-*fen?*

Today

We are leaving today.

Wir reisen heute ab.

veer RYE-*zen* HOY-*tuh* AHPP.

I need it today.
Ich brauche es heute.
ikh BROW-*khuh ess* HOY-*tuh.*

Toilet Paper
Please bring me some toilet paper.
Bitte bringen Sie mir Toilettenpapier.
bit-tuh BRING-*en zee meer too-ah-*LETT-*ten-pah-*PEER.

Token
Do I need a token?
Brauche ich eine Münze?
BROW-*khuh ikh ine-uh* MÜNT-*suh?*

Where can I buy some tokens?
Wo kann ich Münzen kaufen?
VOH *kahn ikh* MÜNT-*sen* KOW-*fen?*

Tomorrow
We are leaving tomorrow.
Wir reisen morgen ab.
veer RYE-*zen* MOR-*gen* AHPP.

I would like a reservation for tomorrow.
Ich möchte eine Reservierung für morgen.
ikh MÖKH-*tuh ine-uh ray-zehr-*VEER-*oong für* MOR-*gen.*

May I see you tomorrow?
Kann ich Sie morgen sehen?
kahnn ikh zee MOR-*gen* ZAY-*en?*

I need it tomorrow.
Ich brauche es morgen.
ikh BROW-*khuh ess* MOR-*gen.*

Tonight
A room for tonight only, please.
Ein Zimmer nur für heute Nacht, bitte.
ine TSIMM-*mehr noorr für* HOY-*tuh* NAHKHT, BIT-*tuh.*

May I see you tonight?
Kann ich Sie heute abend sehen?
KAHNN *ikh zee hoy-tuh* AH-*bent* ZAY-*en?*

Toothache – see also Dentist
I have a toothache.
Ich habe Zahnschmerzen.
ikh hah-beh TSAHN-*shmehrts-tsen.*

Tough

This meat is too tough; please take it back.

Dieses Fleisch ist zu zäh; bitte tragen Sie es zurück.

dee-zes FLYSH *isst tsoo* TSAY; *bit-tuh* TRAH-*gen zee ess tsoo-*RÜCK.

Tour

We would like a tour of the city.

Wir möchten eine Rundfahrt durch die Stadt machen.

veer MÖKH-*ten ine-uh* ROONT-*fahrrt doorrkh dee* SHTAHT *mahkh-en.*

Can you arrange a tour for this morning (this afternoon, this evening)?

Können Sie eine Rundfahrt für heute vormittag (heute nachmittag, heute abend) arrangieren?

könn-en zee ine-uh ROONT-*fahrrt für hoy-tuh* FOR-*mitt-tahg (hoy-tuh* NAHKH-*mitt-tahg, hoy-tuh* AH-*bent) ah-rahng-*ZHEER-*en?*

Where can we get a tour to _____?

Wo können wir eine Rundfahrt nach _____ bekommen?

VOH *könn-en veer ine-uh* ROONT-*fahrrt nahkh* _____ *buh-*KAWMM-*en?*

Do any tours leave from this hotel?

Gehen Rundfahrten vom Hotel ab?

GAY-*en* ROONT-*fahrr-ten fawmm ho-*TELL AHPP?

When do they leave?

Wann gehen Sie ab?

VAHNN GAY-*en zee* AHPP?

Tourist

A ticket in tourist class, please.

Eine Karte Touristen-Klasse, bitte.

ine-uh KAHRR-*tuh too-*RIST-*en-*KLAHSS-*uh,* BIT-*tuh.*

Towels

Please bring me some towels.

Bitte bringen Sie mir Handtücher.

bit-tuh BRING-*en zee meer* HAHNNT-*tü-khehr.*

Town

What town is this?
Wie heisst diese Stadt?
vee HYSST *dee-zuh* SHTAHT*?*

What is the next town?
Wie heisst die nächste Stadt?
vee HYSST *dee* NEXT-*uh* SHTAHT*?*

May I have a ride to town?
Kann ich in die Stadt mitfahren?
KAHNN *ikh inn dee* SHTAHT MITT-*fah-ren?*

Track

What track does it leave from?
Von welchem Gleis geht er ab?
fawnn VELL-*khem* GLICE *gate air* AHPP*?*

Where is track ____?
Wo ist Gleis ____?
VOH *isst* GLICE ____*?*

Trade

Will you trade me that for this?
Würden Sie das gegen das eintauschen?
vürr-den zee DAHSS *gay-gen* DAHSS INE-*tow-shen?*

Train

When does the train arrive?
Wann kommt der Zug an?
vahnn KAWMMT *dair* TSOOK AHNN*?*

When does the train leave?
Wann fährt der Zug ab?
vahnn KAWMMT *dair* TSOOK AHPP*?*

Does this train stop at ____?
Hält dieser Zug in ____?
HELLT *dee-zehr* TSOOK *inn* ____*?*

Is this the train for ____?
Ist das der Zug nach ____?
isst DAHSS *dair* TSOOK *nahkh* ____*?*

Does the train have sleeping accommodations (a dining car)?

Hat der Zug Schlafwagen (Speisewagen)?

hahtt dair TSOOK SHLAHF-*vah-gen* (SHPYE-*zuh-vah-gen*)?

Transfer

A transfer, please.

Eine Umsteigekarte, bitte.

ine-uh OOMM-*shtye-guh-*KAHRR-*tuh,* BIT-*tuh.*

Where do I transfer?

Wo muss ich umsteigen?

VOH *mooss ikh* OOMM-*shtye-gen?*

Transportation

What kind of transportation is there to _____?

Welche Art Transportation gibt es nach _____?

vell-khuh ART *trahnns-por-tahts-*YON *gippt ess nahkh* _____?

Travel Agency

Where is the nearest travel agency?

Wo ist die nächste Reisebüro?

VOH *isst dee* NEXT-*uh rye-zuh-bü-*ROH?

Travelers' Checks − see also Bank

I have travelers' checks.

Ich habe Reiseschecks.

ikh hah-beh RYE-*zuh-shecks.*

Do you accept (cash) travelers' checks?

Akzeptieren (lösen) Sie Reiseschecks (ein)?

*ahk-tsep-*TEER-*en* (LÖ-*zen*) *zee* RYE-*zuh-shecks* (INE)?

Trip

How long does the trip take?

Wie lange dauert die Reise?

vee LAHNNG-*uh* DOW-*ehrt dee* RYE-*zuh?*

This is my (our) first (second, third) trip.

Das ist meine (unsere) erste (zweite, dritte) Reise.

dahss isst mine-uh (OONN-*zehr-uh*) EHRST-*uh* (TSVYE-*tuh,* DRITT-*tuh*) RYE-*zuh.*

Trouble
What is the trouble?
Was ist passiert?
vahss isst PAHSS-*eert?*

True
That is (not) true.
Das ist (nicht) wahr.
dahss isst nikht VAHR.

Trunk
That is my trunk.
Das ist mein Koffer.
dahss isst mine KAWFF-*fehr.*

Please take my trunk to the hotel (to the airport, to my
    room, to the railroad station).
Bitte bringen Sie meinen Koffer ins Hotel (zum Flug-
    hafen, in mein Zimmer, zum Bahnhof).
bit-tuh BRING-*en zee mine-en* KAWFF-*fehr innss ho-*TELL
    (tsoom FLOOCK-*hah-fen, inn mine* TSIMM-*mehr, tsoom*
    BAHN-*hohf).*

Try
May I try this on?
Kann ich das anprobieren?
kahn ikh dahss AHNN-*pro-*BEE-*ren?*

Tub
I would like a bath with a tub.
Ich möchte ein Badezimmer mit einen Badewanne.
ikh mökh-tuh ine BAH-*duh-*TSIMM-*mehr mitt* EYE-*nehr*
    BAH-*duh-vahn-nuh.*

Turn
Where should I turn?
Wo muss ich einbiegen?
VOH *mooss ikh* INE-*bee-gen?*

Typewriter
Where can I rent a typewriter?
Wo kann ich eine Schreibmaschine mieten?
VOH *kahn ikh ine-uh* SHRIBE-*mah-*SHEE-*nuh* MEE-*ten?*

Umbrella
Where can I buy an umbrella?
Wo kann ich einen Regenschirm kaufen?
VOH *kahnn ikh eye-nen* RAY-*gen-sheerm* KOW-*fen?*

Undercooked
This is undercooked; please take it back.
Das ist nicht gar; bitte tragen Sie es zurück.
dahss isst nikht GAHR; *bit-tuh* TRAH-*gen zee ess tsoo-*
RÜCK.

Understand
I (don't) understand.
Ich verstehe (nicht).
*ikh fehr-*SHTAY-*uh (*NIKHT*).*

Do you understand?
Verstehen Sie?
*fehr-*SHTAY-*en zee?*

Undertow
Is there an undertow here?
Gibt es eine Gegenströmung?
gippt ess ine-uh GAY-*gen-*SHTRÖ-*moong?*

United States
I am from the United States.
Ich bin aus den Vereinigten Staaten.
*ikh binn owss dane fehr-*INE-*ick-ten* SHTAH-*ten.*

Have you ever been to the United States?
Sind Sie jemals in den Vereinigten Staaten gewesen?
zinnt zee YAY-*mahlss inn dane fehr-*INE-*ick-ten* SHTAH-
*ten guh-*VAY-*zen?*

University
Which is the best way to the University?
Wie kommt man am besten zur Universität?
VEE *kawmmt mahnn ahmm* BESS-*ten tsoor oo-nee-vehr-*
*zee-*TAYT*?*

Do you study (do you teach) at the University?
Studieren (lehren) Sie an der Universität?
*shtoo-*DEER-*en (*LAY-*ren) zee ahnn dair oo-nee-vehr-zee-*
TAYT*?*

Upper

I want an upper berth.
Ich möchte eine obere Koje.
ikh MÖKH-*tuh ine-uh* OH-*behr-uh* KOH-*yuh.*

Urgent

It is urgent.
Es ist dringend.
ess isst DRING-*ent.*

Use

I don't know how to use this.
Ich weiss nicht, wie man das gebraucht.
ikh VICE *nikht vee mahnn dahss guh-*BROWKHT.

That is for my own use.
Das ist für meinen eigenen Gebrauch.
dahss isst für mine-em EYE-*gen-en guh-*BROWKH.

Vacancies

Have you any vacancies?
Haben Sie Zimmer frei?
hah-ben zee TSIMM-*mehr* FRY?

Vacation

I am on my vacation.
Ich bin auf einer Ferienreise.
ikh binn owff EYE-*nehr* FEHR-*yen-*RYE-*zuh.*

Vaccinate

I have been vaccinated for _____.
Ich bin gegen _____ geimpft.
ikh binn gay-gen _____ *guh-*IMPFT.

Vacuum

Please vacuum the rug.
Bitte reinigen Sie den Teppich mit dem Staubsauger.
bit-tuh RINE-*ih-gen zee dane* TEPP-*ikh mitt dame*
   SHTOWB-*zow-gehr.*

Valid

For how long is the ticket valid?
Wie lange ist die Fahrkarte gültig?
vee LAHNNG-*uh isst dee* FAR-*karr-tuh* GÜL-*tick?*

Valuables

Please place my valuables in your safe.

Bitte legen Sie meine Wertsachen in Ihr Safe.

bit-tuh LAY-*gen zee mine-uh* VAIRT-*zahkh-en inn ear* SAFE.

Vegetarian

I am a vegetarian.

Ich bin Vegetarier.

*ikh binn veg-ih-*TAH-*ree-er.*

Vicinity

Are we in the vicinity of _____?

Sind wir in der Nähe von _____?

zinnt veer inn dair NAY-*uh fawnn* _____?

View

I want a room (a table) with a good view.

Ich möchte ein Zimmer (einen Tisch) mit einem guten Ausblick.

ikh mökh-tuh ine TSIMM-*mehr (eye-nen* TISH*) mitt eye-nem goo-ten* OWSS-*block.*

Village

What village is this?

Wie heisst dieses Dorf?

vee hysst dee-zehs DORF?

How far is it to the next village?

Wie weit ist es bis zum nächsten Dorf?

vee VITE *isst ess biss tsoom* NEXT-*en* DORF?

What is the next village?

Wie heisst das nächste Dorf?

VEE HYSST *dahss* NEXT-*uh* DORF?

Visa

Do I need a visa for _____?

Brauche ich ein Visum für _____?

BROW-*khuh ikh ine* VEE-*zoom für* _____?

Here is my visa.

Hier ist mein Visum.

HEER *isst mine* VEE-*zoom.*

I don't have a visa.
Ich habe kein Visum.
ikh HAH-*beh kine* VEE-*zoom.*

Where do I apply for a visa?
Wo muss ich ein Visum beantragen?
VOH *mooss ikh ine* VEE-*zoom buh-*AHNN-*trah-gen?*

Visit
Come visit us when you are in the United States.
Kommen Sie uns besuchen, wenn Sie in den Vereinigten Staaten sind.
kawmm-en zee OONNSS *buh-*ZOOKH-*en venn zee inn dane
fehr-*INE-*ick-ten* SHTAH-*ten zinnt.*

This is our first visit.
Das ist unser erster Besuch.
DAHSS *isst oonn-zehr* EHRST-*ehr buh-*ZOOKH.

We are visiting _____.
Wir besuchen _____.
*veer buh-*ZOOKH-*en* _____.

Visitors
Can visitors come on board?
Können Besucher an Bord kommen?
*könn-en buh-*ZOOKH-*ehr ahnn* BORT *kawmm-en.*

Voltage
What is the voltage?
Wie ist die Voltzahl?
vee isst dee FAWLLT-*tsahl?*

Wait
Wait a moment!
Warten Sie einen Moment!
VAHRR-*ten zee eye-nen moh-*MENT*!*

How long must I wait?
Wie lange muss ich warten?
vee LAHNNG-*uh mooss ikh* VAHRR-*ten?*

Please (don't) wait for me.
Bitte warten Sie (nicht) auf mich.
bit-tuh VAHRR-*ten zee (*NIKHT*) owff* MIKH.

Waiter (Waitress)

Are you our waiter (our waitress)?
Sind Sie unser Kellner (unsere Kellnerin)?
zinnt ZEE *oonn-zehr* KELL-*nehr (oonn-zehr-uh* KELL-*nehr-inn)?*

Please send over our waiter (our waitress).
Bitte schicken Sie unseren Kellner (unsere Kellnerin) zu uns.
bit-tuh SHICK-*en zee oonn-zehr-en* KELL-*nehr (oonn-zehr-uh* KELL-*nehr-inn)* TSOO *oonnss.*

Waiting

Where is the waiting room?
Wo ist der Warteraum?
VOH *isst dair* VAHRR-*tuh-rowm?*

Are you waiting for someone?
Warten Sie auf jemanden?
VAHRR-*ten zee owff* YAY-*mahnn-den?*

Wake

Please wake me at _____.
Bitte wecken Sie mich um _____.
bit-tuh VECK-*en zee mikh oomm* _____.

Walk

Let's walk to _____.
Gehen wir zu Fuss nach _____.
gay-en veer tsoo FOOSS *nahkh* _____.

Is it an easy walk to _____?
Führt ein Spazierweg nach _____?
FÜRT *ine shpah-*TSEER-*veek nahkh* _____?

Want

I want to _____.
Ich möchte _____.
ikh MÖKH-*tuh* _____.

Warm

It is not warm enough.
Es ist nicht warm genug.
ess isst NIKHT VAHRM *guh-*NOOK.

I am (not) warm.
Mir ist (nicht) warm.
*meer isst (*NIKHT*) VAHRM.*

Wash – see Laundry or Automobile

Watch

Watch this!
Passen Sie auf!
PAHSS-*en zee* OWFF*!*

Where is there a watch repair shop?
Wo ist ein Uhren-Reparaturladen?
VOH *isst ine* OOR-*en-reh-par-ah-*TOOR-*lah-den?*

What do you charge to clean and regulate a watch?
Wieviel kostet es, eine Uhr zu reinigen und regulieren?
vee-feel KAWSS-*tet ess ine-uh* OOR *tsoo* RINE-*ih-gen oonnt ray-goo-*LEER-*en?*

My watch is running fast (slow).
Meine Uhr geht vor (nach).
mine-uh OOR *gate* FOR *(*NAHKH*).*

My watch is broken.
Meine Uhr geht nicht.
mine-uh OOR GATE *nikht.*

Water

Please bring me some (more) water.
Bitte bringen Sie mir (mehr) Wasser.
bit-tuh BRING-*en zee meer (*MAIR*)* VAHSS-*ehr.*

Mineral water, plain water, hot water, cold water.
Mineralwasser, frisches Wasser, heisses Wasser, kaltes Wasser.
*mee-nuh-*RAHL-VAHSS-*ehr,* FRISH-*ess* VAHSS-*ehr,* HICE-*ess* VAHSS-*ehr,* KAHLLT-*ess* VAHSS-*ehr.*

There is no hot water.
Es gibt kein heisses Wasser.
ess GIPPT *kine* HICE-*ess* VAHSS-*ehr.*

Waterski

I don't know how to water ski.
Ich kann nicht Wasserski fahren.
*ikh kahnn nikht vahss-ehr-*SHEE FAH-*ren.*

Where can I go water skiing?
Wo kann ich Wasserski fahren?
VOH *kahnn ikh vahss-ehr*-SHEE FAH-*ren?*

Way

Which way is _____?
In welcher Richtung ist _____?
inn vell-khehr RIKH-*toong isst* _____?

Is this the way to _____?
Ist das der Weg nach _____?
isst DAHSS *dair* VECK *nahkh* _____?

Which is the best way to _____?
Welches ist der beste Weg nach _____?
VELL-*khehs isst dair* BESS-*tuh* VECK *nahkh* _____?

Can I go by way of _____?
Kann ich über _____ fahren?
KAHNN *ikh* Ü-*behr* _____ FAH-*ren?*

Wear

What should I wear?
Was soll ich anziehen?
vahss ZAWLL *ikh* AHNN-*tsee-en?*

Weather

What is the weather like in _____?
Wie ist das Wetter in _____?
VEE *isst dahss* VET-*tehr inn* _____?

Week

I want it for one (two) week(s).
Ich möchte es für eine (zwei) Woche(n).
ikh MÖKH-*tuh ess für* INE-*uh* (TSVYE) VAWKH-*e(n).*

Weight

How much weight is allowed?
Wieviel Gewicht ist erlaubt?
vee-feel guh-VIKHT *isst ehr*-LOWPT?

Is my baggage overweight?
Habe ich Übergewicht?
hah-beh ikh Ü-*behr-guh*-VIKHT?

What is the rate for excess weight?
Wieviel kostet Übergewicht pro Kilo?
vee-feel KAWSS-*tet* Ü-*behr-guh*-VIKHT *pro* KEE-*loh?*

Well

I want my meat well done.

Ich möchte das Fleisch gut durchgebraten.

ikh mökh-tuh dahss FLYSH *goot* DOORRKH-*guh*-BRAH-*ten.*

This is too well done; please take it back.

Das ist zu sehr durchgebraten; bitte tragen Sie es zurück.

dahss isst tsoo ZAIR DOORRKH-*guh*-BRAH-*ten; bit-tuh* TRAH-*gen zee ess tsoo*-RÜCK.

I don't feel well.

Ich fühle mich nicht wohl.

ikh FÜ-*luh mikh nikht* VOHL.

What

What do you want?

Was wünschen Sie?

VAHSS VÜN-*shen zee?*

What is it?

Was gibt es?

vahss GIPPT *ess?*

What did you (did he, did she) say?

Was haben Sie (hat er, hat sie) gesagt?

VAHSS *hah-ben zee (hahtt air, hahtt zee) guh*-ZAHKHT?

What is this in _____?

Was ist das auf _____?

VAHSS *isst* DAHSS *owff* _____

When

When will we arrive?

Wann werden wir ankommen?

VAHNN *vair-den veer* AHNN-*kawmm-en?*

When do you open (close)?

Wann öffnen (schliessen) Sie?

vahnn ÖFF-*nen (*SHLEE-*sen) zee?*

When is breakfast (lunch, dinner) served?

Wann wird Frühstück (Mittagessen, Abendessen) serviert?

VAHNN *veert* FRÜ-*shtück (*MITT-*tahg-ess-sen,* AH-*bent-ess-sen zehr*-VEERT?

Please tell me when to get off.
Bitte sagen Sie mir, wenn ich aussteigen muss.
bit-tuh ZAH-*gen zee meer venn ikh* OWSS-*shtye-gen*
MOOSS.

Where

Where is _____?
Wo ist _____?
VOH *isst* _____?

Where can I find (buy) _____?
Wo kann ich _____ finden (kaufen)?
VOH *kahnn ikh* _____ FINN-*den (*KOW-*fen)?*

Where are we?
Wo sind wir?
VOH ZINNT *veer?*

Please tell me where to get off.
Bitte sagen Sie mir, wo ich aussteigen muss.
bit-tuh ZAH-*gen zee meer* VOH *ikh* OWSS-*shtye-gen*
MOOSS.

Widow (Widower)

I am a widow (a widower).
Ich bin Witwe (Witwer).
ikh binn VIT-*vuh (*VIT-*vehr).*

Window

Where is the ticket window?
Wo ist der Fahrkarten-Schalter?
VOH *isst dair* FAR-*karr-ten-*SHAHL-*tehr?*

A seat (a table) by the window, please.
Einen Platz (einen Tisch) beim Fenster, bitte.
eye-nen PLAHTTS *(eye-nen* TISH*) bime* FENN-*stehr,* BIT-
tuh.

Do you mind if I open (close) the window?
Haben Sie etwas dagegen, wenn ich das Fenster öffne
(schliesse)?
HAH-*ben zee ett-vahss dah-*GAY-*gen venn ikh dahss*
FENN-*stehr* ÖFF-*nuh (*SHLEE-*suh)?*

Please (don't) open the window.
Bitte öffnen Sie (nicht) das Fenster.
bit-tuh ÖFF-*nen zee (*NIKHT*) dahss* FENN-*stehr.*

Please (don't) close the window.
Bitte schliessen Sie (nicht) das Fenster.
bit-tuh SHLEE-*sen zee (*NIKHT) *dahss* FENN-*stehr.*

Wine

May I have the wine list, please?
Kann ich die Weinkarte haben, bitte?
KAHNN *ikh dee* VINE-*karr-tuh* HAH-*ben,* BIT-*tuh?*

Which wine do you recommend?
Welchen Wein empfehlen Sie mir?
VELL-*khen* VINE *emp-*FAY-*len zee* MEER?

A glass (a half-bottle, a bottle) of red (white) table
    wine, please.
Ein Glas (eine halbe Flasche, eine Flasche) roten
    (weissen) Tischwein, bitte.
ine GLAHSS (*ine-uh* HAHLL-*buh* FLAHSH-*uh, ine-uh*
    FLAHSH-*uh*) ROH-*ten (*VICE-*en*) TISH-*vine,* BIT-*tuh.*

Woman

Who is that woman?
Wer ist diese Frau?
VAIR *isst dee-zuh* FROW?

Wood

May I have some wood for the fireplace?
Kann ich Holz für den Kamin haben?
kahnn ikh HAWLLTS *für dane kah-*MEEN *hah-ben?*

Word

What does this word mean?
Was bedeutet dieses Wort?
VAHSS *buh-*DOY-*tet dee-zehs* VAWRT?

Work

Where do you work?
Wo arbeiten Sie?
VOH AHR-*by-ten zee?*

The _____ does not work.
Das _____ funktioniert nicht.
DAHSS _____ *foonk-tsee-oh-*NEERT NIKHT.

Can you fix it?
Können Sie es reparieren?
KÖNN-*en zee ess reh-par-*REER-*en?*

Worth
What is it worth?
Was ist es wert?
vahss isst ess VAIRT?

It is worthless.
Es ist wertlos.
ess isst VAIRT-*lohss.*

Wrap
Please wrap this (carefully).
Bitte verpacken Sie das (sorgfältig).
*bit-tuh fehr-*PAHCK-*en zee dahss (*ZAWRK-*fell-tikh).*

Write
Write it down, please.
Schreiben Sie es auf, bitte.
SHRIBE-*en zee ess* OWFF, BIT-*tuh.*

How do you write _____ in _____?
Wie schreibt man _____ auf _____?
VEE SHRIBT *mahnn* _____ owff _____?

Let's write to each other.
Schreiben wir einander.
SHRIBE-*en veer ine-*AHNN-*dehr.*

Writing Paper
I need some (more) writing paper.
Ich brauche (noch) Schreibpapier.
ikh BROW-*khuh (*NAWKH*)* SHRIBE-*pah-*PEER.

Wrong
What is wrong?
Was ist passiert?
VAHSS *isst* PAHSS-*eert?*

Is anything wrong?
Ist etwas nicht in Ordnung?
isst ETT-*vahss* NIKHT *inn* AWRT-*noong?*

Yours

Is that yours?

Gehört das Ihnen?

guh-HÖRT *dahss* EEN-*en?*

That is yours.

Das gehört Ihnen.

dahss guh-HÖRT EEN-*en.*

Youth Hostel – see Hotel

Zoo

Can you direct me to the zoo?

Wie komme ich zum Tiergarten, bitte?

VEE *kawmm-uh ikh tsoom* TEER-*gahrr-ten,* BIT-*tuh?*

Take me to the zoo, please.

Bringen Sie mich zum Tiergarten, bitte.

BRING-*en zee mikh tsoom teer-gahrr-ten,* BIT-*tuh.*

SIGNS AND NOTICES

GERMAN	ENGLISH
ACHTUNG	ATTENTION
AN	ON
AUF	ON
AUS	OFF
AUSFAHRT	EXIT
AUSGANG	OUT
AUSSER BETRIEB	OUT OF ORDER
BAHNÜBERGANG	RAILROAD CROSSING
DAMEN	LADIES (LADIES' ROOM)
DAS GRAS NICHT BETRETEN	KEEP OFF THE GRASS
DOPPELTE KURVE	DOUBLE CURVE
DRÜCKEN	PUSH
EINBAHNSTRASSE	ONE WAY
EINFAHRT	ENTRANCE
EINGANG	IN
EILZUG	EXPRESS (TRAIN)
ENGE STRASSE	NARROW ROAD
FAHRGÄSTE	PASSENGERS
FRAUEN	LADIES (LADIES' ROOM)
GEFAHR	CAUTION
GEFÄHRLICHE KURVE	DANGEROUS CURVE
GEHEN	GO
GESCHLOSSEN	CLOSED

GERMAN	ENGLISH
HALT	STOP
HERREN	MEN (MEN'S ROOM)
HINAUF	UP
HINUNTER	DOWN
HOCHSPANNUNG	HIGH TENSION LINES
HÖCHSTGESCHWIN-DIGKEIT	MAXIMUM SPEED
KEINE DURCHFAHRT	NO THOROUGHFARE
KEIN EINGANG	KEEP OUT
KREUZUNG	CROSS ROADS
KURVE	CURVE
KURVENREICHE STRECKE	WINDING ROAD
LANGSAM	SLOW
LINKS HALTEN	KEEP TO YOUR LEFT
NAHVERKEHR	LOCAL (TRAIN)
NICHT AUSSPUCKEN	NO SPITTING
NICHT DREHEN	NO TURN
NICHT LINKS ABBIEGEN	NO LEFT TURN
NICHT RECHTS ABBIEGEN	NO RIGHT TURN
NICHT ÜBERHOLEN	NO PASSING
NICHT UMDREHEN	NO U TURN
OFFEN	OPEN
ORTSVERKEHR	LOCAL (MAIL, TRAFFIC)

GERMAN	ENGLISH
PARKIEREN VERBOTEN	NO PARKING
PARKPLATZ	PARKING
PERSONENZUG	LOCAL (TRAIN)
PRIVAT	PRIVATE
QUERRINNE	DIP
RAUCHEN VERBOTEN	NO SMOKING
RECHTS HALTEN	KEEP TO YOUR RIGHT
SACKGASSE	DEAD END
SCHARFE KURVE	SHARP TURN
SCHNELLZUG	EXPRESS (TRAIN)
SCHULE	SCHOOL
STEIGUNG	STEEP GRADE
STRASSENBAU	ROAD REPAIR
STUNDENKILOME-TERGESCHWINDIG-KEIT	KILOMETERS PER HOUR
TOILETTE	LAVATORY
UMLEITUNG	DETOUR
VORSICHT	CAUTION
VORSICHTIG FAHREN	DRIVE CAREFULLY
ZIEHEN	PULL
ZU	OFF

ENGLISH	GERMAN	PRONUNCIATION
a (an)	ein, eine	INE, INE-*uh*
able (capable)	aufgeben	OWF-*gay-ben*
aboard	an Bord	AHNN BORT
about	über	Ü-*behr*
abroad (in foreign land)	im Ausland	*imm* OWSS-*lahnt*
absence	Abwesenheit, f.	AHPP-*vay-zen-hite*
absent	abwesen	AHPP-*vay-zen*
accent (speech)	Aussprache, f.	OWSS-*shprah-khuh*
accept, to	annehmen	AHNN-*nay-men*
accident (mishap)	Unfall, m.	OONN-*fahll*
accommodate (have room for), to	unterbringen	*oonn-tehr*-BRING-*en*
accompany (go along with), to	begleiten	*buh*-GLITE-*en*
accord (agreement)	Übereinstim- mung, f.	Ü-*behr*-INE-*shtimm-oong*
according to (in accordance with)	nach	NAHKH
account	Konto, n.	KAWNN-*toh*
accountant	Buchführer, m.	BOOKH-*fü-rehr*
accurate	genau	*guh*-NOW
accuse, to	anklagen	AHNN-*klah-gen*
accustom oneself, to	sich gewöhnen	*zikh guh*-VO-*nen*
ache	Schmerz, m.	SHMEHRTS
ache, to	schmerzen	SHMEHR-*tsen*
acknowledge (note receipt of), to	bestätigen	*buh*-SHTAY-*tih-gen*
acquaintance (person known)	Bekannte, m., f.	*buh*-KAHNN-*tuh*
across (beyond)	jenseits	YANE-*zites*
act (deed)	Tat, f.	TAHT
act (dramatic unit)	Auftritt, m.	OWF-*tritt*
act (behave), to	sich verhalten	*zikh fehr*-HAHLL-*ten*

ENGLISH	GERMAN	PRONUNCIATION
act (do), to	handeln	HAHNN-*deln*
action (deed)	Handlung, f.	HAHNND-*loong*
actor (player)	Schauspieler, m.	SHOW-*shpeel-ehr*
actress	Schauspielerin, f.	SHOW-*shpeel-ehr-in*
add (include), to	hinzufügen	HINN-*tsoo-fü-gen*
address (speech)	Rede, f.	RAY-*duh*
addressee	Adressat, m.	*ah-dress-saht*
admire, to	bewundern	*buh-*VOONN*-dehrn*
adventure	Abenteuer, n.	AH-*ben-toy-ehr*
advertise (give notice of), to	annoncieren	*ahnn-nohn-*SEE-*renn*
advertisement	Anzeige, f.	AHNN-*tsye-guh*
advice	Rat, m.	RAHT
aerial (antenna)	Antenne, f.	*ahn-*TEN-*nuh*
affect (influence)	betreffen	*buh-*TREFF-*fen*
afraid	ängstlich	ENGST-*likh*
after (conj.)	nachdem	NAHKH-*dame*
after (prep.)	nach	NAHKH
afternoon	Nachmittag, m.	NAHKH-*mit-tahk*
afterward (later)	nachher	NAHKH-*hehr*
again	wieder	VEE-*dehr*
against	gegen	GAY-*gen*
agent (representative)	Vertreter, m.	*fehr-*TRAY-*tehr*
agree (assent), to	beistimmen	BY-*shtim-men*
agreeable (pleasing)	angenehm	AHNN-*guh-name*
agreement (mutual understanding)	Übereinkunft, f	*ü-behr-*INE-*koonnft*
agree with, to	mit . . . Einverstanden sein	*mitt . . .* INE-*fehr-shtahn-den* ZINE.
ahead (forward)	vorwärts	FOR-*vehrts*
ahead (in front)	voraus	*for-*OWSS
aim (purpose)	Zweck, m.	TSVECK
air (atmosphere)	Luft, f.	LOOFFT

ENGLISH	GERMAN	PRONUNCIATION
air conditioning	Klimaanlage, f.	KLEE-*mah-ahnn-lah-guh*
air mail	Luftpost, f.	LOOFFT-*pawsst*
airplane	Flugzeug, n.	FLOOK-*tsoyk*
airport	Flughafen, m.	FLOOK-*hah-fen*
aisle (passageway)	Gang, m.	GAHNNG
alcohol	Alkohol, m.	AHLL-*koh-hohl*
alive	lebendig	*lay*-BEN-*dick*
all (entirely) adv.	ganz	GAHNNTS
all (every) adj.	jeder	YAY-*dehr*
all (everything) n.	alles	AHLL-*less*
all (whole of) adj.	ganz	GAHNNTS
allergy (med.)	Allergie, f.	*ahl-lehr*-GEE
allow (permit), to	erlauben	*ehr*-LOW-*ben*
almost	fast	FAHSST
alone	allein	*ahl*-LINE
aloud	laut	LOWT
already	schon	SHONE
also	auch	OWKH
although	obgleich	*ohp*-GLYEKH
altogether (entirely)	ganz	GAHNNTS
always	immer	IMM-*mehr*
ambassador	Botschafter, m.	BOAT-*shahf-tehr*
ambulance	Krankenwagen, m.	KRAHNNG-*ken-vah-gen*
amendment (enacted change)	Zusatzartikel, m.	TSOO-*zahts-ahr-tee-kell*
America	Amerika, m.	*ah*-MAY-*ree-kah*
American (adj.)	amerikanish	*ah-may-ree*-KAH-*nish*
among	unter	OONN-*tehr*
amount	Betrag, m.	*buh*-TRAHK
amount to, to	betragen	*buh*-TRAH-*gen*
amuse, to	unterhalten	*oonn-tehr*-HAHLL-*ten*
amusement	Vergnügung, f.	*fehr*-GNÜ-*goong*

ENGLISH	GERMAN	PRONUNCIATION
ancestor	Vorfahr, m.	FOR-*far*
anchor	Anker, m.	AHNN-*kehr*
ancient	uralt	OOR-*ahlt*
angry	zornig	TSAWR-*nick*
animal	Tier, n.	TEER
ankle	Knöchel, m.	KNÖCK-*el*
anniversary	Jahrestag, m.	YAH-*ress-tahk*
announce, to	melden	MELL-*den*
announcement	Meldung, f.	MELL-*doong*
annoy (irk), to	ärgern	EHR-*gehrn*
annual	jährlich	YEHR-*likh*
another (different one), pron.	ein anderer	INE AHNN-*dehr-ehr*
another (one more) adj.	noch ein	NAWKH INE
answer	Antwort, f.	AHNNT-*vort*
answer	antworten	AHNNT-*vor-ten*
anticipate (expect), to	erwarten	*ehr*-VAR-*ten*
antiquity (ancientness)	Altertümlichkeit, f.	AHLL-*tehr-tüm-likh-kite*
anxious (uneasy)	beunruhigt	*buh*-OONN-*roo-ickt*
any (any at all), adj.	irgendwelche	EAR-*gent*-VELL-*khuh*
anybody (anybody whosoever)	wer immer	VAIR IMM-*mehr*
anybody (not . . . anybody)	niemand	NEE-*mahnnt*
anyhow (in any case)	jedenfalls	YAY-*den-fahlls*
anything (anything whatsoever)	was immer	VAHSS IMM-*mehr*
apartment	Wohnung, f.	VOH-*noong*
apologize, to	sich entschuldigen	*zikh* ent-SHOOL-*dih-gen*
apparent (obvious)	offenbar	AWFF-*fen-bar*

ENGLISH	GERMAN	PRONUNCIATION
appeal to (entreat), to	ersuchen	*ehr*-ZOO-*khen*
appear, to (seem)	scheinen	SHY-*nen*
appearance (aspect)	Aussehen, n.	OWSS-*zay-en*
appendicitis	Blinddarmentzün- dung, f.	BLINNT-*dahrm- ent-tsün-doong*
appetite	Appetit, m.	*ahp-puh*-TEET
apple	Apfel, m.	AHPP-*fel*
application (request)	Gesuch, n.	*guh*-ZOOKH
appointment (meeting)	Verabredung, f.	*fehr*-AHPP-*ray- doong*
appraisal (bus.)	Wertschätzung, f.	VAIRT-*shett-soong*
appreciate (be grateful for), to	schätzen	SHETT-*sen*
approach (come near to) to	sich nähern	*zikh* NAY-*ehrn*
apricot	Aprikose, f.	*ahp-ree*-KOH-*zuh*
arch (curved structure)	Bogen, m.	BOH-*gen*
area (extent)	Grundfläche, f.	GROONNT-*fleh- khuh*
area (region)	Gebiet, n.	*guh*-BEET
argue (maintain), to	behaupten	*buh*-HOWP-*ten*
argument (dispute)	Auseinanderset- zung, f.	OWSS-*ine*-AHNN- *dehr-zet-tsoong*
arm	Arm, m.	ARM
arrange (plan), to	einrichten	INE-*rikh-ten*
arrangement (order)	Einordnung, f.	INE-*ord-noong*
arrest (take into custody), to	verhaften	*fehr*-HAHFF-*ten*
arrival	Ankunft, f.	AHNN-*koonft*
arrive, to	ankommen	AHNN-*kawm-men*
art	Kunst, f.	KOONST
arthritis	Arthritis, f.	*ahr*-TREE-*tiss*
article (literary composition)	Artikel, m.	*ahr*-TEE-*kell*
article (thing)	Sache, f.	ZAHKH-*uh*

ENGLISH	GERMAN	PRONUNCIATION
artificial (synthetic)	künstlich	KÜNNST-*likh*
artist	Künstler, m.	KÜNST-*lehr*
as (in the same way, conj.)	wie	VEE
ascend (go upward along), to	besteigen	*buh*-SHTYE-*gen*
ashamed (mortified)	beschämt	*buh*-SHAYMT
ash tray	Aschenbecher, m.	AHSH-*en-behkh-ehr*
ask (put question to), to	fragen	FRAHG-*en*
ask (request), to	bitten um	BIT-*ten oom*
ask about, to	fragen über	FRAH-*gen* Ü-*behr*
asleep (sleeping)	eingeschlafen	INE-*guh-shlah-fen*
asparagus	Spargel, m.	SHPAHR-*gel*
aspirin	Aspirin, n.	*ahss-pih-*REEN
assent, to	beistimmen	BY-*shtim-men*
assist, to	beistehen	BY-*shtay-en*
assistance	Beistand, m.	BY-*shtahnt*
assistant	Gehilfe, m.	*guh-*HILL-*fuh*
association (body of persons)	Verein, m.	*fehr-*INE
assume (take for granted), to.	annehmen	AHNN-*nay-men*
astonish, to	erstaunen	*ehr-*SHTOW-*nen*
at (in)	bei; in	BY; INN
at (near)	neben	NAY-*ben*
at (on)	auf	OWF
Athens	Athen, n.	*ah-*TAYN
athlete	Athlet, m.	*aht-*LATE
atmosphere (air)	Luft, f.	LOOFFT
attach	anhängen	AHNN-*heng-en*
attack (assault physically) to	angreifen	AHNN-*grife-en*
attempt, to	versuchen	*fehr-*ZOO-*khen*

ENGLISH	GERMAN	PRONUNCIATION
attend (be present at) to	beiwohnen	BY-*voh-nen*
attendance (presence)	Anwesenheit, f.	AHNN-*vay-zen-hite*
attention (heed)	Aufmerksamkeit, f.	OWF-*mehrk-zahmm-kite*
attorney	(Rechts)Anwalt, m.	*(rehkhts-)* AHNN-*vahlt*
attractive	anziehend	AHNN-*tsee-ent*
auction	Versteigerung, f.	*fehr-*SHTYE-*guh-roong*
audience	Publikum, n.	POO-*blee-koomm*
auditorium	Hörsaal, m.	HÖR-*zahl*
aunt	Tante, f.	TAHNN-*tuh*
Austria	Österreich, n.	ÖS-*tuh-ryekh*
Austrian (adj.)	österreichisch	ÖS-*tuh-ryekh-ish*
author	Verfasser, m.	*fehr-*FAHSS-*sehr*
authority (power)	Vollmacht, f.	FAWLL-*mahkht*
authorization	Bevollmächtigung, f.	*buh-*FAWLL-*mehkh-tih-goong*
automobile	Auto, n.	OW-*toh*
autumn	Herbst, m.	HEHRPST
available	zur Verfügung stehen	*tsoor fehr-*FU-*goong* SHTAY-*en*
avenue (street)	Allee, f.	*ahl-*LAY
average (ordinary, adj.)	durchschnittlich	DOORRKH-*shnitt-likh*
avert (prevent), to	abwenden	AHPP-*venn-den*
aviator	Flieger, m.	FLEE-*gehr*
avoid, to	vermeiden	*fehr-*MY-*den*
await, to	erwarten	*ehr-*VAR-*ten*
awful	furchtbar	FOORRKHT-*bar*
awkward	ungeschickt	OONN-*guh-shickt*
baby	Kindlein, n.	KINNT-*line*

ENGLISH	GERMAN	PRONUNCIATION
back (rearward, adv.)	zurück	*tsoo*-RÜCK
back (reverse side)	Rückseite, f.	RÜCK-*zite-uh*
bacon	Speck, m.	SHPECK
bad, worse, worst	schlimm, schlimmer, (der) schlimmst(e)	SHLIMM, SHLIMM-*mehr* SHLIMMST(E)
bag (purse)	Handtasche, f.	HAHNNT-*tahsh-uh*
bag (sack)	Sack, m.	ZAHCK
baggage (luggage)	Gepäck, n.	*guh*-PECK
bake (be cooking), to	backen	BAHK-*ken*
baker	Bäcker, m.	BECK-*ehr*
bald (hairless)	kahl	KAHL
ball-point pen	Kugelschreiber, m.	KOO-*gel-shrye-behr*
banana	Banane, f.	*bah*-NAH-*nuh*
band (ribbon)	Band. n. (pl. Bänder)	BAHNNT (BEND-*ehr*)
bandage	Verband, m.	*fehr*-BANNT
bank (shore)	Ufer, n.	OO-*fehr*
bank (treasury)	Bank, f.	BAHNNK
banker	Bank, f.	*bahnnk*-YAY
bankruptcy	Bankier, m.	*bahnnk*-RAWTT
banner	Banner, n.	BAHNN-*nehr*
bar (barroom)	Bar, f.	BAR
barber	Frisör, m.	*frih*-ZOR
bare (nude)	nackt	NAHKT
bargain (advantageous purchase)	Gelegenheitskauf, m.	*guh*-LAY-*gen-hites-kowf*
bargain (agreement)	Abmachung, f.	AHPP-*mahkh-oong*
bargain (negotiate), to	verhandeln	*fehr*-HAHNN-*deln*
barrier	Schranke, f.	SHRAHNN-*kuh*
baseball	Baseball, m.	BASE-*ball*
basement	Keller, m.	KELL-*ehr*

ENGLISH	GERMAN	PRONUNCIATION
bashful	schüchtern	SHÜKH-*tehrn*
basket	Korb, m.	KAWRP
bathe (take a bath), to	baden	BAH-*den*
bathing suit	Badeanzug, m.	BAH-*duh-ahnn-tsook*
bathroom	Badezimmer, n.	BAH-*duh-tsimm-mehr*
bathtub	Badewanne, f.	BAH-*duh-vahn-nuh*
battery (primary cell)	Batterie, f.	*baht-teh-*REE
battle	Schlacht, f.	SHLAHKHT
Bavaria	Bayern, n.	BY-*ehrn*
be, to	sein	ZINE
beach (strand)	Strand, m.	SHTRAHNNT
bead (jewelry)	Perle, f.	PEHR-*luh*
beam (ray)	Strahl, m.	SHTRAHL
bean (string bean)	(grüne) Bohne, f.	(GRÜ-*nuh*) BOH-*nuh*
bear (carry), to	tragen	TRAH-*gen*
beard	Bart, m.	BAHRRT
beautiful	schön	SHÖN
beauty	schönheit, f.	SHÖN-*hite*
because (conj.)	weil	VILE
because of	wegen	VAY-*gen*
become, to	werden	VAIR-*den*
bed	Bett, n.	BET
bedroom	Schlafzimmer, n.	SHLAHF-*tsimm-mehr*
bee	Biene, f.	BEE-*nuh*
beef	Rindfleisch	RINNT-*flysh*
beer	Bier, n.	BEER
before (ahead, adv.)	vorn(e)	FORN(-*uh*)
before (earlier, adv.)	früher	FRÜ-*ehr*
beg (solicit alms), to	betteln	BET-*teln*
beggar	Bettler, m.	BET-*lehr*
begin (start to do), to	anfangen	AHNN-*fahnng-en*

ENGLISH	GERMAN	PRONUNCIATION
beginning	Anfang, m.	AHNN-*fahnng*
behave (conduct oneself), to	sich benehmen	*zikh buh-*NAY-*men*
behavior	Benehmen, n.	*buh-*NAY-*men*
behind (prep.)	hinter	HINN-*tehr*
Belgium	Belgien, n.	BELG-*ee-en*
believe (accept), to	glauben	GLOW-*ben*
belly (abdomen)	Bauch, m.	BOWKH
belong to (be the property of), to	gehören	*guh-*HÖR-*en*
belt	Gürtel, m.	GÜRR-*tel*
bend (make bend), to	biegen	BEE-*gen*
benefit (advantage)	Vorteil, m.	FOR-*tile*
berry (fruit)	Beere, f.	BARE-*ruh*
berth (train bunk)	(Schlafwagen) Bett, n.	(SHLAHF-*vahg-en-*) BET
beside (other than, prep.)	ausser	OWSS-*ehr*
bet, to	wetten	VET-*ten*
between (prep.)	zwischen	TSVISH-*en*
beyond (farther on than, prep.)	über. . . . hinaus	*ü-behr . . . hin-*OWSS
Bible	Bibel, f.	BEE-*bel*
bicycle	(Fahr)Rad, n.	(FAR-)RAHT
bill (currency)	Geldschein, m.	GELT-*shine*
bill (invoice)	Rechnung, f.	REHKH-*noong*
bill of sale	Verkaufschein, m.	*fehr-*KOWFS-*shine*
billiards	Billard, n.	BILL-*yart*
bird	Vogel, m.	FOH-*gel*
birthday	Geburtstag, m.	*guh-*BOORTS-*tahk*
bit (small part)	Bisschen, n.	BISS-*khen*
bite, to	beissen	BICE-*en*
bitter	bitter	BIT-*tehr*
black	schwarz	SHVAHRRTS
blackberry	Brombeere, f.	BRAWMM-*bare-uh*
blackboard	Wandtafel, f.	VAHNNT-*tah-fel*

ENGLISH	GERMAN	PRONUNCIATION
bladder	Harnblase, f.	HAHRN-*blah-zuh*
blame, to	tadeln	TAH-*deln*
blanket	Decke, f.	DECK-*uh*
bleach (make white), to	bleichen	BLYE-*khen*
bleed (loose blood), to	bluten	BLOO-*ten*
blind (lacking sight)	blind	BLINNT
blister	Blase, f.	BLAH-*zuh*
blond	blond	BLAWNNT
blood	Blut, n.	BLOOT
bloom, to	blühen	BLÜ-*en*
blouse (shirtwaist)	Bluse, f.	BLOO-*zuh*
blow	blasen	BLAH-*zen*
blue	blau	BLOW
blush, to	erröten	*ehr*-RO-*ten*
boarding house	Pension, f.	*pahn-see*-YOHNG
boat	Boot, n.	BOAT
body	Körper, m.	KÖR-*pehr*
boil (bubble up), to	kochen	KAW-*khen*
bolt	Riegel, m.	REE-*gel*
bone	Knochen, m.	KNAW-*khen*
book	Buch, n.	BOOKH
book (engage space), to	bestellen	*buh*-SHTELL-*en*
boot	Stiefel, m.	SHTEE-*fel*
boredom	Lang(e)weile, f.	LAHNG(-*uh*)-*vye-luh*
borrow, to	borgen	BOR-*gen*
bosom	Busen, m.	BOO-*zen*
boss (master)	Chef, m.	SHEFF
both (adj.)	beide	BY-*duh*
both (pron.)	beide	BY-*duh*
bother (annoy), to	stören	SHTÖ-*ren*
bottle	Flasche, f.	FLAHSH-*uh*
bottom	Boden, m.	BOH-*den*
boundary (limit line)	Grenze, f.	GRENT-*suh*

ENGLISH	GERMAN	PRONUNCIATION
bow (nod)	Verbeugung, f.	*fehr-*BOY*-goong*
bowels	Eingeweide, n.	INE*-guh-vye-duh*
bowl (dish)	Schüssel, f.	SHUSS*-sel*
box (container)	Schachtel, f.	SHAHKH*-tel*
boy (lad)	Junge, m.	YOONNG*-uh*
bracelet	Armband, n.	ARM*-bahnt*
brain	Gehirn, n.	*guh-*HEERN
brake	Bremse, f.	BREMM*-zuh*
brand (trade mark)	Marke, f.	MAHRR*-kuh*
brandy	Kognak, m.	KAWNN*-yahck*
brass (metal, n.)	Messing, n.	MESS*-ing*
brassiere	Büstenhalter, m.	BUSS*-ten-hahl-tehr*
bread	Brot, n.	BROHT
breadth (width)	Breite, f.	BRIGHT*-uh*
break (come apart), to	brechen	BREH*-khen*
breakfast	Fruhstück, n.	FRÜ*-shtück*
breast	Brust, f.	BROOSST
breath	Atem, m.	AH*-tem*
breeze	Lüftchen, n.	LUFFT*-khen*
bribe, to	bestechen	*buh-*SHTEHKH*-en*
bridge	Brücke, f.	BRUK*-uh*
briefcase	Aktenmappe, f.	AHK*-ten-mah-puh*
bright (shining)	hell	HELL
bring, to	bringen	BRING*-en*
British (adj.)	britisch	BREE*-tish*
broad (wide)	breit	BRIGHT
broadcasting (rad.)	Rundfunkübertragung, f.	ROONNT*-foonk-ü-behr-trah-goong*
bronchitis	Bronchitis, f.	*brawn-*KHEE*-tiss*
bronze (n.)	Bronze, f.	BRAWNG*-zuh*
brooch	Brosche, f.	BRAWSH*-uh*
broom	Besen, m.	BAY*-zen*
brother	Bruder, m.	BROO*-dehr*

ENGLISH	GERMAN	PRONUNCIATION
brother-in-law	Schwager, m.	SHVAH-*gehr*
brown	braun	BROWN
bruise	Quetschung, f.	KVET-*shoong*
budget (n.)	Budget, n.	bü-JAY
bug (insect)	Kerbtier, m.	KEHRP-*teer*
building	Gebäude, n.	guh-BOY-*duh*
bulb (light bulb)	Glühbirne, f.	GLÜ-*beer-nuh*
bundle (parcel)	Paket, n.	pah-KATE
bureau (chest)	Kommode, f.	kawmm-MOH-*duh*
bureau (office)	Büro, n.	bü-ROH
burglar	Einbrecher, m.	INE-*brehkh-ehr*
burial	Begräbnis, n.	buh-GRAYP-*niss*
burn (to be on fire), to	brennen	BRENN-*en*
bury	begraben	buh-GRAH-*ben*
bus	Omnibus, m.	AWMM-*nee-booss*
bush (plant)	Busch, m.	BUSH
business (commerce)	Geschäft, n.	guh-SHEFFT
businessman	Geschäftsmann, m.	guh-SHEFFTS-*mahnn*
busy (occupied)	beschäftigt	buh-SHEFF-*tickt*
but (yet, conj.)	aber	AH-*behr*
butcher	Fleischer, m.	FLYSH-*ehr*
butter	Butter, f.	BOOTT-*tehr*
button	Knopf, m.	KNAWPF
buy, to	kaufen	KOW-*fen*
by (near, prep.)	bei	BY
by (prior to, prep.)	vor	FOR
cab (taxi)	Taxe, f.	TAHCKS-*uh*
cabbage	Kohl, m.	KOLE
cabin (of ship)	Kabine, f.	kah-BEE-*nuh*
cablegram	Kabelgramm, n.	KAH-*bel-grahmm*
cake (dessert)	Kuchen, m.	KOO-*khen*
calendar	Kalender, m.	kah-LEN-*dehr*
call (shout), to	rufen	ROO-*fen*
call (summon), to	rufen lassen	ROO-*fen* LAHSS-*en*

ENGLISH	GERMAN	PRONUNCIATION
camera	Kamera, f.	KAH-*muh-rah*
can (tin)	(Conserven)	(*kawn-*ZEHR-*ven-*)
	Büchse, f.	BÜKH-*suh*
canal	Kanal, m.	*kah-*NAHL
cancel (revoke), to	aufheben	OWF-*hay-ben*
cancer	Krebs, m.	KRAYBSS
candle	Kerze, f.	KEHR-*tsuh*
candy	Süssigkeit, f.	ZÜ-*sick-kite*
cane (walking stick)	Spazierstock, m.	*shpah-*TSEER-*shtawck*
cap	Mütze, f.	MÜTT-*suh*
capital (city)	Haupstadt, f.	HOWPT-*shtaht*
captain (officer)	Kapitän, m.	*kah-pee-*TAYN
car (auto)	Auto, n.	OW-*toh*
car, railroad	(Eisenbahn-)	(EYE-*zen-bahn-*)
	Wagen, m.	VAH-*gen*
carbon copy	Durchschlag, m.	DOORRKH-*shlahk*
card, calling	Visitenkarte, f.	*vee-*ZEE-*ten-kahr-tuh*
card, playing	Spielkarte, f.	SHPEEL-*kahr-tuh*
card, postal	Postkarte, f.	PAWSST-*kahr-tuh*
cardboard	Pappe, f.	PAHPP-*puh*
care (custody)	Fürsorge, f.	FUR-*zor-guh*
care (be concerned), to	sich kümmern	*sikh* KUMM-*ehrn*
careful (cautious)	vorsichtig	FOR-*zikh-tick*
cargo	Ladung, f.	LAH-*doong*
carpet	Teppich, m.	TEPP-*ikh*
carriage (horse-drawn vehicle)	Wagen, m.	VAH-*gen*
carrot	Mohrrübe, f.	MORE-*rü-buh*
carry (bear), to	tragen	TRAH-*gen*
cart	Karren, m.	KAHRR-*en*
case (instance)	Fall, m.	FAHLL
cash (money)	Bargeld, n.	BAR-*gellt*
cashier	Kassierer, m.	*kahss-*SEER-*ehr*
castle	Schloss, n.	SHLAWSS

ENGLISH	GERMAN	PRONUNCIATION
cat	Katze, f.	KAHT-*suh*
cathedral	Dom, m.	DOME
Catholic (adj.)	katholisch	*kah-*TOH-*lish*
cattle	Rindvieh, n.	RINNT-*fee*
cauliflower	Blumenkohl, m.	BLOO-*men-kole*
cause	Ursache, f.	OOR-*zahkh-uh*
caution (warn), to	warnen	VAHRR-*nen*
ceiling (of room)	Decke, f.	DECK-*uh*
celery	Sellerie, m.	ZELL-*uh-ree*
cellar	Keller, m.	KELL-*ehr*
cemetery	Friedhof, m.	FREET-*hohf*
center	Mittelpunkt, m.	MITT-*tel-poonkt*
century	Jahrhundert, n.	*yahr-*HOONN-*dehrt*
ceremony	Zeremonie, f.	*tsehr-uh-moh-nee*
certain (sure)	sicher	ZIKH-*ehr*
certainly (of course! interj.)	selbstverständlich	ZELLPST-*fehr-*SHTENNT-*likh*
certify, to	beglaubigen	*buh-*GLOW-*bee-gen*
chair	Stuhl, m.	SHTOOL
chance (opportunity)	Gelegenheit, f.	*guh-*LAY-*gen-hite*
chance (possibility)	Aussicht, f.	OWS-*zikht*
change (become different), to	sich ändern	ZIKH ENN-*dehrn*
channel (strait)	Kanal, m.	*kah-*NAHL
chapel	Kapelle, f.	*kah-*PELL-*uh*
character (person portrayed)	Person, f.	*pehr-*ZOHN
charge (price)	Preis, m.	PRICE
charge account	laufende Rechnung, f.	LOW-*fenn-duh* REHKH-*noong*
charming	reizend	RYE-*tsent*
chat, to	plaudern	PLOW-*dehrn*
cheap (inexpensive)	billig	BILL-*ikh*
cheat (defraud), to	betrügen	*buh-*TRÜ-*gen*
check (bank check)	Scheck, m.	SHECK

ENGLISH	GERMAN	PRONUNCIATION
cheek	Backe, f.	BAHK-*uh*
cheer (applaud), to	Beifall rufen	BY-*fahll* ROO-*fen*
cheerful (joyful)	heiter	HYE-*tehr*
cheese	Käse, m.	KAY-*zuh*
cherry (fruit)	Kirsche, f.	KEERR-*shuh*
chess	Schach, n.	SHAHKH
chest	Brust, f.	BROOSST
chew, to	kauen	KOW-*en*
chicken	Huhn, n.	HOON
chicken pox	Windpocken, f.	VINNT-*pawkenn*
chief (leading)	Haupt-. . .	HOWPT-
child	Kind, n.	KINNT
chimney	Schornstein, m.	SHORN-*shtine*
chocolate	Schokolade, f.	*shoh-koh-*LAH-*duh*
choke, to	(er)würgen	*(ehr)*VURR-*gen*
cholera	Cholera, f.	KOHL-*uh-rah*
choose (select), to	wählen	VAY-*len*
Christmas	Weihnachten, f.	VYE-*nahkh-ten*
church	Kirche, f.	KEERRKH-*uh*
cigar	Zigarre, f.	*tsee-*GAHRR-*uh*
cigarette	Zigarette, f.	*tsee-gah-*RET-*tuh*
citizen	(Staats)Bürger, m.	(SHTAHTS-)BÜR-*gehr*
city	Stadt, f.	SHTAHTT
claim, to	beanspruchen	*buh-*AHNN-*shprookh-en*
clap (applaud), to	klatschen	KLAHTCH-*en*
class (kind)	Klasse, f.	KLAHSS-*uh*
classroom	Klassenzimmer, n.	KLAHSS-*en-tsimm-mehr*
clean	rein	RINE
clear	klar	KLAHR
clearance (customs clearance)	Zollabfertigung, f.	TSAWLL-*ahpp-fehr-tee-goong*
clerk (salesperson)	Verkäufer, m.	*fehr-*KOY-*fehr*
clever	klug	KLOOK

ENGLISH	GERMAN	PRONUNCIATION
climate (weather)	Klima, n.	KLEE-*mah*
climb (scale), to	steigen	SHTYE-*gen*
cloak (apparel)	Umhang, m.	OOMM-*hahng*
clock	Uhr, f.	OOR
close (shut), to	schliessen	SHLEE-*sen*
cloth	Stoff, m.	SHTAWFF
clothing	Kleidung, f.	KLYE-*doong*
cloud	Wolke, f.	VAWLL-*kuh*
cloudy (overcast)	wolkig	VAWLL-*kick*
coach, railroad	Personenwagen, m.	*pehr*-ZOHN-*en-vah-gen*
coal	Kohle, f.	KOLE-*uh*
coarse	grob	GRAWPP
coast (seaboard)	Küste, f.	KUSS-*tuh*
coat (man's overcoat)	Mantel, m.	MAHNN-*tell*
coat (woman's overcoat)	Mantel, m.	MAHNN-*tell*
cocktail	Cocktail, m.	KOCK-*tehl*
cocoa	Kakao, m.	*kah*-KAH-*oh*
coffee	Kaffee, m.	KAHFF-*ay*
coffin	Sarg, m.	ZARK
coin	Münze, f.	MÜNT-*suh*
cold (adj.)	kalt	KAHLLT
cold (disease)	Erkältung, f.	*ehr*-KELL-*toong*
collar	Kragen, m.	KRAH-*gen*
color	Farbe, f.	FAR-*buh*
column (pillar)	Säule, f.	ZOY-*luh*
comb (for hair)	Kamm, m.	KAHMM
combine (make join), to	verbinden	*fehr*-BINN-*den*
come, to	kommen	KAWMM-*en*
comedy (comic play)	Komödie, f.	*koh*-MÖD-*yuh*
comfort (ease)	Bequemlichkeit, f.	*buh*-KVAYM-*likh-kite*
comfort (console), to	trösten	TROS-*ten*
comfortable (affording comfort)	behaglich	*buh*-HAHG-*likh*

ENGLISH	GERMAN	PRONUNCIATION
command (order), to	befehlen	*buh-*FAIL*-en*
comment, to	Bemerkungen machen	*buh-*MEHR*-koong-en* MAH*-khen*
commercial	kommerziell	*kawmm-ehrts-*YELL
common (usual)	gewöhnlich	*guh-*VÖN*-likh*
communism	Kommunismus, m.	*kawmm-moo-*NISS*-mooss*
community (neighborhood)	Gemeinde, f.	*guh-*MINE*-duh*
companion	Gefährte, m.	*guh-*FAIR*-tuh*
company (bus.)	Gesellschaft, f.	*guh-*ZELL*-shahfft*
compare (consider relatively), to	vergleichen	*fehr-*GLYEKH*-en*
comparison	Vergleich, m.	*fehr-*GLYEKH
compartment (of train)	Abteil, n.	AHPP*-tile*
compass (drawing instrument)	Zirkel, m.	TSEERR*-kel*
complain, to	klagen	KLAH*-gen*
complaint	Klage, f.	KLAH*-guh*
complete (entire)	vollständig	FAWLL*-shtenn-dick*
compliment	Kompliment, n.	*kawmm-plee-*MENT
comrade	Kamerad, m.	*kah-muh-*RAHT
conceal, to	verbergen	*fehr-*BEHR*-gen*
concern (business firm)	Unternehmen, n.	*oonn-tehr-*NAY*-men*
concern (affect), to	angehen	AHNN*-gay-en*
concert (musical performance)	Konzert, n.	*kawnn-*TSEHRRT
condition (state)	Zustand, m.	TSOO*-shtahnnt*
conductor (mus.)	Dirigent, m.	*deer-rih-*GENT
conductor (ticket colector)	Schaffner, m.	SHAHFF*-nehr*

ENGLISH	GERMAN	PRONUNCIATION
confident (self-assured)	selbstbewusst	ZELLPST-*buh-voost*
confidential (private)	vertraulich	*fehr*-TROW-*likh*
confirm (corroborate), to	bestätigen	*buh*-SHTAY-*tih-gen*
confirmation (corroboration)	Bestätigung, f.	*buh*-SHTAY-*tih-goong*
confusion (disorder)	Verwirrung, f.	*fehr*-VEERR-*roong*
congregation (religious community)	Gemeinde, f.	*guh*-MINE-*duh*
connection (relationship)	Zusammenhang, m.	*tsoo*-ZAHMM-*en-hahng*
conquer, to	erobern	*ehr*-OH-*behrn*
conscious (aware)	bewusst	*buh*-VOOSST
consequently	infolgedessen	*inn-fawll-guh-*DESS-*en*
consider (reflect on), to	sich überlegen	*zikh ü-behr*-LAY-*gen*
consist of (comprise), to	bestehen aus	*buh*-SHTAY-*en* OWSS
constitute (make up), to	bilden	BILL-*den*
construct, to	(er)bauen	*(ehr-)*BOW-*en*
consul	Konsul, m.	KAWNN-*zooll*
consult (seek professional advice of), to	zu Rate ziehen	*tsoo* RAH-*tuh tsee-en*
contain, to	enthalten	*ent*-HAHLL-*ten*
contemporary (modern)	heutig	HOY-*tick*
contempt (scorn)	Verachtung, f.	*fehr*-AHKH-*toong*
content (satisfied)	zufrieden	*tsoo*-FREE-*den*
continent (geog.)	Weltteil, m.	VELT-*tile*
continual	dauernd	DOW-*ehrnt*
continuation	Fortsetzung, f.	FORT-*zetts-soong*

ENGLISH	GERMAN	PRONUNCIATION
cosmetic (n.)	Schönheitsmittel, n.	SHÖN-*hites-mit-tel*
cost (price)	Preis, m. (pl. Kosten)	PRICE
cost, to	kosten	KAWSS-*ten*
cot (bed)	Feldbett, n.	FELD-*bet*
cotton (fabric)	Baumwolle, f.	BOWM-*vawll-uh*
cough	Husten, m.	HOO-*sten*
counsel (advice)	Rat(schlag), m.	RAHT(-*shlahk*)
counsel (lawyer)	Anwalt, m.	AHNN-*vahlt*
count (enumerate), to	zählen	TSAY-*len*
counterfeit (adj.)	gefällscht	*guh*-FELSHT
country (countryside)	Land, n.	LAHNNT
country (nation)	Land, n.	LAHNNT
couple (pair, n.)	Paar, n.	PAHR
court (of law)	Gericht, n.	*guh*-RIKHT
courteous (polite)	höflich	HÖF-*likh*
cousin	Vetter, m.	FEH-*tehr*
cover, to	(be)decken	(*buh*-)DECK-*en*
cow	Kuh, f.	KOO
crab (shellfish)	Krebs, m.	KRAYBSS
cradle	Wiege, f.	VEE-*guh*
cramp (med.)	Krampf, m.	KRAHMMPF
crazy	verrückt	*fehr*-RÜCKT
cream	Sahne, f.	ZAH-*nuh*
create, to	(er)schaffen	(*ehr*-)SHAHFF-*en*
credit (bus.)	Kredit, m.	*kray*-DEET
crew	Mannschaft, f.	MAHNN-*shahfft*
crime	Verbrechen, n.	*fehr*-BREHKH-*en*
criminal (n.)	Verbrecher, m.	*fehr*-BREHKH-*ehr*
crisp (brittle)	knusperig	KNOOSS-*puh-rick*
criticism (judgment)	Kritik, f.	*krih*-TEEK
cross (crucifix)	Kreuz, n.	KROYTS
cross (traverse), to	überschreiten	*ü-behr*-SHRYE-*ten*

ENGLISH	GERMAN	PRONUNCIATION
contraband	Konterbande, f.	*kaunn-tehr-*BAHNN-*duh*
contradict (deny), to	widersprechen	*vee-dehr-*SHPREHKH-*en*
contrary (opposite)	entgegengesetzt	*ent-*GAY-*gen-guh-zettst*
contibute, to	beitragen	BY-*trah-gen*
contribution	Beitrag, m.	BY-*trahk*
convenience	Bequemlichkeit, f.	*buh-*KVAYM-*likh-kite*
convenient	bequem	*buh-*KVAYM
conversation	Unterhaltung, f.	*oonn-tehr-*HAHLL-*toong*
convince, to	überzeugen	*ü-behr-*TSOY-*gen*
cook	Koch, m.	KAWKH
cook (heat food), to	kochen	KAW-*khen*
cook (prepare meals), to	kochen	KAW-*khen*
cool (having low temperature)	kühl	KÜL
cool (make less hot), to	kühlen	KÜ-*len*
cooperation	Mitwirkung, f.	MIT-*veer-koong*
copper	Kupfer, n.	KOOPP-*fehr*
copy (duplicate)	Kopie, f.	*kow-*PEE
copy (of a publication)	Exemplar, n.	*ex-emm-*PLAHR
copy (imitate), to	nachahmen	NAHKH-*ah-men*
cord (rope)	Strick, m.	SHTRICK
cork (stopper)	Kork, m.	KAWRK
corn (maize)	Mais, m.	MICE
correct	richtig	RIKH-*tick*
correspondence (letters)	Briefwechsel, m.	BREEF-*vexel*
correspond with (write to), to	korrespondieren	*kaw-res-pawnn-*DEE-*ren*

ENGLISH	GERMAN	PRONUNCIATION
crossing (ocean voyage)	Überfahrt, f	*ü-behr-fahrrt*
crossroads	Strassenkreuzung, f.	SHTRAH-*sen-kroyts-soong*
crowd	Menge, f.	MENNG-*uh*
cruel	grausam	GROW-*zahm*
cruise (voyage)	Vergnügungsreise, f.	*fehr-*GNÜ-*goongs-*RYE-*zuh*
crumb	Krume, f.	KROO-*muh*
crutch	Krücke, f.	KRÜCK-*kuh*
cry (weep), to	weinen	VINE-*en*
cucumber	Gurke, f.	GOORR-*kuh*
cuff (of sleeve)	Manschette, f.	*mahnn-*SHETT-*uh*
cuff (of trouser)	Umschlag, m.	*oomm-*SHLAHK
cup	Tasse, f.	TAHSS-*suh*
curb (edge of street)	Prellstein, m.	PRELL-*shtine*
cure (healing)	Heilung, f.	HYE-*loong*
cure (heal), to	heilen	HYE-*len*
curious	neugierig	NOY-*gear-ick*
currency (money)	Währung, f.	VARE-*oong*
current (contemporary, adj.)	laufend	LOWF-*ent*
curse	fluch	FLOOKH
curse (swear), to	fluchen	FLOO-*khen*
curtain (drape)	Vorhang, m.	FOR-*hahng*
custom (habit)	Sitte, f.	ZITT-*tuh*
customer (buyer)	Kunde, m.	KOONN-*duh*
customhouse	Zollamt, n.	TSAWLL-*ahmmt*
customs (tax)	Zoll, m.	TSAWLL
cut (divide into parts), to	schneiden	SHNYE-*den*
daily (adj.)	täglich	TAYG-*likh*
dairy	Molkerei, f.	*mawl-kuh-*RYE
damage (injury)	Schaden, m.	SHAH-*den*
damage (injure), to	beschädigen	*buh-*SHAY-*dih-gen*
damp (moist)	feucht	FOYKHT
danger	Gefahr, f.	*guh-*FAR

ENGLISH	GERMAN	PRONUNCIATION
dangerous	gefährlich	*guh*-FAIR-*likh*
dark (in color, adj.)	dunkel	DOONNG-*kell*
darkness	Dunkelheit, f.	DOONNG-*kel-hite*
darn (mend), to	stopfen	SHTAWP-*fen*
date (appointment)	Verabredung, f.	*fehr*-AHPP-*ray-doong*
date (fruit)	Dattel, f.	DAHTT-*tel*
daughter	Tochter, f.	TAWRH-*tehr*
daughter-in-law	Schwiegertoch-ter, f.	SHVEE-*gehr-tawkht-ehr*
dawn (daybreak)	Morgendäm-merung, f.	MOR-*gen*-DEM-*muh-roong*
day (24-hour period)	Tag, m.	TAHK
day (daytime)	Tag, m.	TAHK
dead	tot	TOTE
deaf	taub	TOWP
dealer (trader)	Händler, m.	HENND-*lehr*
dear (beloved, adj.)	lieb	LEEP
death	Tod, m.	TOTE
debt	Schuld, f.	SHOOLLT
debtor (bus.)	Schuldner, m.	SHOOOLLD-*nehr*
deceive (delude), to	betrügen	*buh*-TRÜ-*gen*
decent (respectable)	anständig	AHNN-*stehn-dick*
decide (make up one's mind), to	sich entschlies-sen	*zikh* ent-SHLEE-*sen*
decision (judgment)	Entscheidung, f.	ent-SHY-*doong*
deck (of cards)	Pack, n.	PAHCK
deck (of ship)	Deck, n.	DECK
declare (state), to	erklären	*ehr*-KLAIR-*ren*
decorate (adorn), to	schmücken	SHMÜCK-*en*
decoration (décor)	Dekoration, f.	*day-ko-rahts-*YOHN
deed (act)	Tat, f.	TAHT
deep (in extent)	tief	TEEF
defect (flaw)	Mangel, m.	MAHNNG-*el*
defend (protect), to	verteidigen	*fehr*-TYE-*dih-gen*
definite	bestimmt	*buh*-SHTIMMT

ENGLISH	GERMAN	PRONUNCIATION
degree (unit of measure)	Grad, m.	GRAHT
delay	Verzögerung, f.	*fehr-*TSÖ-*guh-roong*
delay (postpone), to	verzögern	*fehr-*TSÖ-*gehrn*
deliberate (intentional)	absichtlich	AHPP-*zikht-likh*
delicious	köstlich	KÖST-*likh*
delightful	entzückend	*ent-*TSÜK-*ent*
demand (ask for), to	verlangen	*fehr-*LAHNNG-*en*
demonstrate (show), to	vorführen	FOR-*für-en*
demonstration (proof)	Beweis, m.	*buh-*VICE
dentist	Zahnarzt, m.	TSAHN-*artst*
department store	Warenhaus, n.	VAHR-*en-house*
departure (setting out)	Abfahrt, f.	AHPP-*fahrt*
depend (rely) on, to	sich verlassen	*zikh fehr-*LAHSS-*sen*
deposit, to (fin.)	einzahlen	INE-*tsah-len*
depot (station)	Bahnhof, m.	BAHN-*hohf*
depth (deepness)	Tiefe, f.	TEE-*fuh*
descend (move downward), to	herabsteigen	*hehr-*AHPP-*shyte-gen*
descendant (offspring)	Nachkomme, m.	NAHKH-*kawmm-muh*
describe (portray), to	beschreiben	*buh-*SHRY-*ben*
description (account)	Beschreibung, f.	*buh-*SHRY-*boong*
desert	Wüste, f.	VÜ-*stuh*
deserve, to	verdienen	*fehr-*DEE-*nen*
design (intention)	Absicht, f.	AHPP-*zikht*
design (pattern)	Entwurf, m.	*ent-*VOORRF
desire (long for), to	begehren	*buh-*GAY-*ren*
desk	Schreibtisch, m.	SHRIPE-*tish*
despite (prep.)	trotz	TRAWTTS
dessert	Nachtisch, m.	NAHKH-*tish*

ENGLISH	GERMAN	PRONUNCIATION
destination	Bestimmungs-ort, m.	*buh*-SHTIMM-*oongs-ort*
destiny	Schicksal, n.	SHICK-*zahl*
detail (minor item)	Einzelheit, f.	INE-*tsell-hite*
determine (make up one's mind), to	sich entschlies-sen	*zikh* ent-SHLEE-*sen*
detour	Umleitung, f.	OOMM-*lye-toong*
dew	Tau, m.	TOW
diabetes	Zuckerkrank-heit, f.	TSOOCK-*ehr-krahnnk-hite*
dice (marked cubes)	Würfel, m. pl.	VÜRR-*fel*
dictate (for transcription), to	diktieren	*dick*-TEER-*ten*
dictionary	Wörterbuch, n.	VÖR-*tehr-bookh*
die, to	sterben	SHTEHR-*ben*
diet (restricted food allowance)	Diät, f.	*dee*-ATE
difference (dissimilarity)	Unterschied, m.	OONN-*tehr-sheet*
different (unlike)	verschieden	*fehr*-SHEE-*den*
difficult	schwer	SHVAIR
difficulty (hardness)	Schwierigkeit, f.	SHVEE-*rick-kite*
difficulty (obstacle)	Schwierigkeit, f.	SHVEE-*rick-kite*
dig (excavate), to	graben	GRAH-*ben*
digest, to	verdauen	*fehr*-DOW-*en*
dim	trübe	TRÜ-*buh*
dine, to	(zu Mittag) essen	*(tsoo* MITT-*tahk)* ESS-*en*
diner (railway dining car)	Speisewagen, m.	SHPYE-*zuh-vah-gen*
dining room	Speisezimmer, n.	SHPYE-*zuh-tsimm-ehr*
dinner	Mittagessen, n.	MITT-*tagh-ess-senn*
direct (immediate)	unmittelbar	OONN-*mitt-tell-bar*
direction (course)	Richtung, f.	RIKH-*toong*

ENGLISH	GERMAN	PRONUNCIATION
director	Direktor, m.	*dee-*RECK*-tor*
dirt (unclean matter)	Schmutz, m.	SHMOOTTS
dirty (soiled)	schmutzig	SHMOOTTS-*ick*
disagree (differ), to	nicht überein- stimmen	NIKHT *ü-behr-* INE-*shtimm-en*
disagreeable	unangenehm	OONN-*ahnn-guh- name*
disappear, to	verschwinden	*fehr-*SHVINN-*den*
disappoint, to	enttäuschen	*ent-*TOY-*shen*
disappointment	Enttäuschung, f.	*ent-*TOY-*shoong*
discover, to	entdecken	*ent-*DECK-*en*
discuss, to	besprechen	*buh-*SHPRREHKH- *en*
discussion	Besprechung, f.	*buh-*SHPREHKH- *oong*
disease	Krankheit, f.	KRAHNNK-*hite*
dish (food)	Gericht, n.	*guh-*RIKHT
dishes (tableware)	Geschirr, n.	*guh-*SHEERR
dislike, to	nicht mögen	NIKHT MÖ-*gen*
dispatch (communication)	Meldung, f.	MELL-*doong*
display (exhibit), to	ausstellen	OWSS-*shtell-len*
dispute	Streit, m.	SHTRITE
distance	Entfernung, f.	*ent-*FEHR-*noong*
distant (far off)	entfernt	*ent-*FEHRNT
distinct (different)	verschieden	*fehr-*SHEE-*den*
distinction (difference)	Unterschied, m.	OONN-*tehr-sheet*
distinguish (differentiate), to	unterscheiden	OONN-*tehr-*SHY- *den*
distinguished notable)	ausgezeichnet	OWSS-*guh-tsyekh- net*
distress	Not, f.	NOTE
distribute (allot), to	verteilen	*fehr-*TILE-*en*
district (locale)	Bezirk, m.	*buh-*TSEERRK
disturb, to	stören	SHTÖ-*ren*

ENGLISH	GERMAN	PRONUNCIATION
dive, to	einen Kopfsprung machen	*eye-nen* KAWPPF-*shproong mahkh-en*
divine (adj.)	göttlich	GÖTT-*likh*
division (portion)	Abteilung, f.	AHPP-*tile-oong*
divorce (law)	Ehescheidung, f.	AY-*uh-shy-doong*
dizzy (unsteady)	schwindlig	SHVINND-*lick*
do, to	tun; machen	TOON; MAHKH-*en*
dock	Dock, n.	DAWCK
doctor	Doktor, m.	DAWCK-*tohr*
dog	Hund, m.	HOONNT
domestic (not foreign)	einheimisch	INE-*hime-ish*
donkey	Esel, m.	AY-*zel*
door	Tür, f.	TÜRR
doubt	Zweifel, m.	TSVIFE-*el*
doubt (be uncertain about), to	bezweifeln	*buh-*TSVYE-*feln*
doubtful	zweifelhaft	TSVIFE-*el-hahfft*
doubtless	zweifellos	TSVIFE-*el-lohss*
down (downward, adv.)	hinab; herab	*hinn-*AHPP; *hehr-*AHPP
down payment	Anzahlung, f.	AHNN-*tsah-loong*
downstairs (on a lower floor)	unten	OONN-*ten*
dozen	Dutzend, n.	DOOT-*sent*
draft (air current)	Zug, m.	TSOOK
draft (check)	Tratte, f.	TRAHT-*tuh*
draw (pull along), to	ziehen	TSEE-*en*
draw (sketch), to	zeichnen	TSYEKH-*nen*
drawing (sketch)	Zeichnung, f.	TSYEKH-*noong*
dreadful	furchtbar	FOORRKHT-*bar*
dream	Traum, m.	TROWM
dream, to	träumen	TROY-*men*
dress (frock)	Kleid, n.	KLITE
dress (clothe), to	anziehen	AHNN-*tsee-en*

ENGLISH	GERMAN	PRONUNCIATION
dress (get dressed), to	sich anziehen	*zikh* AHNN-*tsee-en*
dresser (bureau)	Komode, f.	*kawmm*-MOH-*duh*
dressing (salad)	Salatsosse, f.	*zah*-LAHT-*zoh-suh*
drink (beverage)	Getränk, n.	*guh*-TRENGK
drink, to	trinken	TRING-*ken*
drive (a vehicle), to	fahren	FAH-*ren*
driver (of automobile)	Fahrer, m.	FAR-*ehr*
drop (droplet)	Tropfen, m.	TRAWPP-*fen*
drown (die by drowning), to	ertrinken	*ehr*-TRING-*ken*
drug (medicine)	Droge, f.	DROH-*guh*
drunk (intoxicated)	betrunken	*buh*-TROONG-*ken*
dry	trocken	TRAWCK-*en*
dry (make dry), to	austrocknen	OWSS-*trawk-nen*
duck	Ente, f.	ENN-*tuh*
duplicate (copy, n.)	Kopie, f.	*kow*-PEE
during	während	VAY-*rent*
dust	Staub, m.	SHTOWP
dusty	staubig	SHTOW-*bick*
duty (obligation)	Pflicht, f.	PFLIKHT
duty (tax)	Zoll, m.	TSAWLL
duty-free	zollfrei	TSAWLL-*fry*
dwell (reside)	wohnen	VOH-*nen*
dwelling	Wohnung, f.	VOH-*noong*
dye, to	färben	FARE-*ben*
dysentery	Ruhr, f.	ROOR
each (every, adj.)	jeder	YAY-*dehr*
each one (pron.)	jeder	YAY-*dehr*
ear (external ear)	Ohr, n.	OAR
earache	Ohrenschmerzen, pl.	OAR-*en-shmehr-tsen*
earn (be paid), to	verdienen	*fehr*-DEE-*nen*
earnest	ernst	EHRNST
earring	Ohrring, m.	OAR-*ring*
earth (land)	Boden, m.	BOH-*den*

ENGLISH	GERMAN	PRONUNCIATION
earthquake	Erdbeben, n.	AIRT-*bay-ben*
east	Osten, m.	OHSS-*ten*
Easter	Ostern, n.	OHSS-*tehrn*
easy (not difficult)	leicht	LYEKHT
eat, to	essen	ESS-*sen*
economical (thrifty)	sparsam	SHPAHR-*zahm*
economy (thrift)	Sparsamkeit, f.	SHPAHR-*zahm-kite*
edge (border)	Rand, m.	RAHNNT
edge (sharp side)	Schneide, f.	SHNYE-*duh*
edition	Ausgabe, f.	OWSS-*gah-buh*
educate, to	erziehen	*ehr*-TSEE-*en*
education (schooling process)	Erziehung, f.	*ehr*-TSEE-*oong*
effort	Anstrengung, f.	AHNN-*shtreng-oong*
egg	Ei, n.	EYE
either (one or the other, adj.)	einer (von beiden)	EYE-*nehr (fun* BY-*den)*
either . . . or (conj.)	entweder . . . oder	ENT-*vay-dehr* . . . OH-*dehr*
elbow	Ellbogen, m.	ELL-*boh-gen*
elect, to	wählen	VAY-*len*
electric	elektrisch	*el*-LECK-*trish*
electricity	Elektrizität, f.	*el-leck-trih-tsih*-TATE
element	Element, n.	*el-luh*-MENT
elevator (passenger lift)	Fahrstuhl, m.	FAR-*shtool*
else (different, adj.)	anders	AHNN-*dehrss*
else (instead, adv.)	sonst	ZAWNNST
elsewhere	anderswo	AHNN-*dehrss-voh*
embarrassment	Verlegenheit, f.	*fehr*-LAY-*gen-hite*
emergency (n.)	Notfall, m.	NOTE-*fahll*
emotion	Gefühl, n.	*guh*-FÜL
employ (hire), to	anstellen	AHNN-*shtell-len*
employ (use), to	verwenden	*fehr*-VENN-*den*

ENGLISH	GERMAN	PRONUNCIATION
employee	Angestellte, m., f.	AHNN-*guh-shtell-tuh*
employer (boss)	Arbeitsgeber, m.	AHR-*bites-gay-behr*
employment (work)	Beschäftigung, f.	buh-SHEFF-*tih-goong*
empty	leer	LAIR
empty (remove contents of), to	(ent)leeren	(ent-)LAIR-*en*
enclose (include in envelope), to	beilegen	BY-*lay-gen*
encourage, to	ermutigen	*ehr*-MOO-*tih-gen*
end (conclusion)	Schluss, m.	SCHLOOSS
endeavor, to	sich bemühen	*zikh buh*-MÜ-*en*
endure (bear), to	ertragen	*ehr*-TRAH-*gen*
enema	Klistier, n.	*kliss*-TEER
enemy	Feind, m.	FINET
energy	Energie, f.	*enn-ehr*-GEE
engagement (appointment)	Verabredung, f.	*fehr*-AHPP-*ray-doong*
engagement (betrothal)	Verlobung, f.	*fehr*-LOH-*boong*
engine (locomotive)	Lokomotive, f.	*loh-kuh-moh*-TEE-*vuh*
engine (motor)	Motor, m.	MOH-*tor*
English (adj.)	englisch	ENG-*lish*
enjoy (derive joy from), to	geniessen	*guh*-NEE-*senn*
enough (adv.)	genug	*guh*-NOOK
enter (come or go into), to	in . . . eintreten	*inn* . . . INE-*tray-ten*
enterprise (undertaking)	Unternehmen, n.	*oonn-tehr*-NAY-*men*
entertain (amuse), to	unterhalten	*oonn-tehr*-HAHLL-*ten*
entertain (be host to), to	bewirten	*buh*-VEERR-*ten*

ENGLISH	GERMAN	PRONUNCIATION
entertainment	Unterhaltung, f.	*oonn-tehr-*HAHLL-*toong*
entrance	Eingang, m.	INE-*gahng*
epidemic	Epidemie, f.	*eh-pih-duh-*MEE
equal (adj.)	gleich	GLYEKH
errand (commission)	Auftrag, m.	OWF-*trahk*
escape, to	entgehen	*ent-*GAY-*en*
especially	besonders	*buh-*ZAWNN-*dehrss*
establishment (firm)	Unternehmen, n.	*oonn-tehr-*NAY-*men*
evening	Abend, m.	AH-*bent*
ever (at all times)	immer	IMM-*mehr*
ever (at any time)	je(mals)	YAY(*-mahlss*)
every	jeder	YAY-*dehr*
everybody	jeder(mann)	YAY-*dehr (-mahnn)*
everyone	jeder(mann)	YAY-*dehr (-mahnn)*
everything (pron.)	alles	AHLL-*less*
everywhere	überall	*übehr-*AHLL
evident	offenbar	AWFF-*fen-bar*
exact (precise)	genau	*guh-*NOW
examination (test)	Prüfung, f.	PRÜ-*foong*
example	Beispiel, n.	BY-*shpeel*
excellent	vortrefflich	*for-*TREFF-*likh*
except (prep.)	ausser	OWSS-*ehr*
exchange (barter)	(Aus)Tausch, m.	(OWSS-)TOWSH
exclude, to	ausschliessen	OWSS-*shlee-sen*
exclusive (not including)	ausschliesslich	OWSS-*shleess-likh*
excuse (pardon), to	entschuldigen	*ent-*SHOOL-*dih-gen*
exempt (adj.)	befreit	*buh-*FRITE
exercise (physical exertion)	Leibesübungen, f. pl.	LYE-*bess-ü-boong-en*
exist, to	bestehen	*buh-*SHTAY-*en*

ENGLISH	GERMAN	PRONUNCIATION
exit	Ausgang, m.	owss-*gahng*
expedition (journey)	Expedition, f.	*ex-pay-deets-* YOHN
expense (cost)	Unkosten, pl.	OONN-*kawss-ten*
expensive	teuer	TOY-*ehr*
experience (conscious event)	Erlebnis, n.	*ehr-*LAPE-*niss*
expire (become void), to	erklären	*ehr-*KLAIR-*ren*
explanation	erklärung	*ehr-*KLAIR-*roong*
export, to	ausführen	owss-*fü-ren*
express (state), to	ausdrücken	owss-*drück-en*
expression (sign of feeling; word or phrase)	Ausdruck, m.	owss-*droock*
extent (stretch out), to	ausstrecken	owss-*shtreck-en*
extensive	ausgedehnt	owss-*guh-danet*
extent (magnitude)	Ausmass, n.	owss-*mahss*
exterior (adj.)	äusserlich	OYSS-*ehr-likh*
extra (additional)	extra	EX-*trah*
extraordinary	ausserordentlich	owss-*ehr-or-dent-* *likh*
extreme (farthest)	äusserst	OYSS-*ehrst*
eye	Auge, n.	ow-*guh*
eyebrow	Augenbraue, f.	ow-*gen-brow-uh*
eyelash	Wimper, f.	VIMM-*pehr*
eyelid	Augenlid, n.	ow-*gen-leet*
fabric (cloth)	Stoff, m.	SHTAWFF
face	Gesicht, n.	*guh-*ZIKHT
fact	Tatsache, f.	TAHT-*zahkh-uh*
factor (element)	Faktor, m.	FAHK-*tor*
factory	Fabrik, f.	*fah-*BREEK
fade (loose color), to	verblassen	*fehr-*BLAHSS-*sen*
fail (be unsuccess- ful), to	misslingen	*miss-*LING-*en*
fail (neglect) to, to	versäumen	*fehr-*ZOY-*men*

ENGLISH	GERMAN	PRONUNCIATION
failure (lack of success)	Misslingen, n.	*miss*-LING-*en*
faint, to	in Ohnmacht fallen	*in* OHN-*mahkht* FAHLL-*en*
fair (impartial)	fair	FARE
fair (not cloudy)	schön	SHÖN
faith (creed)	Glaubensbekenntnis, n.	GLOW-*bens-buh-kennt-niss*
faith (trust)	Vertrauen, n.	*fehr*-TROW-*en*
fall (autumn, n.)	Herbst, m.	HEHRPST
fall, to	fallen	FAHLL-*en*
false (erroneous)	falsch	FAHLLSH
falsehood (lie)	Unwahrheit, f.	OONN-*vahr-hite*
familiar (well-known)	bekannt	*buh*-KAHNNT
family	Familie, f.	*fah*-MEEL-*yuh*
famous	berühmt	*buh*-RÜMT
fan, electric	Ventilator, m.	*ven-tee*-LAH-*tor*
fancy (imagine), to	sich einbilden	*zikh* INE-*bill-den*
fancy (ornamental, adj.)	gemustert	*guh*-MOOSS-*tehrt*
far (afar, adv.)	weit	VITE
far (distant, adj.)	weit	VITE
fare (transp.)	Fahrgeld, n.	FAR-*gelt*
farewell (leave-taking)	Abschied, m.	AHPP-*sheet*
farm	Bauerngut, n.	BOW-*ehrn-goot*
farmer	Bauer, m.	BOW-*er*
fashion (current style)	Mode, f.	MOH-*duh*
fast (quick, adj.)	schnell	SHNELL
fast (quickly, adv.)	geschwind	*guh*-SHVINNT
fat (obese, adj.)	dick	DICK
fate	Schicksal, n.	SHICK-*zahl*
father	Vater, m.	FAH-*tehr*
father-in-law	Schwiegervater, m.	SHVEE-*gehr-fah-tehr*

ENGLISH	GERMAN	PRONUNCIATION
faucet	Wasserhahn, m.	VAHSS-*ehr-hahn*
favorite-	Lieblings-. . .	LEEB-*lingss-*
fear	Furcht, f.	FOORRKHT
fear (be afraid of), to	fürchten	FÜRKH-*ten*
feather	Feder, f.	FAY-*dehr*
feature (part of face)	(Gesichts)Zug, m.	*(guh-*ZIKHTS-*)* TSOOK
fee	Gebühr, f.	*guh-*BÜR
feed (give food to), to	füttern	FÜTT-*ehrn*
feel (experience), to	sich fühlen	*zikh* FÜ-*len*
feel (touch), to	fühlen	FÜ-*len*
feel (grope) for, to	nach . . . tasten	NAHKH . . . TAHSS-*ten*
feeling (emotion)	Gefühl, n.	*guh-*FÜL
feeling (sensation)	Empfindung, f.	*emp-*FINN-*doong*
female (adj.)	weiblich	VIBE-*likh*
female (zool., n.)	Weibchen, n.	VIBE-*khen*
fence (barrier)	Zaun, m.	TSOWN
ferry (boat)	Fähre, f.	FARE-*uh*
festival	Fest, n.	FEST
fever	Fieber, n.	FEE-*behr*
few (not many, adj.)	wenige	VAIN-*ih-guh*
few, a	ein paar	INE PAHR
fig	Feige, f.	FYE-*guh*
fight	Kampf, m.	KAHMMPF
figure (human form)	Gestalt, f.	*guh-*SHTAHLLT
figure (numeral)	Zahl, f.	TSAHL
fill (make full), to	füllen	FÜLL-*en*
film (photog.)	Film, m.	FILM
fine (good)	schön	SHÖN
fine (penalty, n.)	Geldstrafe, f.	GELT-*shtrah-fuh*
finger	Finger, m.	FING-*ehr*
finish (complete), to	vollenden	*fawll-*ENN-*den*
fire	Feuer, n.	FOY-*ehr*
fireplace	Kamin, m.	*kah-*MEEN

ENGLISH	GERMAN	PRONUNCIATION
firm (business company)	Firma, f.	FEERR-*muh*
first (adj.)	erst	EHRST
fish (food)	Fisch, m.	FISH
fish, to	fischen	FISH-*en*
fix (repair), to	reparieren	*reh-par*-REER-*en*
flag	Fahne, f.	FAH-*nuh*
flashlight	Taschenlampe, f.	TAHSH-*en-lahm-puh*
flat (level, adj.)	Flach	FLAHKH
flavor (savor)	Geschmack, m.	*guh*-SCHMAHCK
flesh	Fleisch n.	FLYSH
flight (journey by air)	Flug, m.	FLOOCK
flood	Uberschwemmung, f.	*ü-behr*-SHVEMM-*moong*
floor (bottom surface)	(Fuss)Boden, m.	(FOOSS-)BOH-*den*
floor (story)	Stock, m.	SHTAWCK
flour	Mehl, m.	MAIL
flow (circulate), to	fliessen	FLEE-*sen*
flower (blossom)	Blume, f.	BLOO-*muh*
fly (housefly)	Fliege, f.	FLEE-*guh*
fly, to	Fliegen	FLEE-*gen*
fog (mist)	Nebel, m.	NAY-*bel*
food	Nahrung, f.	NAH-*roong*
foolish	Töricht	TÖ-*rikht*
foot	Fuss, m.	FOOSS
forbidden	verboten	*fehr*-BOH-*ten*
force (coercion)	Gewalt, f.	*guh*-VAHLLT
force, to	zwingen	TSVING-*en*
forehead	Stirn, f.	SHTEERN
foreign	ausländisch	OWSS-*len-dish*
foreigner	Ausländer, m.	OWSS-*len-der*
forest	Wald, m.	VAHLLT
forever	für immer	*für* IMM-*mehr*
forget, to	vergessen	*fehr*-GESS-*en*

ENGLISH	GERMAN	PRONUNCIATION
forgive, to	verzeihen	*fehr*-TSYE-*en*
forgotten	vergessen	*fehr*-GESS-*en*
fork (eating utensil)	Gabel. f.	GAH-*bel*
form (shape)	Form, f.	FORM
form (shape), to	bilden	BILL-*den*
former (first of two, adj.)	erstere	EHRSS-*teh-ruh*
former (preceding, adj.)	früher	FRÜ-*ehr*
fort	Fort, n.	FORT
fortunate	glücklich	GLÜCK-*likh*
foul (filthy)	schmutzig	SHMOOTS-*ick*
fountain	Springbrunnen, m.	SHPRING-*broonn-en*
fowl (poultry)	Geflügel, n.	*guh*-FLÜ-*gel*
fracture (med.)	Bruch, m.	BROOKH
free (gratuitous)	unentgeltlich	OONN-*ent*-GELT-*likh*
free (independent)	frei	FRY
freeze (turn to ice), to	(ge)frieren	(*guh*-)FREE-*ren*
freight	Fracht, f.	FRAHKHT
French (adj.)	französisch	*frahn*-TSÖ-*zish*
fresh (not stale)	frisch	FRISH
friend	Freund, m.	FROYNT
friendly	Freundlich	FROYNT-*likh*
friendship	Freundschaft, f.	FROYNT-*shahft*
from	von; aus	FAWNN; OWSS
front (forward part)	Vonderseite, f.	FOR-*dehr-zite-uh*
frontier	Grenze, f.	GRENT-*suh*
frost	Frost, m.	FRAWSST
frown, to	die Stirn runzeln	*dee* SHTEERN-ROONTS-*eln*
fry (be cooked in fat), to	sich braten	*zikh* BRAH-*ten*
fuel	Brennstoff, m.	BRENN-*shtawf*

ENGLISH	GERMAN	PRONUNCIATION
full (complete)	vollkommen	FAWLL-*kawm-men*
full (filled)	voll	FAWLL
fun	Spass, m.	SHPAHSS
fund	Fonds, m.	FOHNG
funds	Kapital, n.	*kah-pee-*TAHL
funeral	Begräbnis, n.	*buh-*GRAYP-*niss*
funny(comical)	komisch	KOH-*mish*
furious	wütend	VÜ-*tent*
furnace (home heater)	Ofen, m.	OH-*fen*
furniture	Möbel, n. pl.	MÖ-*bel*
fuse (elec.)	Sicherung, f.	ZIKH-*ehr-roong*
fuss (ado)	Lärm, m.	LAIRM
future (adj.)	(zu)künftig	(TSOO-)KÜNNF-*tick*
gain (increase)	Gewinn, m.	*guh-*VINN
gain (get), to	gewinnen	*guh-*VINN-*nen*
galoshes	Gummischuhe, m. pl.	GOOMM-*ee-shoo-uh*
game (contest)	Spiel, n.	SHPEEL
garage	Garage, f.	*gah-*RAH-*zhuh*
garbage	Abfall, m.	AHPP-*fahll*
garden	Garten, m.	GAHRR-*ten*
garlic	Knoblauch, m.	KNAWP-*lowkh*
garment	Kleidungsstück, n.	KLYE-*doongs-shtük*
garter	Strumpfband, n.	SHTROOMPF-*bahnnt*
gas	Gas, n.	GAHSS
gasoline	Benzin, n.	*ben-*TSEEN
gate	Tor, n.	TOHR
gather (bring together), to	zusammenbringen	*tsoo-*ZAHMM-*en-bring-en*
gather (congregate), to	sich (ver)sammeln	*zikh (fehr-)* ZAHMM-*meln*

ENGLISH	GERMAN	PRONUNCIATION
gear (mech.)	Gang, m.	GAHNNG
general (adj.)	allgemein	AHLL-*guh-mine*
generous	freigebig	FRY-*gay-bick*
gentle (soothing)	sanft	ZAHNFFT
gentleman	Herr, m.	HEHRR
genuine	echt	EHKHT
German (adj.)	deutsch	DOYTSH
get (obtain), to	bekommen	*buh*-KAWMM-*en*
gift (present)	Geschenk, n.	*guh*-SHENK
girl	Mädchen, n.	MAID-*khen*
give (bestow), to	geben	GAY-*ben*
glad	froh	FRO
glass (material)	Glas, n.	GLAHSS
glass (vessel)	(Trink)Glas, n.	(TRINGK-)GLAHSS
glasses (spectacles)	Brille, f.	BRILL-*uh*
glide, to	gleiten	GLITE-*en*
gloomy (melancholy)	trübsinnig	TRÜB-*zin-ick*
glorious (resplendent)	herrlich	HEHRR-*likh*
glove	Handschuh, m.	HAHNNT-*shoo*
go (ride), to	fahren	FAH-*ren*
go (walk), to	gehen	GAY-*en*
God	Gott, m.	GAWTT
gold	Gold, n.	GAWLT
good, better, best	gut, besser, (der) beste	GOOT, BESSER, (DEHR) BESS-*tuh*
good-bye	auf Wiedersehen	OWFF VEE-*dehr-zay-en*
goods	Waren, f. pl.	VAHR-*en*
government	Regierung, f.	ray-GEAR-*oong*
governor	Gouverneur, m.	goo-vehr-NÖR
grade (school division)	Klasse, f.	KLAHSS-*uh*
grain (cereal)	Getreide, n.	*guh*-TRY-*duh*
grammar	Grammatik, f.	grahm-MAH-*tick*
grand (imposing)	grossartig	GROHSS-*ahr-tick*

Preface

Webster's Travelers Phrase Book is designed to offer quick, efficient assistance to the traveler who does not speak German—businessman, student, tourist. The book's unique four-part arrangement makes it easy to find the information needed in any situation.

I Guide to pronunciation
Assistance in pronouncing the language is provided in a compact guide that uses the regular alphabet.

II Essential phrases
All phrases are grouped under more than 700 key finding words, which are arranged alphabetically. If you are in a restaurant, for example, and want the check, or if you are in need of cash and want to cash a check, there is no need to figure out whether the phrase you need is under *Eating, Restaurant, Money,* or *Bank.* You go directly to the key word **Check.** Moreover, under many key words, additional related phrases are provided. Under **Automobile,** for example, you will find the phrases needed to 'fill it up,' rent a car, deal with a flat tire, and ask about the next gas station.

III Signs and Notices
More than 60 vital signs and notices are translated.

IV Basic vocabulary
More than 3,000 individual words are listed alphabetically for quick reference.

Guide to Pronunciation

After quickly finding the necessary phrase, you will need to pronounce it easily with a minimum of hesitation. Here again, this new guide offers rapid assistance by showing pronunciation in symbols that are familiar. The pronunciation of all sentences in this book is indicated by use of the English alphabet. Capital letters are used to indicate the stressed syllables. When you become accustomed to hearing German spoken, you will find it easier to imitate and your pronunciation will improve rapidly so that you will seldom need to refer to the pronunciation guide.

Vowels

Symbol	Approximate Sound	German Example	
ah	f*a*ther	fahren	FAH-*ren*
ai	p*ai*r	er	AIR
aw	c*or*n	kommen	KAWMM-*en*
a +Consonant +e	l*ate*	den	DANE
ay	m*ay*	gegen	GAY-*gen*
e	b*e*d	Gepäck	*guh*-PECK
eh	*e*rror	erst	EHRST
ee	f*ee*t	Musik	*moo*-ZEEK
ea	h*ea*r	ihr	EAR
i	st*i*ll	nicht	NIKHT
i +Consonant +e	k*i*te	Leid	LITE
ye	d*ye*	eine	EYE-*nuh*
y	m*y*	bei	BY

(continued)

Vowels—continued

Symbol	Approximate Sound	German Example	
o +Consonant +e	home	widerholen	*vee-dehr-*HOLE-*en*
oa	coat	Botschaft	BOAT-*shafft*
oh	tonal	Monat	MOH-*naht*
ö	no English equivalent; round lips as for oo and try to say ay	Öl	ÖL
oo	boot	Fuss	FOOSS
ow	cow	auf	OWF
oy	toy	euer	OY-*ehr*
uh	sofa	betragen	*buh-*TRAH-*gen*
ü	no English equivalent; round lips as for oo and try to say ee	Münze	MÜNT-*suh*

Consonants

Symbol	Approximate Sound	German Example	
p	park	hinab	*hin-*AHPP
b	beat	Bahnhof	BAHN-*hohf*
t	tall	tief	TEEF
d	dog	Doktor	DAWCK-*tohr*
k; ck	key	Käse	KAY-*zuh*
g	green	ganz	GAHNNTS
f	fair	Frucht	FROOKHT
v	very	wieder	VEE-*dehr*

(continued)

Consonants—continued

Symbol	Approximate Sound	German Example	
s	*sort*	Nuss	NOOSS
z	*zoo*	sehen	ZAY-*en*
sh	*show*	Scheck	SHECK
zh	*rouge*	Garage	*gah*-RAH-*zhuh*
m	*most*	Mund	MOONNT
n	*near*	noch	NAWKH
l	*leaf*	Licht	LIKHT
r	rolled or trilled	rund	ROONNT
y	*yet*	ja	YAH
h	*house*	Hund	HOONNT
kh	no English equivalent:		
after *a, o, u*	as *ch* in the Scottish word *loch*	Koch	KAWKH
otherwise	try to say English *h* while pressing the tip of the tongue against the lower front teeth	ich	IKH

ENGLISH	GERMAN	PRONUNCIATION
granddaughter	Enkelin, f.	ENG-*kell-lin*
grandfather	Grossvater, m.	GROHSS-*fah-tehr*
grandmother	Grossmutter, f.	GROHSS-*moott-tehr*
grandson,	Enkel, m.	ENG-*kell*
grape	Traube, f.	TROW-*buh*
grass	Gras, n.	GRAHSS
grateful	dankbar	DAHNNK-*bar*
gratitude	Dankbarkeit, f.	DAHNNK-*bar-kite*
grave (serious)	ernst	EHRNST
gray	grau	GROW
grease (cooking fat)	Fett, n.	FETT
great	gross	GROHSS
greatness (eminence)	Grösse, f.	GRÖ-*suh*
greedy	gierig	GEAR-*ick*
Greek (adj.)	griechisch	GREEKH-*ish*
green (color)	grün	GRÜN
greet (salute), to	(be)grüssen	(*buh-*)GRUSS-SEN
greeting	Begrüssung, f.	*buh*-GRÜ-*soong*
grief	Kummer, m.	KOOMM-*ehr*
grin, to	grinsen	GRIN-*zen*
grocery	Lebensmittel-geschäft, n.	LAY-*bens-mit-tell-guh-sheft*
ground (earth)	Boden, m.	BOH-*den*
group	Gruppe, f.	GROOPP-*uh*
grow (expand), to	wachsen	VAHX-*en*
growth (development)	Wachstum, n.	VAHX-*toom*
guard (watcher)	Wache, f.	VAHKH-*uh*
guardian	Vormund, m.	FOR-*moonnt*
guess (suppose), to	vermuten	*fehr-moo-ten*
guest (visitor)	Gast, m.	GAHSST
gulf (large bay)	Golf, m.	GAWLF
gum (chewing gum)	Zahnfleisch, n.	TSAHN-*flysh*
gum (chewing gum)	Kaugummi, m.	KOW-*goomm-mee*
gun	Gewehr, n.	*guh*-VARE

ENGLISH	GERMAN	PRONUNCIATION
gutter (of street)	Rinnstein, m.	RINN-*shtine*
gymnasium (athletic arena)	Turnhalle, f.	TOORRN-*hahll-luh*
habit (custom)	Gewohnheit, f.	*guh*-VOHN-*hite*
hail (ice)	Hagel, m.	HAH-*gel*
hail (precipitate hail), to	hageln	HAH-*geln*
hair	Haar, n.	HAHR
half (adj.)	halb	HAHLLP
half (n.)	Hälfte, f.	HELFF-*tuh*
hall (corridor)	Gang, m.	GAHNNG
hall (meeting room)	Saal, m.	ZAHL
halt (come to a stop), to	(an)halten	(AHNN-)HAHLL-*ten*
handkerchief	Taschentuch, n.	TAHSH-*en-tookh*
handle	Griff, m.	GRIFF
happen (occur), to	geschehen	*guh*-SHAY-*en*
happiness	Glück, n.	GLÜCK
happy (glad)	glücklich	GLÜCK-*likh*
harbor	Hafen, m.	HAH-*fen*
hard (difficult)	schwer	SHVAIR
hard (not soft)	hart	HAHRT
hardly (barely)	kaum	KOWM
hardship (privation)	Not, f.	NOTE
hardware	Metallwaren, pl.	*may*-TAHL-*vahren*
harm (damage), to	schaden	SHAH-*den*
haste	Hast, f.	HAHSST
hat	Hut, m.	HOOT
hate (hatred)	Hass, m.	HAHSS
hate, to	hassen	HAHSS-*sen*
have, to	haben	HAH-*ben*
he	er	EHR
head	Kopf, m.	KAWPPF
head (leader)	Vorsteher, m.	FOR-*shtay-ehr*
headache	Kopfweh, n.	KAWPPF-*vay*
headquarters	Hauptquartier, n.	HOWPT-*kvahr-teer*
heal (cure), to	heilen	HYE-*len*

ENGLISH	GERMAN	PRONUNCIATION
health	Gesundheit, f.	*guh*-ZOONNT-*hite*
healthy	gesund	*guh*-ZOONNT
hear, to	hören	HÖ-*ren*
heart	Herz, n.	HEHRRTS
hearty (cordial)	herzlich	HEHRRTS-*likh*
heat	Hitze, f.	HIT-*suh*
heat, to	heizen	HITES-*en*
heaven	Himmel, m.	HIMM-*mel*
heavy	schwer	SHVAIR
heel	Ferse, f.	FEHR-*suh*
height (highness)	Höhe, f.	HÖ-*yuh*
helicopter	Hubschrauber, m.	HOOP-*shrow-behr*
help (assistance)	Hilfe, f.	HILL-*fuh*
help, to	helfen	HELL-*fen*
helper	Helfer, m.	HELL-*fehr*
helpful (useful)	hilfreich	HILLF-*ryekh*
helpless	hilflos	HILLF-*lohss*
hem	Saum, m.	ZOWM
hemisphere	Halbkugel, f.	HAHLLP-*koo-gel*
herb	Kraut, n.	KROWT
herring	Hering, m.	HEHR-*ing*
hide (conceal), to	verstecken	*fehr*-SHTECK-*en*
high	hoch	HOHKH
highway	Landstrasse, f.	LAHNNT-*shtrah-suh*
hill	Hügel, m.	HÜ-*gel*
hinder, to	(ver)hindern	*(fehr-)*HINN-*dehrn*
hip	Hüfte, f.	HÜFF-*tuh*
hire (employ), to	anstellen	AHNN-*shtell-en*
history	Geschichte, f.	*guh*-SHIKH-*tuh*
hit (strike), to	schlagen	SHLAH-*gen*
hog (animal)	Schwein, n.	SHVINE
hold, to	halten	HAHLL-*ten*
holiday	Feiertag, m.	FYE-*ehr-tahk*
hollow (adj.)	hohl	HOLE
holy	heilig	HYE-*likh*

ENGLISH	GERMAN	PRONUNCIATION
home	Heim, n.	HIME
homesickness	Heimweh, n.	HIME-*vay*
honest	ehrlich	AIR-*likh*
honesty	Redlichkeit, f.	RAID-*likh-kite*
honey	Honig, m.	HOH-*nick*
honor	Ehre, f.	AY-*ruh*
honor (respect), to	(ver)ehren	(*fehr-*)AIR-*en*
hood (auto.)	Motorhaube, f.	MOH-*tor-how-buh*
hook	Haken, m.	HAH-*ken*
hope	Hoffnung, f.	HAWFF-*noong*
hope, to	hoffen	HAWFF-*en*
horn (auto.)	Hupe, f.	HOO-*puh*
horn (mus.)	Horn, n.	HORN
horse	Pferd, n.	PFAIRT
hospital	Krankenhaus, n.	KRAHNNG-*ken-house*
host	Gastgeber, m.	GAHSst-*gay-behr*
hot	heiss	HICE
hotel	Hotel, n.	ho-TELL
hour	Stunde, f.	SHTOONN-*duh*
house	Haus, n.	HOWSS
how (interrog. adv.)	wie	VEE
however (nevertheless)	jedoch	YAY-*dawkh*
human (adj.)	menschlich	MENNSH-*likh*
hunger	Hunger, m.	HOONNG-*gehr*
hungry	hungrig	HOONNG-*rick*
hungry, to be	Hunger haben	HOONN-*gehr* HAH-*ben*
hunting (sport)	Jagd, f.	YAHGT
hurry (haste)	Eile, f.	EYE-*luh*
hurry (hasten), to	sich beeilen	zikh buh-EYE-*len*
hurt (be painful), to	schmerzen	SHMEHR-*tsen*
husband	Mann, m.	MAHNN
I	ich	IKH
ice (frozen water)	Eis, n.	ICE

ENGLISH	GERMAN	PRONUNCIATION
icebox	Eisschrank, m.	ICE-*shrahnk*
ice-cream	(Speise)Eis, n.	(SHPYE-*zuh-*)ICE
idea	Idee, f.	ee-DAY
idle (not busy)	müssig	MÜ-*sick*
if (supposing that)	wenn	VENN
if (whether)	ob	OHP
ignorance	Unwissenheit, f.	OONN-*viss-en-hite*
ill (sick)	krank	KRAHNNK
illegal	ungesetzlich	OONN-*guh-zetts-likh*
illness	Krankheit, f.	KRAHNNK-*hite*
illuminate (light up), to	beleuchten	*buh-*LOYKH-*ten*
imagination	Einbildungskraft, f.	INE-*bill-doongs-krahft*
imagine (picture mentally), to	sich vorstellen	*zikh* FOR-*shtell-en*
immediately (instantly)	(so)gleich	(*zoh-*)GLYEKH
impatient	ungeduldig	OONN-*guh-dooll-dick*
importance	Wichtigkeit, f.	VIKH-*tick-kite*
important	wichtig	VIKH-*tick*
impossibility	Unmöglichkeit, f.	OONN-MÖG-*likh-kite*
impossible	unmöglich	OONN-MÖG-*likh*
improvement (betterment)	Verbesserung, f.	*fehr-*BESS-*ehr-oong*
in (during, prep.)	bei	BY
in (inside, prep.)	in	INN
in (into, prep.)	in	INN
include (contain), to	einschliessen	INE-*shlee-sen*
income	Einkommen, n.	INE-*kawmm-en*
income tax	Einkommen-steuer, f.	INE-*kawmm-en-shtoy-ehr*
inconvenience	Lästigkeit, f.	LEHSS-*tick-kite*

ENGLISH	GERMAN	PRONUNCIATION
indeed (adv.)	zwar	TSVAHR
independence	Unabhängigkeit, f.	OONN-*ahpp-heng-ick-kite*
independent	unabhängig	OONN-*ahpp-heng-ick*
indicate (point out), to	(an)zeigen	(AHNN-)TSYE-*gen*
indigestion	Verdauungsstörung, f.	*fehr*-DOW-*oongs-shtör-oong*
individual (person, n.)	Individuum, n.	*in-dih*-VEE-*doo-oomm*
indoors (adv.)	drinnen	DRINN-*en*
inevitable (adj.)	unvermeidlich	OONN-*fehr-mide-likh*
infant (n.)	Säugling, m.	ZOYG-*ling*
infection	Ansteckung, f.	AHNN-*shteck-oong*
inferior (mediocre)	minderwertig	MINN-*dehr-vare-tick*
inflammation	Entzündung, f.	*ent*-TSÜN-*doong*
inform (apprise), to	Auskunft geben	OWSS-*koonft*-GAY-*ben*
information (knowledge)	Auskunft, f.	OWSS-*koonft*
inhabit, to	bewohnen	*buh*-VOH-*nen*
inhabitant	Einwohner, m.	INE-*voh-ner*
initial (letter)	Anfangsbuchstabe, m.	AHNN-*fahnngs-bookh-shtah-buh*
injection (med.)	Einspritzung, f.	INE-*shprits-oong*
injury	Verletzung, f.	*fehr*-LET-*soong*
ink	Tinte, f.	TINN-*tuh*
inn	Gasthof, m.	GAHSST-*hof*
innocent (guiltless)	unschuldig	OONN-*shooll-dick*
inquire (ask), to	nachfragen	NAHKH-*frah-gen*
inquire (question)	Nachfrage, f.	NAHKH-*frah-guh*
insect	Kerbtier, n.	KEHRP-*teer*

ENGLISH	GERMAN	PRONUNCIATION
inspection (scrutiny)	Kontrolle, f.	*kawnn*-TRAWLL-*uh*
install (set up for use), to	aufstellen	OWF-*shtell-en*
installment (payment, bus.)	Rate, f.	RAH-*tuh*
instance (example)	Beispiel, n.	BY-*shpeel*
instead of	statt	SHTAHTT
instruct (teach), to	unterrichten	*oonn-tehr*-RIKH-*ten*
instruction (teaching)	Unterricht, m.	OONN-*tehr-rikht*
instrument (implement)	Instrument, n.	*in-stroo*-MENT
insurance	Versicherung, f.	*fehr*-ZIKH-*ehr-oong*
intelligence (understanding)	Verstand, m.	*fehr*-SHTAHNNT
intelligent	verständig	*fehr*-SHTENN-*dick*
intend (propose), to	beabsichtigen	*buh*-AHPP-*zikh-tih-gen*
intention	Absicht, f.	AHPP-*zikht*
interest (attention)	Interesse, n.	*in-tehr*-ESS-*uh*
interest (money rate)	Zinsen, m. pl.	TSIN-*zen*
interest, to	interessieren	*in-tehr-ruh*-SEE-*ren*
interesting	interessant	*in-tehr-ruh*-SAHNNT
interfere (meddle), to	sich einmischen	*zikh* INE-*mish-en*
interior (inside, n.)	Innere, n.	INN-*ehr-uh*
interpret (explain), to	deuten	DOY-*ten*
interrupt, to	unterbrechen	*oonn-tehr*-BREHKH-*en*
interval (period of time)	Zwischenraum, m.	TSVISH-*en-rowm*

ENGLISH	GERMAN	PRONUNCIATION
intimate (personal)	vertraut	*fehr*-TROWT
into (to the inside)	in	INN
introduce (make acquainted), to	vorstellen	FOR-*shtell-en*
invest, to (bus.)	anlegen	AHNN-*lay-gen*
invitation	Einladung, f.	INE-*lah-doong*
invite, to	einladen	INE-*lah-den*
involve (entail), to	zur Folge haben	*tsoor* FAWLL-*guh hah-ben*
iodine (antiseptic)	Jodtinktur, f.	YOHT-*tink-toor*
Irish (adj.)	irisch	EERR-*ish*
iron (metal)	Eisen, n.	EYE-*zen*
iron (electric)	Bügeleisen, n.	BÜ-*gel-eye-zen*
island (geog.)	Insel, f.	INN-*zel*
isthmus	Landenge, f.	LAHNND-*eng-uh*
Italian (adj.)	italienisch	*ee-tahl-*YAY-*nish*
jacket (short coat)	Jacke, f.	YAHCK-*uh*
jail	Gefängnis, n.	*guh-*FENG-*niss*
Japanese (adj.)	japanisch	*yah-*PAH-*nish*
jar (vessel)	Krug, m.	KROOK
jaw	Kiefer, m.	KEE-*fehr*
jelly	Gelee, n.	*zhuh-*LAY
Jew (n.)	Jude, m.	YOO-*duh*
jewel	Juwel, n.	*yoo-*VALE
jewelry	Schmuck, m.	SHMOOCK
Jewish (adj.)	jüdisch	YÜ-*dish*
job (employment)	Arbeit, f.	AHR-*bite*
job (task)	Aufgabe, f.	OWF-*gah-buh*
joke (jest)	Witz, m.	VITTS
joke (jest), to	Spass machen	SHPAHSS MAHKH-*en*
journey	Reise, f.	RYE-*zuh*
joy	Freude, f.	FROY-*duh*
judge	richter, m.	RIKH-*tehr*
judge, to	(be)urteilen	*(buh-)*OOR-*tie-len*
juice	saft, m.	ZAHFFT
jump (bound), to	springen	SHPRING-*en*

ENGLISH	GERMAN	PRONUNCIATION
jury	Geschworenen, pl.	*guh*-SHVOR-*uh-nen*
just (merely)	bloss	BLOHSS
keep (retain), to	behalten	*buh*-HAHLL-*ten*
kettle	Kessel, m.	KESS-*el*
key (for lock)	Schlüssel, m.	SHLÜSS-*el*
kidney	Niere, f.	NEAR-*uh*
kill, to	töten	TÖ-*ten*
kind (adj.)	gütig	GÜ-*tick*
kind (n.)	Art, f.	ART
kindness (goodness)	Güte, f.	GÜ-*tuh*
king	König, m.	KÖ-*nig*
kiss	Kuss, m.	KOOSS
kiss, to	küssen	KÜSS-*en*
kitchen	Küche, f.	KÜ-*khuh*
knee	Knie, f.	KNEE
knife	Messer, n.	MESS-*ehr*
knock (hit), to	klopfen	KLAWPP-*fen*
knot	Knoten, m.	KNOH-*ten*
know (be acquainted with), to	kennen	KENN-*nen*
know (have knowledge), to	wissen	VISS-*en*
knowledge (information)	(Er)Kenntnisse, f. pl.	*(ehr)*KENNT-*niss-uh*
known (familiar)	bekannt	*buh*-KAHNNT
label	Etikett, n.	*eh-tee-*KETT
lace (fabric)	Spitze, f.	SHPITT-*suh*
lace (shoelace)	Schnürsenkel, m.	SHNÜR-*zeng-kel*
lack (be without), to	fehlen	FAY-*len*
lady	Dame, f.	DAH-*muh*
lake	See, m.	ZAY
lamb	Lamm, n.	LAHMM
lamb chop	Hammelkotelett, n.	HAHMM-*mel-kaw-tell-let*
lamp	Lampe, f.	LAHMM-*puh*

ENGLISH	GERMAN	PRONUNCIATION
land (ground)	Land, n.	LAHNNT
land (property)	Grundstück, n.	GROONNT-*shtück*
land (region)	Landschaft, f.	LAHNNT-*shahfft*
land (from a ship), to	landen	LAHNN-*den*
landscape (scenery)	Landschaft, f.	LAHNNT-*shahfft*
language	Sprache, f.	SHPRAHKH-*uh*
large	gross	GROHSS
last (final, adj.)	letzte	LETTS-*tuh*
last (most recent, adj.)	vorig	FO-*rick*
late (at relative time, adv.)	spät	SHPATE
late (tardily, adv.)	spät	SHPATE
latter (second of two, adv.)	letztere	LETTS-*teh-ruh*
laugh, to	lachen	LAHKH-*en*
laughter	Gelächter, n.	*guh*-LEKH-*tehr*
laundry (articles laundered)	Wäsche, f.	VESH-*uh*
law (statute)	Gesetz, n.	*guh*-ZETTS
lawful	gesetzmässig	*guh*-ZETTS-*may-sick*
lawyer	Advokat, m.	*ahd-voh*-KAHT
lay (put down), to	legen	LAY-*gen*
lead (guide), to	führen	FÜ-*ren*
learn (acquire knowledge), to	lernen	LEHR-*nen*
least (adv.)	am wenigsten	AHMM-VAY-*nick-sten*
leather (n.)	Leder, n.	LAY-*dehr*
leave (depart), to	abreisen	AHPP-*rye-zenn*
leave (let remain), to	(übrig)lassen	(*ü-brick-*)LAHSS-*senn*
left (adj.)	links	LINKS
left (adv.)	links	LINKS
leg	Bein, n.	BINE
legal	gesetzlich	*guh*-ZETTS-*likh*

ENGLISH	GERMAN	PRONUNCIATION
leisure	Muse, f.	MOO-*suh*
lemon	Zitrone, f.	*tsee*-TROH-*nuh*
lend, to	(ver)leihen	*(fehr-)*LYE-*en*
length	Länge, f.	LENG-*uh*
less (adv.)	weniger	VAIN-*ih-gehr*
less (minus, prep.)	weniger	VAIN-*ih-gehr*
lesson (assignment)	Aufgabe, f.	OWF-*gah-buh*
let (permit), to	lassen	LAHSS-*senn*
letter (character)	Buchstabe, m.	BOOKH-*shtah-buh*
letter (epistle)	Brief, m.	BREEF
level (flat)	eben	AY-*ben*
liability (responsiblity)	Haftpflicht, f.	HAHFFT-*pflikht*
liable (responsible)	haftbar	HAHFFT-*bar*
liberty (freedom)	Freiheit, f.	FRY-*hite*
library	Bibliothek, f.	*bee-blee-oh*-TAKE
license (permit)	Bescheinigung, f.	*buh*-SHY-*nee-goong*
lid (cover)	Deckel, m.	DECK-*el*
lie (be located), to	liegen	LEE-*gen*
lie (be prone), to	liegen	LEE-*gen*
lie (prevaricate), to	lügen	LÜ-*gen*
lie down, to	sich hinlegen	*zikh* HINN-*lay-gen*
life	Leben, n.	LAY-*ben*
lift (raise), to	(auf)heben	*(*OWF-*)*HAY-*ben*
light (illumination)	Licht, n.	LIKHT
light (of little weight)	leicht	LYEKHT
light (set fire to),	anzünden	AHNN-*tsün-den*
lightning	Blitz, m.	BLITTS
like (adj.)	gleich	GLYEKH
like (adv.)	wie	VEE
like (be fond of), to	gern haben	GEHRN *hah-ben*
likely (probable, adj.)	wahrscheinlich	*vahr*-SHINE-*likh*
limb	Glied, n.	GLEET
limit	Grenze, f.	GRENT-*suh*

ENGLISH	GERMAN	PRONUNCIATION
limit, to	beschränken	*buh*-SHRENG-*ken*
line (row)	Reihe, f.	RYE-*uh*
linen (fabric)	Leinen, n.	LINE-*nen*
liner, ocean	Überseedampfer, m.	*ü-behr-zay-*DAHMMP-*fehr*
lip	Lippe, f.	LIP-*puh*
lipstick	Lippenstift, m.	LIP-*en-shtifft*
listen (hearken), to	zuhören	TSOO-*hö-ren*
litter (stretcher)	Tragbahre, f.	TRAHK-*bar-uh*
little (not much, adj.)	wenig	VAY-*nick*
little (small, adj.)	klein	KLINE
live (adj.)	lebendig	*lay-*BEN-*dick*
live (be alive), to	leben	LAY-*ben*
liver	Leber, f.	LAY-*behr*
living (livelihood)	(Lebens)Unterhalt, m.	(LAY-*bens-*)OONN-*tehr-hahlt*
load (burden)	Last, f.	LAHSST
loaf	Laib, m.	LIPE
lobster	Hummer, m.	HOOMM-*mehr*
local (regional)	örtlich	ÖRT-*likh*
locality (place)	Ort, m.	ORT
locate (find), to	ausfindig machen	OWSS-*fin-dikh* MAHKH-*en*
lock (fastening)	Schloss, n.	SHLAWSS
lock (fasten with key), to	(ver)schliessen	(*fehr-*)SHLEE-*sen*
lodging (temporary quarters)	Unterkunft, f.	OONN-*tehr-koonnft*
lone (solitary)	einsam	INE-*zahm*
lonely (unfrequented)	verlassen	*fehr-*LAHSS-*sen*
lonesome	einsam	INE-*zahm*
long (not short)	lang	LAHNNG
long for, to	sich sehnen	*zikh* ZAY-*nen*

ENGLISH	GERMAN	PRONUNCIATION
plane (airplane)	Flugzeug, n.	FLOOK-*tsoyk*
plant (flora)	Pflanze, f.	PFLAHNN-*tsuh*
plate (shallow dish)	Teller, m.	TELL-*ehr*
platform, railroad	Bahnsteig, m.	BAHN-*shtyek*
play (stage presentation)	Schauspiel, n.	SHOW-*shpeel*
play (engage in recreation), to	spielen	SHPEE-*len*
play (perform music upon), to	spielen	SHPEE-*len*
playmate	Spielgefährte, m.	SHPEEL-*guh-fair-tuh*
pleasant	angenehm	AHNN-*guh-name*
please (satisfy), to	belieben	*buh*-LEEB-*en*
pleasure	Vergnügen, n.	*fehr*-GNÜ-*gen*
plenty (n.)	Fülle, f.	FÜLL-*uh*
plug (elec.)	Stecker, m.	SHTECK-*ehr*
plum (fruit)	Pflaume, f.	PFLOW-*muh*
pneumonia	Lungenentzündung, f.	LOONNG-*en-ent-tsün-doong*
pocket	Tasche, f.	TAHSH-*uh*
poem	Gedicht, n.	*guh*-DIKHT
poet	Dichter, m.	DIKH-*tehr*
poetry	Dichtung, f.	DIKH-*toong*
point (indicate), to	hinweisen	HINN-*vye-zen*
poison	Gift, n.	GIFT
poison, to	vergiftern	*fehr*-GIFF-*ten*
police	Polizei, f.	*poh-lee*-TSYE
policeman	Polizist, m.	*poh-lee*-TSIST
polish, to	polieren	*poh*-LEE-*ren*
polite	höflich	HÖF-*likh*
political	politisch	*poh*-LEE-*tish*
politician	Politiker, m.	*poh*-LEE-*tee-kehr*
politics	Politik, f.	*poh-lee*-TEEK
pool (standing water)	Pfuhl, m.	PFOOL
poor (needy)	dürftig	DÜRF-*tick*

ENGLISH	GERMAN	PRONUNCIATION
poor (unfortunate)	arm	ARM
pope	Papst, m.	PAHPST
popular (prevalent)	verbreitet	*fehr*-BRYE-*tet*
population (number of people)	Bevolkerung, f.	*buh*-FOL-*kehr-oong*
porcelain (n.)	Porzellan, n.	*por*-tsell-LAHN
pork	Schweinefleisch, n.	SHVINE-*uh-flysh*
pork chop	Schweinsripp-chen, n. pl.	SHVINES-*rip-khen*
port (harbor)	Hafen, m.	HAH-*fen*
porter (baggage carrier)	Gepäckträger, m.	*guh*-PECK-*tray-gehr*
possess, to	besitzen	*buh*-ZITT-*sen*
possession (ownership)	Besitz, m.	*buh*-ZITTS
possibility	Möglichkeit, f.	MÖG-*likh-kite*
possible	möglich	MÖG-*likh*
postal (postal charge)	Porto, n.	POR-*toh*
post office	Postamt, n.	PAWSST-*ahmmt*
postpone, to	verschieben	*fehr*-SHEE-*ben*
potato (white)	Kartoffel, f.	*kahr*-TAWFF-*fell*
poverty	Armut, f.	AHR-*moot*
powder (cosmetic)	Puder, m.	POO-*dehr*
power (authority)	Macht, f.	MAHKHT
powerful	mächtig	MEHKH-*tick*
practice (custom)	Brauch, m.	BROWKH
praise, to	loben	LOH-*ben*
pray, to	beten	BAY-*ten*
prayer (petition)	Gebet, n.	*guh*-BATE
prefer (like better), to	vorziehen	FOR-*tsee-en*
prejudice	Vorurteil, n.	FOR-*oor-tile*
prescription (med.)	Rezept, n.	*ray*-TSEPT
present (give), to	überreichen	*ü-behr*-RYE-*khen*
present (introduce), to	vorstellen	FOR-*shtell-en*

ENGLISH	GERMAN	PRONUNCIATION
press (newspapers and periodicals)	Presse, f.	PRESS-*uh*
press (iron), to	bügeln	BU-*geln*
pretend (feign), to	heucheln	HOY-*kheln*
pretty	hübsch	HÜPSH
prevent (stop), to	verhüten	*fehr*-HÜ-*ten*
previous	vorhergehend	*for*-HAIR-*gay-ent*
price	Preis, m.	PRICE
priest	Priester, m.	PREESS-*tehr*
principal (main)	hauptsächlich	HOWPT-*zehkh-likh*
principle	Grundsatz, m.	GROONNT-*zahtts*
print (printed reproduction)	Abdruck, m.	AHPP-*drook*
print, to	drucken	DROOCK-*en*
prison	Gefängnis, n.	*guh*-FENG-*niss*
prisoner	Gefangene, m., f.	*guh*-FAHNNG-*en-uh*
private (personal)	privat	*pree*-VAHT
privilege	Vorrecht, n.	FOR-*rehkht*
prize (trophy)	Preis, m.	PRICE
probable (likely)	wahrscheinlich	*vahr*-SHINE-*likh*
product	Erzeugnis, n.	*ehr*-TSOYG-*niss*
profession (occupation)	Beruf, m.	*buh*-ROOF
professor (teacher)	Professor, m.	*pro*-FESS-*ohr*
profit (bus.)	Gewinn, m.	*guh*-VINN
prohibition	Verbot, m.	*fehr*-BOAT
prominent (eminent)	hervorragend	*hehr*-FOR-*rahg-ent*
promise (pledge)	Versprechen, n.	*fehr*-SHPREHKH-*en*
promise (pledge), to	versprechen	*fehr*-SHPREHKH-*en*
prompt (quick)	unverzüglich	OONN-*fehr*-TSUG-*likh*
proper (acceptable)	geziehmend	*guh*-TSEE-*ment*
property (possession)	Eigentum, n.	EYE-*gen-toom*
propose (suggest), to	vorschlagen	FOR-*shlah-gen*
prosperity	Wohlstand, m.	VOHL-*shtahnnt*

ENGLISH	GERMAN	PRONUNCIATION
prosperous	gedeihlich	*guh*-DYE-*likh*
protect, to	schützen	SHÜTT-*sen*
proud (taking pride in)	stolz	SHTAWLLTS
prove (verify), to	beweisen	*buh*-VIZE-*en*
prune	Backpflaume, f.	BAHK-*pflow-muh*
public (common, adj.)	öffentlich	ÖFF-*ent-likh*
publication (published work)	Veröffenlichung, f.	*fehr*-ÖFF-*ent-likh-oong*
publish, to	herausgeben	*hehr*-OWSS-*gay-ben*
publisher	Verleger, m.	*fehr*-LAY-*gehr*
pudding (dessert)	Pudding, m.	POOD-*ing*
pull (draw), to	ziehen	TSEE-*en*
punctual	pünktlich	PUNKT-*likh*
punish, to	strafen	SHTRAH-*fen*
punishment	Strafe, f.	SHTRAH-*fuh*
pupil (student)	Schüler, m.	SHÜ-*lehr*
purchase (act of buying)	Kauf, m.	KOWF
pure (unadulterated)	rein	RINE
purpose (aim)	Absicht, f.	AHPP-*zikht*
purse (coin pouch)	Geldbeutel, m.	GELT-*boy-tel*
pursue (chase), to	verfolgen	*fehr*-FAWLL-*gen*
push (shove), to	stossen	SHTOH-*sen*
put (place), to	stellen	SHTELL-*en*
quaint (unusual)	seltsam	ZELLT-*zahm*
quantity (amount)	Menge, f.	MENNG-*uh*
quarrel (dispute)	Streit, m.	SHTRITE
quarrel (dispute), to	streiten	SHTRYE-*ten*
quarter (one-fourth)	Viertel, n.	FEERR-*tel*
queen	Königin, f.	KÖ-*nig-in*
queer	sonderbar	ZAWNN-*dehr-bar*
question (query)	Frage, f.	FRAH-*guh*
question (doubt), to	bezweifeln	*buh*-TSVYE-*feln*
question (query), to	befragen	*buh*-FRAHG-*en*
quick (rapid)	schnell	SHNELL

ENGLISH	GERMAN	PRONUNCIATION
quiet (silent, adj.)	still	SHTILL
quiet (stillness)	Ruhe, f.	ROO-*uh*
quite (considerably)	ganz	GAHNNTS
rabbi	Rabbiner, m.	*rah*-BEE-*nehr*
rabbit	Kaninchen, n.	*kah*-NEEN-*khen*
race (contest)	Wettlauf, m.	VET-*lowf*
radiator (heater)	Heizkörper, m.	HITES-*kör-pehr*
radio (receiving set)	Radio, n.	RAHD-*yoh*
rag (piece of cloth)	Lumpen, m.	LOOM-*pen*
rail (bar on track)	Schiene, f.	SHEE-*nuh*
railroad	Eisenbahn, f.	EYE-*zen-bahn*
rain	Regen, m.	RAY-*gen*
rain, to	regnen	RAYG-*nen*
rainbow	Regenbogen, m.	RAY-*gen-boh-gen*
raincoat	Regenmantel, m.	RAY-*gen-mahnn-tel*
rainy	regnerisch	RAYG-*nuh-rish*
raisin	Rosine, f.	*roh*-ZEE-*nuh*
range (of mountains)	Bergkette, f.	BEHRK-*ket-tuh*
rapid (adj.)	schnell	SHNELL
rare (uncommon)	selten	ZELL-*ten*
raspberry	Himmbeere, f.	HIMM-*bay-ruh*
rat	Ratte, f.	RAHTT-*tuh*
rate (degree of speed)	Geschwindigkeit, f.	*guh*-SHVINN-*dick-kite*
rate (exchange)	Kurs, m.	KOORRSS
rather (somewhat)	ziemlich	TSEEM-*likh*
raw (in natural state)	roh	ROH
ray (beam)	Strahl, m.	SHTRAHL
rayon	Kunstseide, f.	KOONST-*zye-duh*
razor	Rasiermesser, n.	*rah*-ZEER-*mess-ehr*
razor blade	Rasierklinge, f.	*rah*-ZEER-*kling-uh*
reach (arrive at), to	erreichen	*ehr*-RYE-*khen*
read, to	lesen	LAY-*zen*
ready (prepared)	bereit	*buh*-RITE

ENGLISH	GERMAN	PRONUNCIATION
real (actual)	wirklich	VEERR-*klikh*
really (actually)	wirklich	VEERR-*klikh*
reason (ground)	Grund, m.	GROONNT
reason (intellect)	Vernunft, f.	*fehr*-NOONNFT
reasonable (rational)	vernünftig	*fehr*-NÜNF-*tick*
recall (remember), to	sich erinnern	*zikh* ehr-IN-*ehrn*
receipt (voucher)	Quittung, f.	KVITT-*toong*
recent	neu	NOY
recently	unlängst	OONN-*lengst*
recipe	Rezept, n.	*ray*-TSEPT
reckon (compute), to	rechnen	REHKH-*nen*
recognition (acknowledgement)	Anerkennung, f.	AHNN-*ehr-ken-noong*
recognize (identify), to	wiedererkennen	VEE-*dehr-ehr-ken-nen*
recommend (advise), to	empfehlen	emp-FAY-*len*
recommendation	Empfehlung, f.	emp-FAY-*loong*
recover (get well), to	sich erholen	*zikh* ehr-HOLE-*en*
red	rot	ROHT
refer (allude), to	sich beziehen	*zikh* buh-TSEE-*en*
reference (allusion)	Verweisung, f.	*fehr*-VIE-*zoong*
reflection (meditation)	Überlegung, f.	*ü-behr*-LAY-*goong*
refresh, to	erfrischen	ehr-FRISH-*shen*
refreshments	Erfrischungen, f.	ehr-FRISH-*shoong-en*
refrigerator	Eisschrank, m.	ICE-*shrahnk*
regard (consider), to	betrachten	*buh*-TRAHKH-*ten*
regarding (concerning)	betreffs	*buh*-TREFFS
region (area)	Gegend, f.	GAY-*gent*
register, to	einschreiben	INE-*shribe-en*
registered (postal designation)	eingeschrieben	INE-*guh-shree-ben*

ENGLISH	GERMAN	PRONUNCIATION
regret, to	bedauern	*buh-*DOW*-ehrn*
regular (normal)	regelmässig	RAY*-gel-may-sick*
reimburse, to	entschädigen	*ent-*SHAY*-dih-gen*
related (connected)	verwandt	*fehr-*VAHNNT
relation (connection)	Beziehung, f.	*buh-*TSEE*-oong*
relative (kinsman)	Verwandte, m., f.	*fehr-*VAHNNT*-tuh*
reliable	zuverlassig	TSOO*-fehr-less-ick*
relieve (ease), to	erleichtern	*ehr-*LYEKH*-tehrn*
religion	Religion, f.	*ray-lig-*YOHN
religious (adj.)	religiös	*ray-lig-*YÖS
remain (be left), to	übrigbleiben	ÜB*-rick-blibe-en*
remain (stay behind), to	bleiben	BLIBE*-en*
remainder	Rest, m.	REST
remark (comment)	Bemerkung, f.	*buh-*MEHR*-koong*
remark (say), to	bemerken	*buh-*MEHR*-ken*
remedy	Hilfsmittel, n.	HILLFS*-mitt-tel*
remember (recollect), to	sich erinnern	*zikh ehr-*IN*-ehrn*
remind, to	erinnern	*ehr-*IN*-ehrn*
remit (send payment), to	überweisen	*ü-behr-*VIZE*-en*
remittance	(Geld)Sendung, f.	(GELLT-)ZENN*-doong*
remote (far-off)	entlegen	*ent-*LAY*-gen*
remove (take away), to	beseitigen	*buh-*ZITE*-tih-gen*
renew, to	erneuern	*ehr-*NOY*-ehrn*
rent (payment)	Miete, f.	MEE*-tuh*
rent (charge rent for), to	vermieten	*fehr-*MEE*-ten*
rent (pay rent for), to	mieten	MEE*-ten*
repair (fix), to	ausbessern	OWSS*-bess-ehrn*
repay (reimburse), to	zurückzahlen	*tsoo-*RÜCK*-tsah-len*
repeat (reiterate), to	wiederholen	*vee-dehr-*HOLE*-en*

ENGLISH	GERMAN	PRONUNCIATION
repent, to	bereuen	*buh-*ROY-*en*
reply	Erwiderung, f.	*ehr-*VEE-*duh-roong*
reply, to	erwidern	*ehr-*VEE-*dehrn*
represent (act for), to	vertreten	*fehr-*TRAY-*ten*
representation (pol.)	Vertretung, f.	*fehr-*TRAY-*toong*
representative (deputy)	Vertreter, m.	*fehr-*TRAY-*tehr*
reproach	Vorwurf, m.	FOR-*voorrf*
reproach, to	vorwerfen	FOR-*vehr-fen*
reputation	Ruf, m.	ROOF
request	Bitte, f.	BIT-*tuh*
request, to	ersuchen	*ehr-*ZOO-*khen*
resemble, to	ähneln	AY-*neln*
reserve (order in advance), to	vorausbestellen	*for-*OWSS-*buh-stell-en*
residence (abode)	Wohnsitz, m.	VOHN-*zitts*
resident (n.)	Ansässige, m., f.	AHNN-*zess-egg-uh*
resist, to	widerstehen	*vee-dehr-*SHTAY-*en*
resistance	Widerstand, m.	VEE-*dehr-shtahnnt*
resort (spa)	Kurort, m.	KOOR-*ort*
respect (esteem)	Achtung, f.	AHKH-*toong*
respect (esteem), to	achten	AHKH-*ten*
respectable	anständig	AHNN-*shten-dick*
respective (adj.)	jeweilig	YAY-*vile-ick*
respond (reply), to	antworten	AHNNT-*vor-ten*
response (reply)	Antwort, f.	AHNNT-*vort*
responsibility (accountablility)	Verantwortung, f.	*fehr-*AHNNT-*vort-toong*
responsible (answerable)	verantwortlich	*fehr-*AHNNT-*vort-likh*
rest (remainder)	Rest, m.	REST
rest (repose)	Ruhe, f.	ROO-*uh*
rest (repose), to	ruhen	ROO-*en*
restaurant	Restaurant, n.	*ress-toh-*RAHNG
result (consequence)	Ergebnis, n.	*ehr-*GAPE-*niss*

ENGLISH	GERMAN	PRONUNCIATION
retire (stop working), to	sich zurückziehen	*zikh* tsoo-RÜCK-*tsee-en*
return (coming or going back)	Rückkehr, f.	RÜCK-*kair*
return (give back), to	zurückgeben	*tsoo*-RUCK-*gay-ben*
return (go back), to	zurückkehren	*tsoo*-RÜCK-*kay-ren*
reverence (respect)	Verehrung, f.	*fehr*-AIR-*oong*
revolution (pol.)	Revolution, f.	*ray-voh-loots-*YOHN
reward (recompense)	Belohnung, f.	*buh*-LOAN-*oong*
reward, to	belohnen	*buh*-LOAN-*en*
rheumatism	Rheumatismus, m.	*roy-mah*-TISS-*mooss*
rib	Rippe, f.	RIP-*puh*
ribbon	Band, n.	BAHNNT
rice	Reis, m.	RICE
riches	Reichtum, m.	RYEKH-*toom*
ride (in a car)	Fahrt, f.	FAHRRT
ride (in a car), to	fahren	FAH-*ren*
ridiculous	lächerlich	LEHKH-*ehr-likh*
right (correct)	richtig	RIKH-*tick*
right (on the right, adj.)	recht	REHKHT
right (right-hand side)	Rechte, f.	REHKHT-*tuh*
right (to the right, adv.)	rechts	REHKHTS
ring (jewelry)	Ring, m.	RING
ring (resound), to	klingen	KLINNG-*en*
ripe	reif	RIFE
rise (ascend), to	steigen	SHTYE-*gen*
rise (stand up), to	aufstehen	OWF-*shtay-en*
risk (danger)	Gefahr, f.	*guh*-FAR
river	Fluss, m.	FLOOSS
road	Strasse, f.	SHTRAH-*suh*
roast	Braten, m.	BRAH-*ten*

ENGLISH	GERMAN	PRONUNCIATION
roast (be roasted), to	sich braten	*zikh* BRAH-*ten*
rob (steal from), to	berauben	*buh*-ROWB-*en*
robber	Räuber, m.	ROY-*behr*
robe (dressing gown)	Schlafrock, m.	SHLAHF-*rawck*
rock (large stone)	Felsen, m.	FELL-*zen*
rocky (rock-covered)	felsig	FELL-*zikh*
role	Rolle, f.	RAWLL-*luh*
roll (bread)	Brötchen, n.	BRÖT-*khen*
romantic	romantisch	*roh*-MAHNN-*tish*
roof	Dach, n.	DAHKH
room (of house)	Zimmer, n.	TSIMM-*mehr*
room (space)	Raum, m.	ROWM
rope	Tau, n.	TOW
rotten (decayed)	faul	FOWL
rouge	Schminke, f.	SHMINN-*kuh*
rough (harsh)	grob	GRAWPP
rough (uneven)	rauh	ROW
round (adj.)	round	ROONNT
rouse (awaken), to	wecken	VECK-*en*
royal	königlich	KÖ-*nig-likh*
rubber	Gummi, n.	GOOMM-*ee*
rubbers (overshoes)	Gummischuhe, pl.	GOOMM-*ee-shoo-uh*
rubbish (litter)	Abfall, m.	AHPP-*fahll*
rude (impolite)	grob	GRAWPP
rug	Teppich, m.	TEPP-*ikh*
ruins (remains)	Ruine, f.	*roo*-EE-*nuh*
rule (regulation)	Regel, f.	RAY-*gel*
rule (govern), to	herrschen	HEHRR-*shen*
ruler (measuring instrument)	Lineal, n.	*lenn*-YAHL
run (extent), to	sich erstrecken	*zikh ehr*-SHTRECK-*en*
run (flow), to	fliessen	FLEE-*sen*
run (sprint), to	rennen	REN-*nen*
rural	ländlich	LEND-*likh*

ENGLISH	GERMAN	PRONUNCIATION
rush (dash), to	sich stürzen	*zikh* SHTUR-*tsen*
Russian (adj.)	russisch	ROOSS-*ish*
rust	Rost, m.	RAWSST
rusty	rostig	RAWSS-*tick*
sack (bag)	Sack, m.	ZAHCK
sacred	heilig	HYE-*lick*
sad (sorrowful)	traurig	TROW-*rick*
sadness	Schwermut, f.	SHVAIR-*moot*
safe (unharmed)	heil	HILE
safe (without risk)	sicher	ZIKH-*ehr*
safety (n.)	Sicherheit, f.	ZIKH-*ehr-hite*
safety pin	Sicherheitsnadel, f.	ZIKH-*ehr-hites-nah-del*
saint	Heilige, m., f.	HILE-*ee-guh*
salad	Salat, m.	*zah-*LAHT
sale (exchange)	Verkauf, m.	*fehr-*KOWF
salesman	Verkäufer, m.	*fehr-*KOY-*fehr*
salmon	Lachs, m.	LAHKHS
salt	Salz, n.	ZAHLLTS
same (adj.)	der-, die-, dasselbe	DAIR-, DEE-, DAHSS- ZEHL-*buh*
sample	Muster, n.	MOOSS-*tehr*
sandwich	Butterbrot, n.	BOOTT-*tehr-broht*
sane	vernünftig	*fehr-*NÜNF-*tick*
satin	Atlas, m.	AHT-*lahss*
satisfactory	befriedigend	*buh-*FREE-*dee-gent*
satisfied (contented)	zufrieden	*tsoo-*FREE-*den*
satisfy, to	befriedigen	*buh-*FREE-*dee-gen*
saucer	Untertasse, f.	OONN-*tehr-tahss-suh*
sausage	Wurst, f.	VOORRST
save (rescue), to	retten	RET-*ten*
save (store up), to	sparen	SHPAH-*ren*
savings (money)	Ersparnis, n.	*ehr-*SHPAHR-*niss*
saw (tool)	Säge, f.	ZAY-*guh*

ENGLISH	GERMAN	PRONUNCIATION
say, to	sagen	ZAH-*gen*
scarce	knapp	KNAHPP
scare (frighten), to	erschrecken	*ehr*-SHRECK-*en*
scarf (neck cloth)	Schal, m.	SHAHL
scarlet (adj.)	scharlachrot	SHAHRR-*lahkh-rote*
scarlet fever	Scharlachfiieber, n.	SHAHRR-*lahkh-fee-behr*
scene (dramatic unit)	Auftritt, m.	OWF-*tritt*
scent (odor)	Geruch, m.	*guh*-ROOKH
schedule (timetable)	Stundenplan, m.	SHTOONN-*den-plahn*
school	Schule, f.	SHOO-*luh*
schooling (instruction)	Schulunterricht, m.	SHOOL-*oonn-tehr-rikht*
science	Wissenschaft, f.	VISS-*en-shahfft*
scientific	wissenschaftlich	VISS-*en-shahfft-likh*
scissors	Schere, f.	SHAY-*ruh*
Scotch (adj.)	schottisch	SHAWTT-*ish*
scrambled eggs	Rührei, n.	RÜR-*eye*
scrap (fragment)	Brocken, m.	BRAWCK-*en*
scratch, to	kratzen	KRAHTT-*sen*
screen (partition)	Schirm, m.	SHEERM
screw	Schraube, f.	SHROW-*buh*
screw driver	Schraubenzieher, m.	SHROW-*ben-tsee-ehr*
scrub, to	scheuern	SHOY-*ehrn*
sculptor	Bildhauer, m.	BILLT-*how-ehr*
sea	Meer, n.	MAIR
search (hunt)	Suche, f.	ZOOKH-*uh*
season (of year)	Jahreszeit, f.	YAH-*ress-tsite*
second (adj.)	zweite	TSVYE-*tuh*
second (time unit)	Sekunde, f.	*zay*-KOONN-*duh*
secret (n.)	Geheimnis, n.	*guh*-HIME-*niss*

ENGLISH	GERMAN	PRONUNCIATION
secretary (stenographer)	Sekretärin, f.	*zeck-ray-*TAIR-*een*
secure (safe)	sicher	ZIKH-*ehr*
security (safety)	Sicherheit, f.	ZIKH-*ehr-hite*
seldom	selten	ZELL-*ten*
select, to	wählen	VAY-*len*
selection (things chosen)	Auswahl, f.	OWWSS-*vahl*
sell, to	verkaufen	*fehr-*KOW-*fen*
send, to	senden	ZENN-*den*
sense (intelligence)	Vernunft, f.	*fehr-*NOONNFT
sense (signification)	Sinn, m.	ZINN
sensible (reasonable)	vernünftig	*fehr-*NÜNF-*tick*
sensitive (susceptible)	empfindlich	*emp-*FINND-*likh*
sentence (gram.)	Satz, m.	ZAHTTS
separate	getrennt	*guh-*TRENT
separate (disconnect), to	trennen	TRENN-*en*
series	Reihe, f.	RYE-*uh*
serious	ernst	EHRNST
servant (in a household)	Dienstbote, m.	DEENST-*boh-tuh*
serve, to	dienen	DEE-*nen*
service	Dienst, m.	DEENST
set (put), to	setzen	ZET-*zen*
settle (agree on), to	abmachen	AHPP-*mahkh-en*
several (a few, adj.)	mehrere	MAY-*ruh-ruh*
severe (strict)	streng	SHTRENG
sew, to	nähen	NAY-*en*
sewing machine	Nähmaschine, f.	NAY-*mah-shee-nuh*
sex	Geschlecht, n.	*guh-*SHLEHKHT
shade (window blind)	Rouleau, n.	*roo-*LOH

ENGLISH	GERMAN	PRONUNCIATION
shadow	Schatten, m.	SHAHTT-*en*
shake, to	schütteln	SHÜTT-*teln*
shallow	seicht	ZYEKHT
shame	Schande, f.	SHAHNN-*duh*
shape (contour)	Form, f.	FORM
share, to	teilen	TIE-*len*
sharp	scharf	SHAHRRF
shave (oneself), to	sich rasieren	*zikh rah-*ZEE-*ren*
shaver, electric	elektrischer Rasierapparat	*eh-*LECK-*trish-ehr rah-*ZEER-*ahp-pah-raht*
shaving cream	Rasiercreme, f.	*rah-*ZEER-*kray-muh*
she	sie	ZEE
sheet (bedding)	Bettuch, n.	BET-*tookh*
sheet (of paper)	Bogen, m.	BOH-*gen*
shelf	Fach, n.	FAHKH
shell (covering)	Schale, f.	SHAH-*luh*
shine (gleam), to	glänzen	GLENNT-*sen*
shine (polish), to	blank putzen	BLAHNNK POOTT-*sen*
ship	Schiff, n.	SHIFF
ship (send goods), to	versenden	*fehr-*ZEND-*en*
shipping agent	Spediteur, m.	*shpay-dee-*TÖR
shirt	Hemd, n.	HEMMT
shoe (footwear)	Schuh, m.	SHOO
shoemaker	Schuster, m.	SHOOSS-*tehr*
shop (store)	Laden, m.	LAH-*den*
shop, to	einkaufen	INE-*kow-fen*
shore	Ufer, n.	OO-*fehr*
short (brief)	kurz	KOORTS
shoulder	Schulter, f.	SHOOLL-*tehr*
show (exhibit)	Ausstellung, f.	OWSS-*shtell-oong*
show (make visible), to	zeigen	TSYE-*gen*
shower (bath)	Dusche, f.	DOO-*shuh*

ENGLISH	GERMAN	PRONUNCIATION
shower (rainfall)	Regenschauer, m.	RAY-*gen-show-ehr*
shrill	schrill	SHRILL
shrimp	Garnele, f.	*gar*-NAY-*luh*
shudder, to	schaudern	SHOW-*dehrn*
shut (make close), to	schliessen	SHLEE-*sen*
shy (bashful)	schüchtern	SHÜKH-*tehrn*
sick (ailing)	krank	KRAHNNK
sickness	Krankheit, f.	KRAHNNK-*hite*
side	Seite, f.	ZITE-*tuh*
sidewalk	Bürgersteig, m.	BUR-*gehr-shtike*
sigh, to	seufzen	ZOYF-*tsen*
sight (eyesight)	Sehkraft, f.	ZAY-*krahfft*
sight (spectacle)	Anblick, m.	AHNN-*blick*
sign (indication)	Zeichen, n.	TSYE-*khen*
sign (endorse), to	unterschreiben	OONN-*tehr*-SHRIBE-*en*
signature (name)	Unterschrift, f.	OONN-*tehr-shrift*
silk	Seide, f.	ZIDE-*uh*
silly	albern	AHLL-*behrn*
silver	Silber, n.	ZILL-*behr*
similar	ähnlich	AYN-*likh*
similarity	Ähnlichkeit, f.	AYN-*likh-kite*
simple (uninvolved)	einfach	INE-*fahkh*
since (after, prep.)	seit	ZITE
since (because, conj.)	da	DAH
since (from then to now, adv.)	seitdem	*zite*-DAME
sing, to	singen	ZING-*en*
single (unmarried)	ledig	LAY-*dick*
singular (peculiar)	einzigartig	INE-*tsick-ahr-tick*
sink (n.)	Ausguss, m.	OWSS-*gooss*
sir	Herr, m.	HEHRR
sister (n.)	Schwester, f.	SHVESS-*tehr*
sister-in-law	Schwägerin, f.	SHVAY-*guh-rin*

ENGLISH	GERMAN	PRONUNCIATION
sit (be sitting), to	sitzen	ZITT-*sen*
sit down, to	sich setzen	*zikh* ZET-*sen*
size (of hats)	Grösse, f.	GRÖ-*suh*
size (of shoes, gloves)	Grösse, f.	GRÖ-*suh*
size (of suits, dresses, coats)	Grösse, f.	GRÖ-*suh*
skate(ice)	Schlittschuh, m.	SHLITT-*shoo*
ski, to	skilaufen	SHEE-*low-fen*
skin (animal hide)	Fell, n.	FELL
skin (human skin)	Haut, f.	HOWT
skirt (garment)	Rock, m.	RAWCK
sky	Himmel, m.	HIMM-*mel*
skyscraper	Wolkenkratzer, m.	VAWLL-*ken-krahtt-sehr*
sled	Schlitten, m.	SHLITT-*en*
sleep	Schlaf, m.	SHLAHFF
sleep, to	schlafen	SHLAH-*fen*
sleeve	Armel, m.	EHR-*mel*
slide, to	gleiten	GLITE-*en*
slipper	Hausschuh, m.	HOWSS-*shoo*
slippery	schlüpfrig	SHLÜPP-*frick*
slow (not fast)	langsam	LAHNNG-*zahm*
smallpox	Blattern, f. pl.	BLAHTT-*ehrn*
smell (odor)	Geruch, m.	*guh*-ROOKH
smell (perceive odor), to	riechen	REE-*khen*
smile	Lächeln, n.	LEHKH-*eln*
smile, to	lächeln	LEHKH-*eln*
smoke	Rauch, m.	ROWKH
smoke, to	rauchen	ROWKH-*en*
smooth (adj.)	glatt	GLAHTT
snail	Schnecke, f.	SHNECK-*kuh*
sneeze, to	niesen	NEE-*zen*
snow	Schnee, m.	SHNAY
so (in order that, conj.)	damit	*dah*-MITT

ENGLISH	GERMAN	PRONUNCIATION
so (therefore, adv.)	also	AHLL-*zoh*
soap	Seife, f.	ZIFE-*uh*
social (societal)	gesellschaftlich	guh-ZELL-*shaft-likh*
society (association)	Gesellschaft, f.	guh-ZELL-*shahfft*
sock (garment)	Socke, f.	ZAWCK-*uh*
soft (not hard)	weich	VYEKH
soil (make dirty), to	beschmutzen	buh-SHMOOTT-*sen*
sole (of shoe)	Sohle, f.	ZOH-*luh*
solemn (grave)	feierlich	FIRE-*likh*
solution (solving)	Lösung, f.	LÖ-*zoong*
solve, to	lösen	LÖ-*zen*
some (a few, adj.)	einige	INE-*ee-guh*
some (unspecified, adj.)	irgend ein	EAR-*gent-ine*
some (a quantity, pron.)	etwas	ETT-*vahss*
some (a quantity of, adj.)	etwas	ETT-*vahss*
somebody	jemand	YAY-*mahnt*
somehow	irgendwie	EERR-*gent-vee*
someone	jemand	YAY-*mahnt*
something	etwas	ETT-*vahss*
son	Sohn, m.	ZONE
song	Lied, n.	LEET
son-in-law	Schwiegersohn, m.	SHVEE-*gehr-zohn*
soon	bald	BAHLLT
sore throat	Halsweh, n.	HAHLLSS-*vay*
sorrow (sadness)	Kummer, m.	KOOMM-*ehr*
sorry, to be	bedauern	buh-DOW-*ehrn*
sort	Sorte, f.	ZAWR-*tuh*
sound (healthy)	gesund	guh-ZOONNT
sound (noise)	Laut, m.	LOWT
soup	Suppe, f.	SOOPP-*uh*
sour (tart)	sauer	ZOW-*ehr*
south (n.)	Süden, m.	ZÜ-*den*

ENGLISH	GERMAN	PRONUNCIATION
southern	südlich	ZÜD-*likh*
space (area)	Raum, m.	ROWM
Spanish (adj.)	spanisch	SHPAH-*nish*
spark	Funke, m.	FOONG-*kuh*
speak (talk), to	sprechen	SHPREHKH-*en*
special	besonder	*buh*-ZAWNN-*dehr*
spectacles (glasses)	Brille, f.	BRILL-*uh*
speed (rapidity)	Geschwindigkeit, f.	*guh*-SHVINN-*dick-kite*
spell, to	buchstabieren	*bookh-shtah*-BEE-*ren*
spirit	Geist, m.	GUYST
spit, to	spucken	SHPOOCK-*en*
spoon (tablespoon)	Esslöffel, m.	ESS-*löff-el*
spoon (teaspoon)	Teelöffel, m.	TAY-*löff-el*
sport (game)	Sport, m.	SHPAWRT
spot (place)	Stelle, f.	SHTELL-*uh*
spot (stain)	Fleck, m.	FLECK
sprain, to	verrenken	*fehr*-RENG-*ken*
square (adj.)	quadratisch	*kvad*-DRAH-*tish*
square (plaza)	Platz, m.	PLAHTTS
squirrel	Eichhörnchen, n.	EYEKH-*hörn-khen*
staff (personnel)	Personal, n.	*pehr-zoh*-NAHL
stage (dais)	Bühne, f.	BÜ-*nuh*
stain	Fleck, m.	FLECK
stairway	Treppe, f.	TREPP-*puh*
stale	altbacken	AHLLT-*bahk-ken*
stall (stop going), to	aussetzen	OWSS-*zett-sen*
stamp (postage)	Marke, f.	MAHRR-*kuh*
stand (bear), to	ertragen	*ehr*-TRAH-*gen*
stand (be upright), to	stehen	SHTAY-*en*
stand up, to	aufstehen	OWF-*shtay-en*
star	Stern, m.	SHTEHRN
start (beginning)	Anfang, m.	AHNN-*fahnng*
start (initiate), to	anfangen	AHNN-*fahnng-en*

ENGLISH	GERMAN	PRONUNCIATION
starve (die of hunger), to	verhungern	*fehr*-HOONNG-*ehrn*
state (condition)	Zustand, m.	TSOO-*shtahnnt*
station, railroad	Bahnhof, m.	BAHN-*hohf*
stationery (writing paper)	Schreibpapier, n.	SHRIPE-*pah*-PEER
statue	Bildsäule, f.	BILLT-*zoy-luh*
stay (sojourn)	Aufenthalt, m.	OWF-*ent-hahlt*
stay (remain), to	bleiben	BLIBE-*en*
steal, to	stehlen	SHTAY-*len*
steam	Dampf, m.	DAHMMPF
steep (adj.)	steil	SHTILE
step	Stufe, f.	SHTOO-*fuh*
step (stride)	Schritt, m.	SHRITT
steward (attendant on ship)	Steward, m.	SHTOO-*art*
stick (small branch)	Stock, m.	SHTAWCK
stick (adhere), to	kleben	KLAY-*ben*
still (adv.)	noch	NAWKH
still (motionless, adj.)	ruhig	ROO-*ick*
stocking	Strumpf, m.	SHTROOMPF
stomach	Magen, m.	MAH-*gen*
stone (piece of rock)	Stein, m.	SHTINE
stop (halt)	Halt, m.	HAHLLT
stop (cease), to	aufhören	OWF-*hö-ren*
stop (come to a stand-still), to	anhalten	AHNN-*hahl-ten*
store (shop)	Laden, m.	LAH-*den*
storm	Sturm, m.	SHTOORM
story (account)	Geschichte, f.	*guh*-SHIKH-*tuh*
story (floor)	Stockwerk, n.	SHTAWCK-*vehrk*
stove (for cooking)	Herd, m.	HEHRT
strange (peculiar)	seltsam	ZELLT-*zahm*
strawberry	Erdbeere, f.	AIRT-*bay-ruh*
stream (rivulet)	Strom, m.	SHTROHM

ENGLISH	GERMAN	PRONUNCIATION
street	Strasse, f.	SHTRAH-*suh*
strength	Kraft, f.	KRAHFFT
stretch (draw out), to	ausdehnen	OWSS-*day-nen*
string (cord)	Schnur, f.	SHNOOR
strip (band)	Streifen, m.	SHTRYE-*fen*
stroll, to	schlendern	SHLENN-*dehrn*
strong	stark	SHTARK
structure (thing built)	Bau, m.	BOW
stubborn	hartnäckig	HAHRT-*neck-ick*
student	Student, m.	*shtoo*-DENT
study (active learning)	Studium, n.	SHTOOD-*yoomm*
study, to	studieren	*shtoo*-DEE-*ren*
stupid	dumm	DOOMM
style (manner)	Stiel, m.	SHTEEL
subject (topic)	Gegenstand, m.	GAY-*gen-shtahnt*
subscription (for periodicals, etc.)	Abonnement, n.	*ah-bawnn-ay-*MAHNG
subsequent	folgend	FAWLL-*gent*
substitute (thing replacing another)	Ersatzmittel, n.	*ehr*-ZAHTTS-*mitt-el*
substitute (put in place of), to	an die Stelle setzen	*ahn dee* SHTELL-*uh zett-sen*
subtract, to	abziehen	AHPP-*tsee-en*
subway (underground railway)	Untergrundbahn, f.	OONN-*tehr-groont-bahn*
succeed (attain goal), to	Erfolg haben	*ehr*-FAWLLK *hah-ben*
success (attainment)	Erfolg, m.	*ehr*-FAWLLK
successful	erfolgreich	*ehr*-FAWLLG-*ryekh*
such (of that kind, adj.)	solch	ZOHLKH
sudden (unexpected)	plötzlich	PLÖTTS-*likh*

ENGLISH	GERMAN	PRONUNCIATION
sue (bring action against), to	verklagen	*fehr*-KLAHG-*en*
suede (n.)	Ziegenleder, n.	TSEE-*gen-lay-dehr*
suffer (undergo), to	leiden	LYE-*den*
sugar	Zucker, m.	TSOOCK-*ehr*
suggestion (proposal)	Vorschlag, m.	FOR-*shlahk*
suit (lawsuit)	Prozess, m.	*pro*-TSESS
suit, man's	Anzug, m.	AHNN-*tsook*
suit, woman's	Kostüm, n.	*kawss*-TÜM
summer (n.)	Sommer, m.	ZAWMM-*ehr*
summit	Gipfel, m.	GIPP-*fel*
sun	Sonne, f.	ZAWNN-*uh*
sunburn	Sonnenbrand, m.	ZAWNN-*en-brahnnt*
sunglasses	Sonnenbrille, f.	ZAWNN-*en-brill-uh*
sunlight	Sonnenlicht, n.	ZAWNN-*en-likht*
sunny	sonnig	ZAWNN-*ick*
sunrise	Sonnenaufgang, m.	ZAWNN-*en-owf-gahnng*
sunset	Sonnenuntergang, m.	ZAWNN-*en-oonn-tehr-gahnng*
sunshine	Sonnenschein, m.	ZAWNN-*en-shine*
superstition	Aberglaube, m.	AH-*behr-glow-buh*
supply (provide), to	versehen	*fehr*-ZAY-*en*
surgeon	Chirurg, m.	*khee*-ROORRK
surname	Zuname, m.	TSOO-*nah-muh*
surprise	Uberraschung, f.	Ü-*behr*-RAHSH-*oong*
surprise (astonish), to	überraschen	Ü-*behr*-RAHSH-*en*
surroundings	Umgebung, f.	*oomm*-GAY-*boong*
suspect (distrust), to	beargwöhnen	*buh*-ARG-*vö-nen*
suspenders	Hosenträger, m. pl.	HOH-*zen-tray-gehr*
suspicion	Verdacht, m.	*fehr*-DAHKHT

ENGLISH	GERMAN	PRONUNCIATION
swallow, to	schlucken	SHLOOCK-*en*
swear (curse), to	fluchen	FLOO-*khen*
sweat	Schweiss, m.	SHVICE
sweater	Sweater, m.	SVAY-*tehr*
Swedish (adj.)	schwedisch	SHVAY-*dish*
sweep (clean), to	fegen	FAY-*gen*
sweet (pleasant tasting)	süss	ZÜSS
sweetheart	Liebchen, n.	LEEP-*khen*
swim, to	schwimmen	SHVIMM-*men*
Swiss (adj.)	schweizerisch	SHVITE-*suh-rish*
syllable	Silbe, f.	ZILL-*buh*
sympathy (compassion)	Mitgefühl, n.	MITT-*guh-fül*
table (furniture)	Tisch, m.	TISH
tablecloth	Tischtuch, n.	TISH-*tookh*
tailor	Schneider, m.	SHNYE-*dehr*
take, to	nehmen	NAY-*men*
talk (conversation)	Gespräch, n.	*guh*-SPREHKH
talk, to	reden	RAY-*den*
tall (of persons)	gross	GROHSS
tall (of things)	hoch	HOHKH
tap (faucet)	Hahn, m.	HAHN
tape recorder	Bandregistrierap-parat, n.	BAHNNT-*ray-geess-treer-ah-pah*-RAHT
tariff (duty)	Zoll, m.	TSAWLL
taste (flavor)	Geschmack, m.	*guh*-SHMAHCK
taste (sample), to	kosten	KAWSS-*ten*
tax (n.)	Steuer, f.	SHTOY-*ehr*
taxi	Taxi, n.	TAHCK-*see*
tea	Tee, m.	TAY
teach, to	lehren	LAY-*ren*
teacher	Lehrer, m.	LAY-*rehr*
tear (rip), to	reissen	RYE-*sen*
tease, to	necken	NECK-*en*

ENGLISH	GERMAN	PRONUNCIATION
telegraph, to	telegraphieren	*tay-luh-grah-*FEE-*ren*
telephone	Fernsprecher, m.	FEHRN-*sprehkh-ehr*
telephone, to	anrufen	AHNN-*roo-fen*
television	Fernsehen, n.	FEHRN-*zay-en*
tell (inform), to	sagen	ZAH-*gen*
temperature	Temperatur, f.	*temm-puh-rah-*TOOR
temporary	vorläufig	FOR-*loy-fick*
tenant	Mieter, m.	MEE-*tehr*
tent	Zelt, n.	TSELT
term (duration)	Frist, f.	FRISST
term (expression)	Ausdruck, m.	OWSS-*droock*
terms (conditions)	Bedingunger, f.	*buh-*DING-*oong-en*
terrible	schrecklich	SHRECK-*likh*
test (educ.)	Prüfung, f.	PRÜ-*foong*
testify, to	bezeugen	*buh-*TSOY-*gen*
testimony	Zeugnis, n.	TSOYK-*niss*
textile (n.)	Webwaren, f. pl.	VAPE-*vah-ren*
than	als	AHLLSS
thank, to	danken	DAHNNG-*ken*
thankful	dankbar	DAHNNK-*bar*
thanks (gratitude)	Dank, m.	DAHNNK
then (at that time)	dann	DAHNN
then (in that case)	dann	DAHNN
then (subsequently)	dann	DAHNN
there (at that place)	dort	DORT
therefore	daher	*dah-*HAIR
thick (not thin)	dick	DICK
thief	Dieb, m.	DEEP
thin (not fat)	mager	MAH-*gehr*
thin (not thick)	dünn	DÜNN
thing (material object)	Ding, n.	DING
think (reason), to	denken	DENG-*ken*

ENGLISH	GERMAN	PRONUNCIATION
thirst	Durst, m.	DOORSST
thirsty	durstig	DOORSST-*tick*
thorough (complete)	gründlich	GRÜNT-*likh*
thought (idea)	Gedanke, m.	*guh*-DAHNNG-*kuh*
thread (sewing thread)	Faden, m.	FAH-*den*
threaten, to	drohen	DROH-*en*
throat	Hals, m.	HAHLLSS
through (by means of, prep.)	durch	DOORRKH
through (from end to end of, prep.)	durch	DOORRKH
throw, to	werfen	VEHR-*fen*
thumb	Daumen, m.	DOW-*men*
thunder	Donner, m.	DAWNN-*ehr*
ticket (entitling card)	Karte, f.	KAHRR-*tuh*
tide, high	Flut, f.	FLOOT
tide, low	Ebbe, f.	EBB-*uh*
tie (necktie)	Krawatte, f.	*krah*-VAHTT-*tuh*
tie (fasten), to	binden	BINN-*den*
time (hour determined by clock)	Zeit, f.	TSITE
time (interval)	Zeit, f.	TSITE
timetable	Fahrplan, m.	FAR-*plahn*
tiny	winzig	VINT-*sick*
tip (gratuity)	Trinkgeld, n.	TRINK-*gelt*
tire	Reifen, m.	RYE-*fen*
tired	müde	MÜ-*duh*
title (name)	Uberschrift, f.	Ü-*behr-shrift*
to (indicating destination, prep.)	nach	NAHKH
to (indicating direction, prep.)	zu	TSOO
toast (bread)	geröstete Brotschnitte, f.	*guh*-RÖ-*shuh-tuh* BROHT-*shnitt-tuh*

ENGLISH	GERMAN	PRONUNCIATION
tobacco	Tabak, m.	TAH-*bahck*
today	heute	HOY-*tuh*
toe	Zehe, f.	TSAY-*uh*
together	zusammen	tsoo-ZAHMM-*en*
toilet (water closet)	Toilette, f.	tooah-LETT-*tuh*
tomorrow	morgen	MOR-*gen*
tongue (anat.)	Zunge, f.	TSOONNG-*uh*
tonight	heute abend	HOY-*tuh* AH-*bent*
too (also)	auch	OWKH
too (overly)	zu	TSOO
tooth	Zahn, m.	TSAHN
toothache	Zahnweh, n.	TSAHN-*vay*
toothbrush	Zahnbürste, f.	TSAHN-*bür-stuh*
tooth paste	Zahnpaste, f.	TSAHN-*pahss-tuh*
top (summit)	Gipfel, m.	GIPP-*fel*
total (complete)	gänzlich	GENTS-*likh*
total (sum)	Gesamtbetrag, m.	guh-ZAHMMT-*buh-trahk*
tough, to	berühren	buh-RU-*ren*
tour	Tour, f.	TOOR
toward	auf; zu	OWF; TSOO
towel, hand	Handtuch, n.	HAHNNT-*tookh*
town	Stadt, f.	SHTAHTT
toy	Spielzeug, n.	SHPEEL-*tsoyk*
track (rails)	Geleise, n.	guh-LYE-*zuh*
trade mark	Handelsmarke, f.	HAHNN-*delss-mahr-kuh*
traffic (flow of vehicles)	Verkehr. m.	fehr-KAIR
train, railroad	Zug, m.	TSOOK
training (instruction)	Erziehung, f.	ehr-TSEE-*oong*
transit (passage)	Transport, m.	trahnns-PORT
transport, to	befördern	buh-FÖR-*dehrn*
travel, to	reisen	RYE-*zen*
traveler	Reisende, m. f.	RYE-*zen-duh*
tray	Tablett, n.	tah-BLETT
treat (behave toward), to	behandeln	buh-HAHNN-*deln*

ENGLISH	GERMAN	PRONUNCIATION
treatment (behavior toward)	Behandlung, f.	*buh*-HAHNND-*loong*
treatment (medical care)	Behandlung, f.	*buh*-HAHNND-*loong*
tree	Baum, m.	BOWM
trial (court proceeding)	Gerichtsverhand-lung, f.	*guh*-RIKHTS-*fehr-hahnnd-loong*
trick (ruse)	Trick, m.	TRICK
trip (journey)	Reise, f.	RYE-*zuh*
trip (stumble), to	stolpern	SHTAWLL-*pehrn*
trolley (street car)	Strassenbahn, f.	SHTRAH-*sen-bahn*
trouble (distress)	Schwierigkeiten, f. pl.	SHVEE-*rick-kye-ten*
trouble (exertion)	Mühe, f.	MÜ-*uh*
trousers	Hose, f. pl.	HOH-*zuh*
truck	Lastwagen, m.	LAHSST-*vah-gen*
true	wahr	VAHR
trunk (baggage)	Koffer, m.	KAWFF-*fehr*
trust (confidence)	Vertrauen, m.	*fehr*-TROW-*en*
trust (rely on), to	vertrauen	*fehr*-TROW-*en*
truth	Wahrheit, f.	VAHR-*hite*
try (attempt), to	versuchen	*fehr*-ZOO-*khen*
tub (bathtub)	Wanne, f.	VAHNN-*nuh*
tuition (school fee)	Schulgeld, n.	SHOOL-*gelt*
tumbler (glass)	Becher, m.	BEHKH-*ehr*
tune (melody)	Melodie. f.	*may-loh*-DEE
turkey	Truthahn, m.	TROOT-*hahn*
turn (face about), to	sich umdrehen	*zikh* OOMM-*dray-en*
turn (make rotate), to	drehen	DRAY-*en*
tweed (cloth)	Tweed, m.	TWEED
twice	zweimal	TSVYE-*mahl*
twilight	Dämmerung, f.	DEM-*muh-roong*
twin (n.)	Zwilling, m.	TSVILL-*ing*
twist (wind), to	winden	VIN-*den*
type (kind)	Art, f.	ART

ENGLISH	GERMAN	PRONUNCIATION
type (typewrite), to	tippen	TIPP-*pen*
typewriter	Schreibmaschine, f.	SHRIBE-*mah-shee-nuh*
typhoid fever	Unterleibstyphus, m.	OONN-*tehr-lipes-tü-fooss*
ugly	hässlich	HESS-*likh*
ulcer	Geschwür, n.	*guh-*SHVÜR
umbrella	(Regen)Schirm, m.	(RAY-*gen-*)SHEERM
uncle	Onkel, m.	AWNG-*kel*
under (prep.)	unter	OONN-*tehr*
underground (belowground, adj.)	unterirdisch	OONN-*tehr-eerr-dish*
underneath (prep.)	unter	OONN-*tehr*
understand (comprehend), to	verstehen	*fehr-*SHTAY-*en*
underwear	Unterkleidung, f.	OONN-*tehr-klye-doong*
uneasy (anxious)	unruhig	OONN-*roo-ick*
unemployed	müssig	MÜ-*sick*
unemployment	Arbeitslosigkeit, f.	AHR-*bites-loh-zikh-kite*
unequal	ungleich	OONN-*glyekh*
unexpected (adj.)	unerwartet	OONN-*ehr-*VAHRR-*tet*
unfortunate	unglücklich	OONN-*glück-likh*
unhappy (sorrowful)	unglücklich	OONN-*glück-likh*
United Nations	Vereinigten Nationen, f. pl.	*fehr-*INE-*ick-ten nahts-*YOH-*nen*
university	Universität, f.	*oo-nee-vehr-zee-*TAYT
unjust (inequitable)	ungerecht	OONN-*guh-rehkht*
unknown	unbekannt	OONN-*buh-kahnnt*
unless (conj.)	wenn nicht	*venn* NIKHT
unlucky	unglücklich	OONN-*glück-likh*
unnecessary	unnötig	OONN-*nötikh*

ENGLISH	GERMAN	PRONUNCIATION
unpaid (due)	unbezahlt	OONN-*buh-tsahlt*
unpleasant	unangenehm	OONN-*ahnn-guh-name*
until (before, prep.)	bis	BISS
until (conj.)	bis	BISS
until (up to the time of, prep.)	bis	BISS
up (adv.)	oben	OH-*ben*
upon	auf	OWF
upstairs (at upper story, adv.)	oben	OH-*ben*
upstairs (to upper story, adv.)	die Treppe hinauf	*dee* TREPP-*puh hin*-OWF
urgent	dringend	DRING-*ent*
use (utilization)	Gebrauch, m.	*guh*-BROWKH
use (utilize); to	benutzen	*buh*-NOOTT-*sen*
useful	nützlich	NÜTTS-*likh*
useless	nutzlos	NOOTTS-*lohss*
usual	gewöhnlich	*guh*-VÖN-*likh*
utility (usefulness)	Nützlichkeit, f.	NÜTTS-*likh-kite*
vacant (untenanted)	leerstehend	LAIR-*shtay-ent*
vacation (work holidays	Ferien, pl.	FEHR-*yen*
vaccination	Impfung, f.	IMP-*foong*
vain (futile)	vergeblich	*fehr*-GABE-*likh*
valuable	wertvoll	VAIRT-*fawll*
value	Wert, m.	VAIRT
value (prize), to	schätzen	SHETT-*sen*
variety (assortment)	Auswahl, f.	OWSS-*vahl*
various (different)	verschieden	*fehr*-SHEE-*den*
veal	Kalbsfleisch, n.	KAHLLPS-*flysh*
veal chop	Kalbskotelett, n.	KAHLLPS-*koht-let*
vegetable	Gemüse, n.	*guh*-MÜ-*zuh*
venture (dare), to	wagen	VAH-*gen*
vertical (adj.)	senkrecht	ZENK-*rekht*
very (extremely)	sehr	ZAIR
vessel (ship)	Schiff, n.	SHIFF

ENGLISH	GERMAN	PRONUNCIATION
vest	Weste, f.	VESS-*tuh*
vicinity	Nähe, f.	NAY-*uh*
victorious	siegreich	ZEEG-*ryekh*
victory	Sieg, m.	ZEEK
Viennese (adj.)	wienerisch	VEE-*nuh-rish*
view (opinion)	Ansicht, f.	AHNN-*zikht*
view (scene)	Aussicht, f.	OWS-*zikht*
village	Dorf, n.	DORF
vine (grapevine)	Weinstock, m.	VINE-*shtawck*
vinegar	Essig, m.	ESS-*ikh*
vineyard	Weingarten, m.	VINE-*gahr-ten*
visible	sichtbar	ZIKHT-*bar*
vision (eyesight)	Sehkraft, f.	ZAY-*kraft*
visit (social call)	Besuch, m.	buh-ZOOKH
visit (call on), to	besuchen	buh-ZOO-*khen*
visitor	Besucher, m.	buh-ZOO-*khehr*
vital (essential)	wesentlich	VAY-*zent-likh*
voice	Stimme, f.	SHTIMM-*muh*
volume (book)	Band, m.	BAHNNT
vomit, to	erbrechen	*ehr*-BREHKH-*en*
vote, to	stimmen	SHTIMM-*men*
vow	Gelübde, n.	*guh*-LÜPP-*duh*
voyage	Reise, f.	RYE-*zuh*
vulgar (ill-bred)	gemein	*guh*-MINE
wages	Lohn, m.	LOHN
waist	Taille, f.	TAHLL-*yuh*
waiter	Kellner, m.	KELL-*nehr*
wait for, to	warten auf	VAHRT-*ten owff*
wake (awaken), to	wecken	VECK-*en*
wake (rouse oneself), too	erwachen	*ehr*-VAHKH-*en*
walk (stroll)	Spaziergang, m.	*shpah*-TSEER-*gahng*
walk, to	gehen	GAY-*en*
wall (inside)	Wand, f.	VAHNNT
wall (outside)	Mauer, f.	MOW-*ehr*
wander, to	wandern	VAHNN-*dehrn*

ENGLISH	GERMAN	PRONUNCIATION
want (desire), to	begehren	*buh-*GAY*-ren*
war	Krieg, m.	KREEK
wardrobe (apparel)	Garderobe, f.	*gahr-duh-*ROH*-buh*
warm	warm	VAHRRM
warm, to	wärmen	VEHR*-men*
warn, to	warnen	VAHRR*-nen*
wash (cleanse), to	waschen	VAHSH*-en*
wash (cleanse onself), to	sich waschen	*zikh* VAHSH*-en*
waste (squander), to	verschwenden	*fehr-*SHVENN*-dehn*
watch (timepiece)	Uhr, f.	OOR
watch (guard), to	bewachen	*buh-*VAHKH*-en*
watch (observe), to	beobachten	*buh-*OHB*-ahkh-ten*
water	Wasser, n.	VAHSS*-ehr*
waterproof	wasserdicht	VAHSS*-ehr-dikht*
way (route)	Weg, m.	VAYK
we	wir	VEER
weak	schwach	SHVAHKH
wear (have on), to	tragen	TRAH*-gen*
weather	Wetter, n.	VET*-tehr*
week	Woche, f.	VAWKH*-uh*
weekend (n.)	Wochenende, n.	VAWKH*-en-en-duh*
weekly (adj.)	wöchentlich	VÖKH*-ent-likh*
weep, to	weinen	VINE*-en*
weigh, to	wiegen	VEE*-gen*
weight (scale weight)	Gewicht, n.	*guh-*VIKHT
welcome (n.)	Willkommen, n.	*vill-*KAWMM*-men*
welcome (receive hospitably), to	begrüssen	*buh-*GRÜ*-sen*
well (in health, adj.)	wohl	VOHL
well (water pit, n.)	Brunnen, m.	BROONN*-nen*
west (n.)	Westen, m.	VESS*-ten*
western	westlich	VEST*-likh*
wet	nass	NAHSS
what (interrog. adj.)	welche	VELL*-kheh*

ENGLISH	GERMAN	PRONUNCIATION
what (interrog. pron.)	was	VAHSS
what (rel. pron.)	was	VAHSS
wheel	Rad, n.	RAHT
when (at the time that, conj.)	als	AHLLSS
when (at what time, adv.)	wann	VAHNN
where (in, at the place that, conj.)	wo	VOH
where (in, at what place, adv.)	wo	VOH
where (to what place, adv.)	wohin	*voh*-HIN
whether (either, conj.)	ob	OHP
whether (if, conj.)	ob	OHP
while (during the time that, conj.)	während	VAY-*rent*
whisper (utter softly), to	flüstern	FLÜSS-*tehrn*
whistle, to	pfeifen	PFIFE-*en*
white (adj.)	weiss	VICE
who (interrog. pron.)	wer	VAIR
whole (entire, adj.)	ganz	GAHNNTS
whooping cough	Keuchhusten, m.	KOYKH-*hooss-ten*
why	warum	*vah*-ROOMM
wide (not narrow)	breit	BRIGHT
widow	Witwe, f.	VIT-*vuh*
widower	Witwer, m.	VIT-*vehr*
width	Breite, f.	BRIGHT-*uh*
wife	Frau, f.	FROW
will (power of choice)	Wille, m.	VILL-*uh*
win (be victor in), to	gewinnen	*guh*-VINN-*nen*
wind	Wind, m.	VINNT
window	Fenster, n.	FENN-*stehr*

ENGLISH	GERMAN	PRONUNCIATION
windshield	Windschutz-scheibe, f.	VINT-*shootts-shy-buh*
wine(beverage)	Wein, m.	VINE
winter	Winter, m.	VIN-*tehr*
wisdom	Weisheit, f.	VIZE-*hite*
wise	weise	VYE-*zuh*
wish	Wunsch, m.	VOONNSH
wish for, to	sich wünschen	*zikh* VÜN-*shen*
wit (humor)	Witz, m.	VITTS
with (prep.)	mit	MITT
without (lacking, prep.)	ohne	OH-*nuh*
woman	Frau, f.	FROW
wood (lumber)	Holz, n.	HAWLLTS
wool (cloth)	Wolle, f.	VAWLL-*uh*
word	Wort, n.	VAWRT
work (labor)	Arbeit, f.	AHR-*bite*
work (labor), to	arbeiten	AHR-*by-ten*
worker	Arbeiter, m.	AHR-*by-tehr*
world	Welt, f.	VELT
worry (feel anxious), to	sich ängstigen	*zikh* ENG-*stee-gen*
worse (adj.)	schlimmer	SHLIMM-*mehr*
worse (adv.)	schlimmer	SHLIMM-*mehr*
worship, to (rel.)	anbeten	AHNN-*bay-ten*
worst (adv.)	am schlimmsten	*ahmm* SHLIMM-*sten*
worst (n.)	Schlimmste, n.	SHLIMM-*stuh*
worthless (valueless)	wertlos	VAIRT-*lohss*
worthy (deserving)	würdig	VÜRR-*dick*
wound (injury)	Wunde, f.	VOONN-*duh*
wrist	Handgelenk, n.	HAHNNT-*guh-lenk*
write, to	schreiben	SHRIBE-*en*
writer (author)	Schriftsteller, m.	SHRIFT-*shtell-ehr*
wrong (amiss, adv.)	verkehrt	*fehr*-KAIRT

ENGLISH	GERMAN	PRONUNCIATION
wrong (erroneous, adj.)	falsch	FAHLLSH
wrong (injustice)	Unrecht, n.	OONN-*rehkht*
wrong (unjust, adj.)	unrecht	OONN-*rehkht*
X-ray (examine), to	durchleuchten	*doorrkh*-LOYKH-*ten*
year	Jahr, n.	YAHR
yearly (adj.)	jährlich	YEHR-*likh*
yellow (adj.)	gelb	GELP
yes	ja	YAH
yesterday	gestern	GUESS-*tehrn*
yet (now, until now, adv.)	noch	NAWKH
young (adj.)	jung	YOONNG
youth (period of life)	Jugend, f.	YOO-*gent*
youthful	jugendlich	YOO-*gent-likh*
zero (n.)	Null, f.	NOOLL

CARDINAL NUMBERS

one	eins	EYENSS
two	zwei	TSVYE
three	drei	DRY
four	vier	FEAR
five	fünf	FÜNF
six	sechs	ZEX
seven	sieben	ZEE-*ben*
eight	acht	AHKHT
nine	neun	NOYN
ten	zehn	TSAYN
eleven	elf	ELF
twelve	zwölf	TSVÖLF
thirteen	dreizehn	DRY-*tsayn*
fourteen	vierzehn	FEERR-*tsayn*
fifteen	fünfzehn	FÜNF-*tsayn*
sixteen	sechzehn	ZEHKH-*tsayn*
seventeen	siebzehn	ZEEP-*tsayn*
eighteen	achtzehn	AHKHT-*tsayn*

ENGLISH	GERMAN	PRONUNCIATION
nineteen	neunzehn	NOYN-*tsayn*
twenty	zwanzig	TSVAHNN-*tsick*
twenty one	einundzwanzig	INE-*oont*-TSVAHNN-*tsick*
twenty-two	zweiundzwanzig	TSVYE-*oont*-TSVAHNN-*tsick*
thirty	dreissig	DRY-*sick*
forty	vierzig	FEERR-*tsick*
fifty	fünfzig	FÜNF-*tsick*
sixty	sechzig	ZEHKH-*tsick*
seventy	siebzig	ZEEP-*tsick*
eighty	achtzig	AHKH-*tsick*
ninety	neunzig	NOYN-*tsick*
one hundred	hundert	HOONN-*dehrt*
one hundred one	hundert und eins	HOONN-*dehrt oont* EYENSS
two hundred	zweihundert	TSVYE-*hoonn-dehrt*
two hundred one	zweihundert und eins	TSVYE-*hoonn-dehrt oonnt* EYENESS
one thousand	(ein) tausend	*(ine)* TOW-*zent*
two thousand	zweitausend	TSVYE-*tow-zent*
two thousand one	zweitausend und eins	TSVYE-*tow-zent oont* EYENSS
one million	eine Million	EYE-*nuh mill-*YOHN
one billion	eine Milliarde	EYE-*nuh mill-*YAHR-*duh*

ORDINAL NUMBERS

first	erste	AIR-*stuh*
second	zweite	TSVYE-*tuh*
third	dritte	DRIT-*tuh*
fourth	vierte	FEAR-*tuh*

ENGLISH	GERMAN	PRONUNCIATION
fifth	fünfte	FÜNF-*tuh*
sixth	sechste	ZEHKH-*stuh*
seventh	siebente	ZEE-*ben-tuh*
eighth	achte	AHKH-*tuh*
ninth	neunte	NOYN-*tuh*
tenth	zehnte	TSAYN-*tuh*
eleventh	elfte	ELF-*tuh*
twelfth	zwölfte	TSVÖLF-*tuh*

DAYS OF THE WEEK

Sunday	Sonntag, m.	ZAWNN-*tahk*
Monday	Montag, m.	MOHN-*tahk*
Tuesday	Dienstag, m.	DEENSS-*tahk*
Wednesday	Mittwoch, m.	MIT-*vawkh*
Thursday	Donnerstag, m.	DAWNN-*ehrss-tahk*
Friday	Freitag, m.	FRY-*tahk*
Saturday	Samstag (Sonnabend), m.	ZAHMMS-*tahk* (ZAWNN-*ah-bent*)

MONTHS OF THE YEAR

January	Januar, m.	YAH-*noo-ahr*
February	Februar, m.	FAY-*broo-ahr*
March	März, m.	MEHRTS
April	April, m.	*ah*-PRILL
May	Mai, m.	MY
June	Juni, m.	YOO-*nee*
July	Juli, m.	YOO-*lee*
August	August, m.	*ow*-GOOST
September	September, m.	*zep*-TEM-*behr*
October	Oktober, m.	*awck*-TOH-*behr*
November	November, m.	*no*-VEM-*behr*
December	Dezember, m.	*day*-TSEM-*behr*

ENGLISH	GERMAN	PRONUNCIATION
perfume (fragrance)	Parfüm, n.	*pahr-*FÜM
perhaps	vielleicht	*feel-*LYEKHT
period (of time)	Zeitraum, m.	TSITE-*rowm*
permanent (adj.)	dauernd	DOW-*ehrnt*
permission	Erlaubnis, f.	*ehr-*LOWP-*niss*
permit (allow), to	erlauben	*ehr-*LOW-*ben*
person	Person, f.	*pehr-*ZOHN
personal	persönlich	*pehr-*ZÖN-*likh*
persuade, to	überreden	Ü-*behr-*RAY-*den*
pet (animal)	Haustier, n.	HOWSS-*teer*
petticoat	Unterrock, m.	OONN-*tehr-rawck*
pharmacist	Apotheker, m.	*ah-poh-*TAY-*kehr*
pharmacy (drug store)	Apotheke, f.	*ah-poh-*TAY-*kuh*
phone, to	telephonieren	*tay-luh-foh-*NEE-*ren*
phonograph	Phonograph, m.	*foh-noh-*GRAHF
photograph	Photographie, f.	*foh-toh-grah-*FEE
physician	Arzt, m.	ARTST
piano	Klavier, n.	*klah-*VEER
pick (choose), to	auswählen	OWSS-*vay-len*
picture (depiction)	Bild, n.	BILLT
pie	Obstkuchen, m.	OHPST-KOO-*khen*
piece (bit)	Stück, n.	SHTÜCK
pig (animal)	Schwein, n.	SHVINE
pigeon	Taube, f.	TOW-*buh*
pill	Pille, f.	PILL-*luh*
pillow	Kissen, n.	KISS-*en*
pin (sewing accessory)	Stecknadel, f.	SHTECK-*nah-del*
pipe (tobacco pipe)	Pfeife, f.	PFIFE-*uh*
pitcher (container)	Krug, m.	KROOK
pity (compassion)	Mitleid, n.	MITT-*lite*
pity, to	bedauern	*buh-*DOW-*ehrn*
place (locality)	Platz, m.	PLAHTTS
place (lay), to	legen	LAY-*gen*
plain (clear)	deutlich	DOYT-*likh*

ENGLISH	GERMAN	PRONUNCIATION
passenger	Passagier, m.	*pahss-sah*-ZHEER
passport	Pass, m.	PAHSS
past (beyond, prep.)	uber	*Ü-behr*
past (bygone adj.)	vergangen	*fehr*-GAHNNG-*en*
past (n.)	Vergangenheit, f.	*fehr*-GAHNNG-*en-hite*
pastor	Pastor, m.	PAHSS-*tohr*
patch (repair)	Flicken, m.	FLICK-*en*
patience	Geduld, f.	*guh*-DOOLLT
patient (forbearing)	geduldig	*guh*-DOOLL-*dick*
patient (invalid)	Kranke, m., f.	KRAHNNG-*kuh*
patron (customer)	Kunde, m.	KOONN-*duh*
pattern (design)	Muster, n.	MOOSS-*tehr*
pavement	Strassenpflaster, n.	SHTRAH-*sen-pflahss-tehr*
pawn, to	verpfänden	*fehr*-PFENN-*den*
pawnshop	Leihhaus, n.	LYE-*howss*
pay, to	bezahlen	*buh*-TSAH-*len*
payable (due)	zahlbar	TSAHL-*bar*
payment	Zahlung, f.	TSAH-*loong*
peace	Frieden, m.	FREE-*den*
peach	Pfirsich, f., m.	PFEER-*zikh*
pear	Birne, f.	BEERR-*nuh*
pearl (gem)	Perle, f.	PEHR-*luh*
peculiar (odd)	eigentümlich	EYE-*gen-tüm-likh*
peel (take skin from), to	(ab)schälen	(AHPP-)SHALE-*len*
pen, fountain	Füllfeder, f.	FÜLL-*fay-dehr*
pencil	Bleistift, m.	BLYE-*shtift*
peninsula	Halbinsel, f.	HAHLLP-*in-zel*
people (persons)	Leute, f. pl.	LOY-*tuh*
pepper (seasoning)	Pfeffer, m.	PFEFF-*ehr*
perfect (flawless)	vollkommen	FAWLL-*kawmm-men*
perform (do), to	verrichten	*fehr*-RIKH-*ten*
performance (stage presentation)	Aufführung, f.	OWF-*fü-roong*

ENGLISH	GERMAN	PRONUNCIATION
pail	Eimer, m.	EYE-*mehr*
pain (ache)	Schmerz, m.	SHMEHRTS
painful	schmerzhaft	SHMEHRTS-*hahfft*
painter (artist)	Maler, m.	MAHL-*ehr*
painting (picture)	Gemälde, n.	*guh*-MEL-*duh*
pair	Paar, n.	PAHR
pajamas	Pyjama, n.	*pee*-JAH-*mah*
pal	Kamerad, m.	*kah-muh*-RAHT
palace	Palast, m.	*pah*-LAHSST
pale (wan)	blass	BLAHSS
pane, window	Fensterscheibe, f.	FENN-*stehr-shy-buh*
paper	Papier, n.	*pah*-PEER
parade (procession)	Parade, f.	*pah*-RAH-*duh*
paragraph	Absatz, m.	AHPP-*zahtts*
parcel (package)	Paket, n.	*pah*-KATE
parcel (post)	Paketpost, f.	*pah*-KATE-*pawsst*
parents	Eltern, pl.	ELL-*tehrn*
park	Park, m.	PAHRRK
park (put in place), to	parken	PAHRR-*ken*
parlor (living room)	Wohnzimmer, n.	VOHN-*tsimm-ehr*
part (portion)	Teil, m.	TILE
part (leave each other), to	sich trennen	*zikh* TRENN-*en*
participate, to	teilnehmen	TILE-*nay-men*
particular (detail, n.)	Einzelheit, f.	INE-*tsell-hite*
particular (specific, adj.)	besonder	*buh*-ZAWNN-*dehr*
partly	teils	TILES
partner (bus.)	Teilhaber, m.	TILE-*hah-behr*
party (pol.)	Partei, f.	*pahr*-TYE
party (social gathering)	Versammlung, f.	*fehr*-SAHMM-*loong*
pass (go by), to	vorbeigehen	*for*-BY-*gay-en*
passage (passageway)	Gang, m.	GAHNNG

ENGLISH	GERMAN	PRONUNCIATION
opposite (prep.)	gegenüber	*gay-gen-ü-behr*
or	oder	OH-*dehr*
orange (fruit)	Orange, f.	*oh-*RAHNZH*-uh*
order (command)	Befehl, m.	*buh-*FAIL
order (purchase)	Auftrag, m.	OWF-*trahk*
order (sequence)	Reihenfolge, f.	RYE-*en-fawl-guh*
order (command), to	befehlen	*buh-*FAIL*-en*
order (purchase), to	bestellen	*buh-*SHTELL*-en*
ordinary (usual)	gewöhnlich	*guh-vön-likh*
original (first)	ursprünglich	OOR-*shprüng-likh*
ornament	Zierde, f.	TSEER-*duh*
orphan (n.)	Waise, m. f.	VIZE-*uh*
other (adj.)	ander	AHNN-*dehr*
other (pron.)	andere	AHNN-*dehr-uh*
otherwise (under other conditions)	sonst	ZAWNNST
out (forth, adv.)	heraus	*hehr-*OWSS
out (not in, adv.)	aus	OWSS
outdoors (adv.)	draussen	DROWSS-*en*
outfit (equipment)	Ausrüstung, f.	OWS-*rüss-toong*
outside (adj.)	äussere	OYSS-*ehr-uh*
outside (adv.)	draussen	DROWSS-*en*
outside (n.)	Aussenseite, f.	OWSS-*en-zite-uh*
oven	Backofen, m.	BAHK-*oh-fen*
over (above, prep.)	über	*ü-behr*
overcoat	Mantel, m.	MAHNN-*tell*
overlook (disregard), to	übersehen	*ü-behr-*ZAY*-en*
oversea(s) (adj.)	überseeisch	Ü-*behr-zay-ish*
owe, to	schuldig sein	SHOOLL-*dick* ZINE
own (adj.)	eigen	EYE-*gen*
own (possess), to	besitzen	*buh-*ZITT*-sen*
owner	Eigentümer, m.	EYE-*gen-tü-mehr*
oyster	Auster, f.	OWSS-*tehr*
pack (wrap), to	verpacken	*fehr-*PAHCK*-en*
package	Paket, n.	*pah-*KATE
page (leaf)	Seite, f.	ZITE-*tuh*

ENGLISH	GERMAN	PRONUNCIATION
oblige (compel), to	verpflichten	*fehr*-PFLIKH-*ten*
observe (remark), to	bemerken	*buh*-MEHR-*ken*
observe (watch), to	beobachten	*buh*-OHB-*ahkh-ten*
obstacle	Hindernis, n.	HINN-*dehr-niss*
obtain (get), to	erhalten	*ehr*-HAHLL-*ten*
obvious	offenbar	AWFF-*fen-bar*
occasion	Gelegenheit, f.	*guh*-LAY-*gen-hite*
occupation (calling)	Beruf, m.	*buh*-ROOF
occupy (make busy), to	beschäftigen	*buh*-SHEFF-*tih-gen*
occur (happen), to	vorkommen	FOR-*kawm-men*
ocean	Ozean, m.	OH-*tsay-ahn*
odor (scent)	Geruch, m.	*guh*-ROOKH
of	von	FAWNN
office (place of business)	Büro, n.	*bü*-ROH
often	oft	AWFFT
oil	Öl, n.	ÖL
old (elderly)	alt	AHLLT
omit (leave out), to	auslassen	OWSS-*lahss-sen*
on (prep.)	auf	OWF
once (one time, adv.)	einmal	INE-*mahl*
once (formerly, adv.)	einst	INEST
onion	Zwiebel, f.	TSVEE-*bel*
only (merely)	bloss	BLOHSS
only (sole)	einzig	INE-*tsick*
open (adj.)	offen	AWFF-*fen*
open (make open), to	öffnen	OFF-*nen*
operate (perform surgery), to	operieren	*aw-peh*-REAR-*en*
operation (med.)	Operation, f.	*aw-pehr-rahts-*YOHN
opinion	Meinung, f.	MINE-*oong*
opportunity	Gelegenheit, f.	*guh*-LAY-*gen-hite*
opposite (n.)	Gegenteil, n.	GAY-*gen-tile*

ENGLISH	GERMAN	PRONUNCIATION
nobody (pron.)	niemand	NEE-*mahnnt*
noise (din)	Lärm, m.	LAIRM
noisy	geräuschvoll	*guh*-ROYSH-*fawll*
none (pron.)	keine	KINE-*uh*
nonsense	Unsinn, m.	OONN-*zin*
noon	Mittag, m.	MITT-*tahk*
nor	noch	NAWKH
normal (adj.)	normal	*nor*-MAHL
north (adv.)	nördlich	NÖRD-*likh*
north (n.)	Norden, m.	NOR-*den*
nose	Nase, f.	NAH-*zuh*
nostril	Nasenloch, n.	NAH-*zen-lawkh*
not	nicht	NIKHT
notary	Notar, m.	*no*-TAR
nothing	nichts	NIKHTS
notice (notification)	ankündigung	AHNN-*kün-dee-goong*
notice (see), to	bemerken	*buh*-MEHR-*ken*
notify, to	benachrichtigen	*buh*-NAHKH-*rikh-tih-gen*
nourish, to	(er)nähren	*(ehr-)*NAIR-*en*
nourishment	Nahrung, f.	NAH-*roong*
novel (book)	Roman, m.	*roh*-MAHN
now (adv.)	jetzt	YETTST
nowhere	nirgends	NEERR-*gents*
number (numeral)	Nummer, f.	NOOMM-*ehr*
number (quantity)	(An)Zahl, f.	(AHNN-)TSAHL
nut (food)	Nuss, f.	NOOSS
oath (vow)	Eid, m.	ITE
obedience (compliance)	Gehorsam, m.	*guh*-HOAR-*zahm*
obedient	gehorsam	*g̀uh*-HOAR-*zahm*
obey, to	gehorchen	*guh*-HOAR-*khen*
object (aim)	Ziel, n.	TSEEL
object (thing)	Gegenstand, m.	GAY-*gen-shtahnt*
objective (aim)	Ziel, n.	TSEEL
obligation (duty)	Verpflichtung, f.	*fehr*-PFLIKH-*toong*

ENGLISH	GERMAN	PRONUNCIATION
near (prep.)	neben; bei	NAY-*ben*; BY
necessary	nötig	NÖ-*tick*
necessity	notwendigkeit,	NOTE-*venn-dick-kite*
neck	Hals, m.	HAHLLSS
necklace	Halskette, f.	HAHLLSS-*kett-tuh*
need	Not, f.	NOTE
need (require), to	brauchen	BROWKH-*en*
needle	Nadel, f.	NAH-*del*
neglect (slight), to	vernachlässigen	*fehr*-NAHKH-*less-ih-gen*
Negro	Neger, m.	NAY-*gehr*
neighbor	Nachbar, m.	NAHKH-*bar*´
neighborhood	Nähe, f.	NAY-*uh*
neither (adj.)	kein	KINE
neither (pron.)	kein	KINE
neither . . . nor (conj.)	weder . . . noch	VAY-*dehr* . . . NAWKH
nephew	Neffe, m.	NEFF-*uh*
nervous (high-strung)	nervös	*nehr*-VÖSS
never	nie(mals)	NEE-(-*mahlss*)
new	new	NOY
newspaper	Zeitung, f.	TSYE-*toong*
newsstand	Zeitungskiosk, m.	TSYE-*toongs-kee-awssk*
New Year's Day	Neujahrstag, m.	NOY-*yahrs-tahk*
next (adv.)	anschliessend	AHNN-*shlee-sent*
next (following, adj.)	nächst	NEXT
next to (alongside of)	neben	NAY-*ben*
nice (agreeable)	nett	NETT
nickname	Spitzname, m.	SHPITTS-*nah-muh*
niece	Nichte, f.	NIKH-*tuh*
night	Nacht, f.	NAHKHT
nightgown	Nachthemd, n.	NAHKHT-*hemmt*
no (nay)	nein	NINE
no (not any, adj.)	kein	KINE

ENGLISH	GERMAN	PRONUNCIATION
mother-in-law	Schwiegermutter, f.	SHVEE-*gehr-moott-ehr*
motor (engine)	Motor, m.	MOH-*tor*
mountain	berg, m.	BEHRK
mountainous	gebirgig	*guh*-BEER-*gick*
mouse	Maus, f.	MOUSE
mouth	Mund, m.	MOONNT
move (change residence), to	umziehen	OOMM-*tsee-en*
move (shift one's position), to	bewegen	*buh*-VAY-*gen*
movement (motion)	Bewegung, f.	*buh*-VAY-*goong*
movies	Kino, n.	KEE-*no*
Mr. (Mister)	Herr, m.	HEHRR
Mrs. (Mistress)	Frau, f.	FROW
much, more, most	viel, mehr, (der) meist(e)	FEEL, MAIR, *(dehr)* MICET *(-uh)*
mud	Schlamm, m.	SHLAHMM
muscle	Muskel, m.	MOOSS-*kel*
museum	Museum, n.	*moo*-ZAY-*oomm*
mushroom (n.)	Pilz, m.	PILLTS
music	Musik, f.	*moo*-ZEEK
musician	Musiker, m.	MOO-*zee-kehr*
mustache	Schnurrbart, m.	SHNOOR-*bahrrt*
mustard	Senf, m.	ZENF
mutton	Hammelfleisch, n.	HAHMM-*mel-flysh*
mutual	gegenseitig	GAY-*gen-zite-tick*
nail	Nagel, m.	NAH-*gel*
nail (hardware)	Nagel, m.	NAH-*gel*
name	Name, m.	NAH-*muh*
namely	nämlich	NAME-*lick*
nap (doze, n.)	Schläfchen, n.	SHLAYFF-*khen*
napkin	Serviette, f.	*zehrv*-YET-*tuh*
narrow	schmal	SHMAHL
national (adj.)	national	*nahts-yoh*-NAHL
natural	natürlich	*nah*-TÜR-*likh*
near (not far, adv.)	nah	NAH

ENGLISH	GERMAN	PRONUNCIATION
mist	Nebel, m.	NAY-*bel*
mistake	Fehler, m.	FAY-*lehr*
mitten	Fausthandschuh, m.	FOWST-*hahnnt-shoo*
mix (make blend), to	mischen	MISH-*en*
mixture	Mischung, f.	MISH-*oong*
mob (disorderly crowd)	pöbel	PÖ-*bel*
model (exemplar)	Muster, n.	MOOSS-*tehr*
model (small copy)	Modell, n.	*moh*-DELL
modest	bescheiden	*buh*-SHY-*den*
moist	feucht	FOYKHT
moldy	schimmelig	SHIMM-*mel-likh*
moment (instant)	Augenblick, m.	ow-*gen-blick*
monastery	Kloster, n.	KLOHSS-*tehr*
money	Geld, n.	GELT
money order	Geldanweisung, f.	GELT-*ahnn-vize-oong*
monk	Mönch, m.	MÖNKH
monkey	Affe, m.	AHFF-*uh*
month	Monat, m.	MOH-*naht*
monthly (every month, adj.)	monatlich	MOH-*naht-likh*
monument	Denkmal, n.	DENGK-*mahl*
mood (humor)	Stimmung, f.	SHTIMM-*oong*
moon	Mond, m.	MÖHNT
more (adj.)	mehr	MAIR
moreover	ausserdem	OWSS-*ehr-dame*
morning	Morgen, m.	MOR-*gen*
morrow	folgender Tag, m.	FAWLL-*gen-dehr* TAHK
mosquito	Moskito, m.	*moss*-KEE-*toh*
most (adv.)	am meisten	*ahm*-MICE-*ten*
most (n.)	(das) Meiste, n.	(*dahss*) MICE-*tuh*
mostly	meistens	MICE-*tenss*
moth	Motte, f.	MAWT-*tuh*
mother	Mutter, f.	MOOTT-*ehr*

ENGLISH	GERMAN	PRONUNCIATION
meet (be introduced to), to	kennenlernen	KENN-*nen-lehr-nen*
meet (come together), to	zusammentreffen	tsoo-ZAHMM-*en-treff-en*
meet (encounter), to	sich treffen,	zikh TREFF-*en*
memory (recollection)	Erinnerung, f.	ehr-IN-*uh-roong*
mend (repair), to	flicken	FLICK-*en*
mention, to	erwähnen	ehr-VAY-*nen*
menu	Speisekarte, f.	SHPYE-*zuh-kahr-tuh*
merchant	Kaufmann, m.	KOWF-*mahnn*
merciful	barmherzig	barm-HEHRT-*sikh*
mercy	Gnade, f.	GNAH-*duh*
merely	bloss	BLOHSS
merit, to	verdienen	fehr-DEE-*nen*
messenger (courier)	Bote, m.	BOH-*tuh*
metal (n.)	Metall, n.	may-TAHLL
middle (center)	Mitte, f.	MITT-*tuh*
midnight	Mitternacht, f.	MITT-*tehr-nahkht*
milk	Milch, f.	MILLKH
mind (opinion)	Meinung, f.	MINE-*oong*
mineral	Mineral, n.	mee-nuh-RAHL
minister (clergyman)	Pfarrer, m.	PFAHRR-*ehr*
minute (unit of time)	Minute, f.	mee-noo-tuh
mirror	Spiegel	SHPEE-*gel*
miscellaneous	vermischt	fehr-MISHT
mischief (harm)	Unfug, m.	OONN-*foock*
miserable (unhappy)	elend	AY-*lent*
misfortune	Unglück, n.	OONN-*glück*
mislay, to	verlegen	fehr-LAY-*gen*
Miss	Fräulein, n.	FROY-*line*
miss (fail to do), to	verfehlen	fehr-FAY-*len*
miss (feel the loss of), to	vermissen	fehr-MISS-*en*

ENGLISH	GERMAN	PRONUNCIATION
manager (administrator)	(Betriebs)Leiter, m.	*(buh-*TREEPS-*)* LYE-*tehr*
manual (small book)	Handbuch, n.	HAHNNT-*bookh*
many, more, most	viele, mehr, (die) meist(en)	FE-*luh*, MAIR, MICET(*en*)
map	(Land)Karte, f.	(LAHNNT-)KAHRR-*tuh*
mark (designate), to	bezeichnen	*buh-*TSYEKH-*nen*
market (trading center)	Markt, m.	MAHRRKT
marriage	Ehe, f.	AY-*uh*
married	verheiratet	*fehr-*HYE-*rah-tett*
marry, to	sich mit . . . vermählen	*zikh mitt . . . fehr-*MAY-*len*
marvelous	wunderbar	VOONN-*dehr-bar*
master (great artist)	Meister, m.	MICE-*tehr*
match (lucifer)	Streichholz, n.	SHTRYEKH-*hawllts*
material (substance)	Stoff, m.	SHTAWFF
matinee (theater performance)	Nachmittags-vorstellung, f.	NAHKH-*mit-tahks-for-shtel-loong*
matter (affair)	Sache, f.	ZAHKH-*uh*
mattress	Matratze, f.	*mah-*TRAHT-*suh*
maybe	vielleicht	*feel-*LYEKHT
mayor	Bürgermeister, m.	BÜR-*gehr-mice-tehr*
meal (repast)	Mahlzeit, f.	MAHL-*tsite*
mean (have in mind), to	meinen	MY-*nen*
meaning (sense)	Sinn, m.	ZINN
meantime (n.)	Zwischenzeit, f.	TSVISH-*en-tsite*
measles	Masern, pl.	MAH-*zehrn*
meat	Fleisch, n.	FLYSH
mechanic	Mechaniker, m.	*muh-*KAHN-*ee-kehr*
medical	ärztlich	EHRTS-*likh*

ENGLISH	GERMAN	PRONUNCIATION
look (gaze), to	ansehen	AHNN-*zay-en*
look (seem), to	aussehen	OWSS-*zah-en*
look for, to	suchen	ZOOKH-*en*
lose, to	verlieren	*fehr*-LEE-*ren*
loss	Verlust, m.	*fehr*-LOOSST
loud (resounding)	laut	LOWT
love	Liebe, f.	LEE-*buh*
love, to	lieben	LEE-*ben*
low	niedrig	NEE-*drick*
luck	Glück, n.	GLÜCK
lucky (fortunate)	glücklich	GLÜCK-*likh*
luggage	Gepäck, n.	*guh*-PECK
lunch (midday meal)	Mittagessen, n.	MITT-*tahg-ess-senn*
lung	Lunge, f.	LOONNG-*uh*
machine	Maschine, f.	*mah*-SHEE-*nuh*
mad (insane)	wahnsinnig	VAHN-*zin-ick*
magazine (periodical)	Zeitschrift, f.	TSITE-*shrift*
maid (servant)	Dienstmädchen, n.	DEENST-*maid-ken*
maiden name	Mädchenname, m.	MAIE-*khen-nah-muh*
mail (letters exchanged)	Post, f.	PAWSST
mail (postal system)	Postdienst, m.	PAWSST-*deenst*
mail (post), to	mit der Post senden	MITT *dehr* PAWSST ZENN-*den*
main (principal)	Haupt-. . .	HOWPT-
make, to	machen	MAHKH-*en*
malaria	Sumpffieber, n.	ZOOMPF-*fee-behr*
male (adj.)	männlich	MEHNN-*likh*
man	Mann, m.	MAHNN
manage (administer), to	leiten	LYE-*ten*
management (administration)	Leitung, f.	LYE-*toong*